Cambridge Studies in French

BECKETT'S FICTION

Cambridge Studies in French

General editor: MALCOLM BOWIE

Recent titles in this series include

A complete list of books in the series will be found at the end of this volume.

BECKETT'S FICTION

IN DIFFERENT WORDS

LESLIE HILL

Lecturer in French Studies, University of Warwick

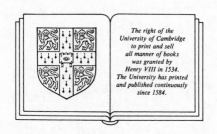

The right of the
University of Cambridge
to print and sell
all manner of books
was granted by
Henry VIII in 1534.
The University has printed
and published continuously
since 1584.

CAMBRIDGE UNIVERSITY PRESS

CAMBRIDGE

NEW YORK   PORT CHESTER

MELBOURNE   SYDNEY

Published by the Press Syndicate of the University of Cambridge
The Pitt Building, Trumpington Street, Cambridge CB2 1RP
40 West 20th Street, New York, NY 10011, USA
10 Stamford Road, Oakleigh, Melbourne 3166, Australia

First published 1990

Printed in Great Britain at the University Press, Cambridge

British Library cataloguing in publication data
Hill, Leslie.
Beckett's fiction: in different words. –(Cambridge studies in French).
1. Fiction in French. Beckett, Samuel, 1906–   .
I. Title.
843′.914

Library of Congress cataloguing in publication data
Hill, Leslie, 1949–
Beckett's fiction in different words / Leslie Hill.
p.   cm. – (Cambridge studies in French)
Includes bibliographical references.
ISBN 0–521–35645–8 (U.S.)
1. Beckett, Samuel, 1906–   – Fiction works.
I. Title.
II. Title: Fiction in different words.
III. Series.
PR6003.E282Z6794   1990
823′.912 – dc20   89–37175 CIP

ISBN 0 521 35645 8

CE

Er hatte etwa sagen wollen: Gott meint die Welt keineswegs wörtlich; sie ist ein Bild, eine Analogie, eine Redewendung, deren er sich aus irgendwelchen Gründen bedienen muß, und natürlich immer unzureichend; wir dürfen ihn nicht beim Worte nehmen, wir selbst müssen die Lösung herausbekommen, die er uns aufgibt.

Robert Musil,
*Der Mann ohne
Eigenschaften*, I, 83

(What he had wanted to say was roughly this: that God does not intend the world to be taken at all literally; it is an image, an analogy, a turn of phrase, which for one reason or another he is obliged to use, and of course always inadequately; we ought not to take him at his word, we must work out for ourselves the solution he gives us the task of finding.)

words have been my only loves, not many . . .

'From an Abandoned Work'

CONTENTS

PREFACE

– Signifier? Nous, signifier! (*Rire bref.*) Ah elle est bonne!

Fin de partie

Beckett's novels and prose texts constitute a verbal labyrinth, and the aim of this book is to chart a course through the labyrinth.

The critical literature on Beckett's fiction and plays is vast, and in recent years, Beckettian exegesis has produced an impressive amount of research into the author's intellectual and literary development, the history of production of his plays, or the evolution of his literary projects from manuscript to published text and French or English translation. But over several decades, in countless books and articles, the search for stable and satisfactory meanings in Beckett's writing has carried on unabated.

Many different approaches have been tried. Critics have gone through the work deciphering mythological, philosophical, literary, Biblical or geographical allusions, in the hope these may reveal influences or covert thoughts and clarify the author's intentions. Other critics have perused and collated Beckett's parallel texts, in French or English, in order to gauge the effect of textual variants on Beckett's meaning or the reasons for the many small and seemingly insignificant changes Beckett makes from one language to another. Others, who are the largest group, have put their confidence in one or other of a host of philosophers or other authorities, from Aristotle to Wittgenstein or Zoroaster, all of whom, at various times, have been pressed into literary critical service by readers of Beckett intent on devising an adequate explanation of the author's literary success.

To write on Beckett after all this implies rashness, obstinacy, even naivety. What remains to be said? This book would not have been written were it not for some frustration or dissatisfaction with much of the commentary and analysis devoted to Beckett's work. For this reader, Beckett's critics – despite exceptions – have often

seemed too willing to domesticate the author's texts and too ready
to recuperate them within well-worn and reductive norms. Set
beside the emotional fervour and intellectual disarray voiced in
Beckett's own writing, the critical response to the task of interpreting Beckett's work has been, to a large degree, bland and
unconvincing.

In this book, no attempt is made to ascribe to the author a
coherent world view, philosophical position or system of belief.
The concern here is not with presumed authorial concepts, but with
textual affects. In Beckett's text there are no valid positions of
transcendence or final stability which might enable the critic to
reconstruct an all-embracing authorial vision with which then to
explain – or explain away – Beckett's writing. What needs to be
elucidated instead, with regard to Beckett's work, is the strange
dispersion which characterises the structure of many of the author's
texts. Reading Beckett in this way, my project is to untangle the
complex relationship between language, meaning and subjectivity
at play in Beckett's texts. In that way, I hope to address directly the
difficulties which readers of Beckett's fiction constantly encounter
and which are at the heart of the disquiet and the rapture which, as
most are ready to admit, run through the author's writings as a
constant but unsettling source of fascination.

Some critics endow Beckett's work with greatness, others think it
self-regarding and bleakly nihilistic. The premise adopted here is
that Beckett speaks to us from the space of our own speaking.
Language, it is sometimes claimed, is what constitutes humans as
subjects, as creative and reflexive agents. In a similar way, language
in Beckett's work would seem to trace a precarious limit between
the human and the non-human, articulateness and engulfment.
Words in Beckett's books are vulnerable, subject to dislocation and
uncertainty, never really sure of what they are nor of what it is they
signify. As a result, Beckett's fiction lives on in a state of constant
self-doubt and textual perplexity. But Beckett's writing draws from
its dilemmas, both private and public, an extraordinary textual
energy and it is this which gives Beckett's work its unmistakable
and provocative singularity, its unique signature. And it is therefore with the question of Beckett's singularity and his signature that
much of what follows is concerned.

This book has undergone many different versions. Portions of
earlier material appeared in *Forum for Modern Language Studies*,
the *Oxford Literary Review*, and *French Studies*, and I wish to
thank the editors of these publications for permission to reproduce

some of that material here. I am also grateful to Beckett's publishers, the Editions de Minuit, John Calder, Faber and Faber, and Grove Press for kindly granting permission to quote from copyright material.

In writing this book, I have contracted many other debts. I could not have done without the friends, students and colleagues who gave me encouragement during what became an unduly protracted gestation period. In particular, I should like to thank for their support and assistance: Yves Abrioux, Andrew Benjamin, Malcolm Bowie, Simon Gaunt, Christopher Prendergast, Mark Treharne and Chris Turner. Anatole also took an interest and Mig Kerr helped redesign the garden. The Department of French Studies at the University of Warwick provided a friendly working environment and Peter Larkin and other members of staff at Warwick University Library gave valuable bibliographical assistance. The Centre for Research in Philosophy and Literature at the University of Warwick gave me the opportunity to develop a number of ideas. I am grateful, too, to the University of Warwick for the generous provision of sabbatical leave which allowed me to carry out some of the research for this project and to complete the final drafts.

Finally, this book is for Melanie, because, she said, nobody ever dedicated a book to her before.

ABBREVIATIONS

Beckett's three best-known novels, *Molloy*, *Malone meurt* and *L'Innommable*, are published in French only as separate, individual texts. However, for clarity and ease of reference, I have adopted the convention of numbering the three novels sequentially and will therefore refer to each text by means of the appropriate numeral. Certain other abbreviations have also been used in this book. These are as follows:

D   Samuel Beckett, *Disjecta*, edited by Ruby Cohn (London, John Calder, 1983)

P   Samuel Beckett, *Proust and Three Dialogues* (London, Calder and Boyars, 1965)

I   Samuel Beckett, *Molloy* (Paris, Editions de Minuit, 1951)

II   Samuel Beckett, *Malone meurt* (Paris, Editions de Minuit, 1951)

III   Samuel Beckett, *L'Innommable* (Paris, Editions de Minuit, 1953).

All further information regarding texts may be found in the notes and the bibliography.

1

MURPHY'S LAW

(Stoop) if you are abcedminded, to this claybook, what curios of
signs (please stoop), in this allaphbed! Can you rede (since We and
Thou had it out already) its world? It is the same told of all. Many.
Miscegenations on miscegenations.
Finnegans Wake (London, Faber & Faber, 1964, p. 18)

Written in English over the period from 1929 to 1938, Beckett's
early work seems restless, nomadic. It straddles two cultures, the
Anglo-Irish and the continental, and interweaves two styles of
discourse, bohemian iconoclasm and academic bookishness. The
effect is of instability, in tone, literary register, genre and idiom,
the result impermeability rather than clarity, and Beckett's language a record of disruption rather than communication.

Beckett's readers have often acknowledged the unsettled character of the author's early prose and poems. One argument is that
Beckett, in the 1930s, was still searching, unsuccessfully, for his own
personal voice and needed to rid himself of an excess of learning.[1]
To say this, however, is immediately to be committed to a series of
problematical assumptions about the status of voice in Beckett's
fiction as a whole. For what the argument inevitably implies is that,
because it came later, Beckett's trilogy, say, is purer, more unified,
more authentic, less discontinuous, than the early writings. Yet
however much one might prefer the trilogy over earlier texts, the
criteria of purity, continuity and authenticity create more problems
than they solve. The later novels require a more sceptical response.
Second, to take Beckett's early work, the essays on Joyce or Proust,
the stories in *More Pricks Than Kicks* or the novel *Murphy*, as being
important for what they tell us about Beckett's better known later
writings, is to grant these early texts secondary status, while still
claiming that they contain more transparent evidence of the author's
underlying intentions and his formative (yet already formed) ideas.
The contradiction seems plainly untenable.

1

In the past Beckett criticism has not always avoided these pitfalls. Repeatedly, the essays on Proust or Joyce have been scoured for statements that might be applied to Beckett's own fiction and *More Pricks Than Kicks* and *Murphy* pillaged for what they say (or may be persuaded to say) about their author's vision of the world or philosophic beliefs. This has tended to obscure to what extent Beckett's early writings possess a coherent, though dislocated rhetoric of their own, which Beckett develops, in various ways, sporadically at times, and at others dogmatically, across both some of his critical pieces and his experiments with novel and short story.

In systematic terms, that rhetoric is most clearly articulated in the 1929 piece on Joyce's future *Finnegans Wake*, the essay 'Dante. . . Bruno. Vico. . Joyce', and in Beckett's 1931 monograph on Proust.[2] This is why it is worth looking closely again at these early essays. The aim is not to begin thinking about Beckett's early fiction as a thematic redrafting of the novels of his two predecessors (once a critical commonplace), nor is it to use the essays as sources for Beckett's own alleged opinions or ideas. More pertinent for the present discussion is an assessment of the method adopted by Beckett in his readings of Joyce and Proust.

One of the distinctive features of the two essays is their preference for criticism as explication rather than as an act of measured evaluation. It is not that the essays are free of value judgements, content with describing neutrally the functioning of the two texts. On the contrary, Beckett is seldom other than peremptory and polemical in his references to received opinion or other literary works. If Beckett makes few value judgements in his text, it is because his whole position is one of assertive though ungrounded evaluation. In refusing to play the detached observer, Beckett identifies himself in a brashly partisan way with the text he is reading. When explicit value judgements do occur, as when Beckett introduces his account of Proust's 'Les Intermittences du cœur' (*P*, 39), it is to castigate the audience and promote the text (even when this might mean, in Beckett's view, defending it against itself).

But Beckett does not use criticism as an excuse for paying homage to a master, and the biographic person of the author is singularly lacking from his essays. *Proust* is prefaced by a short note declining all interest in the 'life and death of Marcel Proust' (*P*, 9), and much the same is true of the Joyce essay, though the collection in which it appeared, initially in *transition*, then in *Our Exagmination round His Factification. . .*, had an obvious celebratory function.[3] Rather, criticism is undertaken by Beckett as an act of submission to the terms of the text he is discussing. The only valid criteria, in the case of Proust and Joyce, are those already contained in the text, and Beckett's essays take it as their central purpose to propound (and extrapolate from) the aesthetic system of the novels concerned. Thus, with Joyce, Beckett concentrates on the relevance of Vico's cyclical theory of history, while with Proust he makes no distinction between Proust the author and the narrator of *A la recherche du temps perdu*, drawing extensively on the comments of the latter as a way of organising his own essay. One effect of this is that when Beckett has the 'impertinence', as he puts it (*P*, 75), to criticise the text (this happens only three times in *Proust*), it is in the name of its own logic, as Beckett construes it, and not extraneous values. To this extent, by illustrating the underlying method of his subjects, what Beckett often ends up doing is pushing the terms of the text into hyperbolic overstatement. Thus the description of Habit as 'the ballast that chains the dog to his vomit' (*P*, 19) mainly serves to underline Beckett's own habit of pugnacious advertisement of a classic Proustian theme.

Beckett's readings are identificatory rather than evaluative, explicative rather than appreciative, synthetic rather than analytic (*Proust* is presented at one point by Beckett as a 'synthesis'), and, as any reader familiar with *A la recherche* will realise, the sheer amount of paraphrase in Beckett's text is overwhelming.[4] The uncompromising nature of Beckett's declared commitment to his subjects is such that he might with good reason pass for little more than an apologist. Beckett brooks no objections on grounds of obscurity or difficulty. Of Proust's novel he declares that 'the complaint that it is an involved style, full of periphrasis, obscure and impossible to follow, has no foundation whatsoever' (*P*, 88). In rebutting a similar reaction to Joyce's 'Work in Progress', Beckett delivers the following, famous tirade:

Here is direct expression – pages and pages of it. And if you don't understand it, Ladies and Gentlemen, it is because you are too decadent to receive it. You are not satisfied unless form is so strictly divorced from content that you can comprehend the one almost without bothering to read the other. This rapid skimming and absorption of the scant cream of sense is made possible by what I may call a continuous process of copious intellectual salivation. (*D*, 26)

The attack on cultural decadence has a familiar ring, recalling many of the claims being made in the 1920s and 1930s by the literary

avant-garde, Futurists, Surrealists, Joycians and others alike. In
the process, Beckett commits himself to a by now routine modern-
ist conception of the autonomy of the literary text and the indissolu-
ble unity of form with content. He dismisses the idea of separating
the two by insisting that 'the one is a concretion of the other, the
revelation of a world' (P, 88) and that, in 'Work in Progress', 'form
is content, content is form' (D, 27). Fusion here results from the
innovative use of language, and in turn Beckett observes 'for Proust
the quality of language is more important than any system of ethics
or aesthetics' (P, 88). The autonomy enjoyed by the work of art
means that the text is not only independent of extraneous value
systems, but also irreducible to a mimetic theory of art (in the
unpublished 'Dream of Fair to Middling Women' Beckett writes off
Balzac as relying on a 'procédé that seems all falsity' [D, 46]).
Instead, according to Beckett, the literary text works as a dynamic
whole in which substance and architecture, theme and structure
come together to form a rhythmic whole. Speaking of Joyce's use of
Vico as a 'structural convenience – or inconvenience', Beckett
explains:

by structural I do not only mean a bold outward division, a bare skeleton
for the housing of material. I mean the endless substantial variation on
these three beats, and interior intertwining of these three themes into a
decoration of arabesques – decoration and more than decoration. (D, 22)

Likewise, Proust's novel is treated as a self-correlating, dynamic
texture of language, in which symbolic relationships are generated
from the sheer density of the language and not imposed by the
author allegorically. In Proust (and the claim originates with
Proust's narrator), there is no divorce between sensible and intelligible, between an impression and its sense. 'Proust does not deal in
concepts', Beckett comments, 'he pursues the Idea, the concrete'
(P, 79). 'For Proust', he adds, 'the object may be a living symbol,
but a symbol of itself' (P, 80). Proust's symbolism is an 'autosymbo-
lism' (P, 80), fusing together the two sides of the linguistic split
between real and ideal, signifier and signified.

The literary texts Beckett is describing transgress the stable
contrasted oppositions of non-literary discourse. This is the second
of Beckett's emphases. As the literary hoists language clear from its
fixed dichotomies, what the text uncovers is not a world of pacific
transcendence, of dualisms incorporated and effaced, but rather its
opposite, an endless circle of interpenetrating differences and
unredeemed contrasts. Prompted by Joyce, Beckett focusses

closely on this motif of the 'coincidence of contraries' (*D*, 21). This
is Bruno's contribution to 'Dante. . . Bruno. Vico. . Joyce', and
Beckett expounds it as follows:

> The principle (minimum) of one contrary takes its movement from the
> principle (maximum) of another. Therefore not only do the minima
> coincide with the minima, the maxima with the maxima, but the minima
> with the maxima in the succession of transmutations. Maximal speed is a
> state of rest. The maximum of corruption and the minimum of generation
> are identical: in principle, corruption is generation. (*D*, 21)

The coincidence of contraries affirms the relativity and instability of
all fixed points. Each position, each meaning becomes answerable
to at least two antagonistic systems, occupying a provisional place
in the round of language, constantly being displaced or undermined
by its opposite (itself similarly unstable). The autonomy of the
literary text is an autonomy without homogeneity: what it describes
is a mobile process of perpetual commingling in which each element
continually passes into its contrary by a sequence of circular
transmutations. Extremes meet: unity disperses into multiplicity.

Beckett's reading of Proust is informed by a similar sense of
duplicity and reversal. His account of *A la recherche* is guided by a
series of self-inverting or self-displacing thematic and structural
figures. These are isolated under the headings: Time, Habit, and
Memory. Proust's novel, says Beckett, is a novel of multiplicities
but the multiplicities behave like dualisms. The presiding divinity
of *A la recherche* is Janus, who always faces both ways and extracts
from apparent unity the divisiveness of perpetual reversal. Thus
Beckett on involuntary memory stresses the crucial dual identity of
Time, Habit and Memory, each poisoning the hero's life precisely
to the extent that it is also, inescapably, a remedy for the symptoms
it creates (*P*, 35).

Proustian memory, then, behaves according to what Derrida,
using the same metaphor, describes as the logic of the *pharmakon*:
poison and remedy, the one because the other, the one despite the
other, retracing and suspending in one movement the bar of
opposition which differentiates the two meanings and allows them
to exist.[5] In Beckett's account, the literary text follows a similar
logic. Like memory, it is predicated on a movement of passage and
transformation by which contraries merge and fuse and unity
reveals its hidden freight of swarming dispersion. Proust's text
bears the mark of this inner reversibility like a dual signature:
'each spear may be a spear of Telephus' (*P*, 11). Undermining

difference, this logic of reversal carries writing towards the infinity of myth and revelation, not myth as a symptom of cultural stability but myth as a process of unending verbal condensation and displacement. Writing redistributes the verbal surface of the world and illuminates its underlying dynamic by dramatising, writes Beckett, in a close paraphrase of Proust, an 'experience [...] at once imaginative and empirical, at once an evocation and a direct perception, real without being merely actual, ideal without being merely abstract, the ideal real, the essential, the extratemporal' (*P*, 75).

Beckett adopts, then, the same method or set of assumptions in approaching both authors. As he does so, Beckett does not compile a personal anthology of commonplaces, nor foist a series of idiosyncratic views on two unwilling authors (as critics have mooted in the past), but rather puts in place an embryonic theory of modern fiction. It is a theory committed to defending the autonomy of literary texts and it defines fiction as an activity of language in which, paradoxically, the foundations of meaning are attacked by the uncontrollable, self-inverting character of meaning itself.

Beckett's approach to Joyce and Proust is not neutral. He defends their break with tradition. This is evident in the stress laid on how both 'Work in Progress' and *A la recherche du temps perdu* respond to crisis by redefining the terms within which writing is legitimated. In a review essay devoted to Denis Devlin in 1938, Beckett speaks of 'social reality' having 'severed the connexion' with art, thus allowing art to rediscover its status as 'pure interrogation, rhetorical question less the rhetoric' (*D*, 91). The response of Joyce and Proust to that severed connection, as Beckett shows, lies in the totalising dynamic which both deploy as a means of giving their writing some foundation or necessity. In *Finnegans Wake* it has the form of a totalising of language and myth within the cyclical theory of history taken from Vico, while in Proust it is articulated by way of what Beckett rightly terms his 'religious' justification of art.

But it is symptomatic that as Beckett begins his account of 'Le Temps retrouvé', he demurs, and impugns the expression, 'le temps retrouvé', declaring it inappropriate. For Beckett the dialectic of art does not culminate, as it did, at least in principle, for Proust's narrator, in an aesthetic 'adoration perpétuelle' (the initial title of Proust's book), but rather in a purgatorial structure which knows no end other than its own infinite circularity and sluggishness. Indeed, for the author of 'Dante. . . Bruno. Vico. . Joyce', the literary text knows no closure nor structure of redemption, no transcendence or term. In its mingling of contraries, its dissolving of unities, what the text embodies is not the world either as paradise or as inferno: it is the world as purgatory. Beckett explains:

In what sense, then, is Mr Joyce's work purgatorial? In the absolute absence of the Absolute. Hell is the static lifelessness of unrelieved viciousness. Paradise the static lifelessness of unrelieved immaculation. Purgatory a flood of movement and vitality released by the conjunction of these two elements. There is a continuous purgatorial process at work, in the sense that the vicious circle of humanity is being achieved, and this achievement depends on the recurrent predomination of one of two broad qualities. No resistance, no eruption, and it is only in Hell and Paradise that there are no eruptions, that there can be none, need be none. On this earth that is Purgatory, Vice and Virtue – which you may take to mean any pair of large contrary human factors – must in turn be purged down to spirits of rebelliousness. Then the dominant crust of the Vicious or Virtuous sets, resistance is provided, the explosion duly takes place and the machine proceeds. And no more than this; neither prize nor penalty; simply a series of stimulants to enable the kitten to catch its tail. And the partially purgatorial agent? The partially purged. (*D*, 33)

The approach Beckett outlines here, displaying paradox and self-contradiction as its motive forces, is not systematic. It is informed by the knowledge that all totalising systems are precarious. Nonetheless the emphasis on the Janal dynamic of writing and its logic of circularity and reversal is indicative of Beckett's own understanding of what constitutes a modern literary text. More importantly, the purgatorial aesthetic set out in these early essays provides Beckett with an initial enabling strategy, a rhetorical framework which he explores at greater length, in the fictional mode, in his most important early work, the collection of stories, or episodic novel, *More Pricks Than Kicks*.[6]

As critics have readily conceded, it is an uneven series of texts, albeit one which in its very dispersion investigates many of the implications of the purgatorial mode. One of the dominant figures of the book, within its uneasy narratorial discourse, but more so on the level of plot construction, is oxymoron, that trope which registers the clash and fusion of contraries within an apparently unified context. 'He had a strong weakness for oxymoron' (41), notes Beckett of his hero, illustrating the trope as well as commenting on it, and it is punningly and literally that the poor figure of Belacqua Shuah, the book's intermittent protagonist, the inverted S.B. of authorial repute, might be described as oxymoronic.

Coupled with oxymoron is an equally rich use of chiasmus, the figure which crosses parallel phrases, or, in Beckett's case, more often plot events, by inverting them along the lines of A:B::B:A. Chiasmus and oxymoron are deployed by Beckett as the principal rhetorical moves of a fiction circulating antithetically from one extreme to the other with the sluggishness of a humankind whose fate is always to be: 'as we were, where we were' (20). Pitting inferno against paradise ('Dante and the Lobster'), fusion against flight ('Fingal'), love against death ('Love and Lethe'), or, chiastically, the laughter at dying against the dying of laughter ('Yellow'), or burial alive against death-bed resurrection ('Draff'), the stories in *More Pricks Than Kicks* explore, by oxymoron and chiasmus, the oscillating and interpenetrating rhythms of a purgatorial round where, if one term is reached, it rapidly turns into its opposite. In this shuttling movement from one extreme to another, the stories highlight not the dialectical unification of contraries, but the evanescence of unity, the movement of constant displacement at the core of apparent stability.

(A parenthesis or digression is necessary here to examine what is at issue in this purgatorial concern for the instability of verbal contrasts and differences. A parenthesis is needed for this because – or so that – what it contains does not form matter for a thesis, but at most – or least – only enough for a fictional text. For Beckett's purgatorial concerns serve to announce a fundamental structure that, in differing guises, is at work in Beckett's writing at virtually every point in its development. What the stories of *More Pricks Than Kicks* display, as the thing they are secretly about as well as the experience from which they come, though it is neither a thing nor an experience, is something which recurs time and again in Beckett's work as though it were indeed the one or the other. One could say it somehow represents the crux of Beckett's writing, its purpose and point, yet it is none of these things, cannot be named, and exists somehow beyond signification, though not beyond words. This something, of which, amongst others, a text like *More Pricks Than Kicks* speaks, is not a transcendental value. Beckett's critics have usually assumed this, and by so doing have consigned much of Beckett's work to being a repetitive endorsement of clichés about the inexpressible nature of the self, the authenticity of being without words, or the role of literature as a quintessential expression of the fate of modern man.

Aside from these commonplaces, the something I want to name in Beckett's writing may be located more effectively in what could be called the figure of indifference or, to borrow a word from the essays of Maurice Blanchot, the neuter.[7] Indifference, the neuter, is that which is in-between positions of meaning, neither positive nor negative, constantly shifting and irreducible to either object or subject. Instead, it is more like the condition of possibility of differences and contrasts, positions and oppositions, theses and parentheses, and of sense as such. To that extent, as Blanchot often phrases it, it is pure affirmation without assertion, or perhaps what Beckett, in his 'Homage to Jack Yeats', calls 'the impetus of need' [*D*, 149]. If the figure of indifference appears as the indeterminate and inexpressible core of meaning, as a shuttling movement of differentiation which is itself without differentiation, it is because the absence of difference is what enables difference as such – which cannot exist 'as such' – to be articulated while at the same time rendering it perpetually unstable and precarious. This preoccupation leaves many trails in Beckett's writing. In *Murphy*,[8] for example, Cooper is described as 'mov[ing] incorruptible between his corruptors with the beautiful indifference of a shuttle, without infamy and without praise' [135], and under cover of the vaudeville burlesque of a man whose 'acathisia was deep-seated and of long standing' [84], this translates exactly what is at issue here: the non-difference, the lack of identity with itself, of a process without subject, location, or object, but which is visible as the fusion and interpenetration of contraries and the teeming movement at the core of sameness.

Indifference has another meaning in Beckett. It also signifies the absence of desire, the suspension of subject–object relations and an abdication from the world's commercial round. Indifference is also a name for that space in which, according to the Geulincxian tag Beckett is fond of quoting [as in *Murphy* (124)], 'ubi nihil vales, ibi nihil velis' ['where you are worth nothing, you should want nothing']. A minor vowel difference – paranomasia – translates here the indifference or non-identity between outside and inside, values and desires. *More Pricks Than Kicks*, among other things, is a portrait of this apathy of indifference, of a protagonist whose life is that of a blank, a void or hiatus in the world, a figure living, oxymoronically, in 'moving pauses' [41], shifting through the world's antinomies as an interval in whom oppositions meet and are annulled as in a 'Beethoven pause' [40], suspended simultaneously and undecidably between sound and silence, meaning and emptiness, difference and indifference.)

If *More Pricks Than Kicks* can be read, then, as a book dedicated to the rhetoric of purgatory and its thematic comminglings and reversals, the same is doubly true of *Murphy*. Like the earlier stories, *Murphy* is, in turn, a singularly recondite text, strewn with numerous self-conscious rhetorical patterns and an array of internal rhyming effects. It displays an extensive repertoire of allusions or direct borrowings which range from the astrological to the psychiatric and the literary to the philosophical. Criticism has responded to the book's complex battery of effects by hunting down the references to their sources, and the novel has been described, variously but consistently in this respect, as a post-Cartesian novel of ideas, Menippean satire, a mythagogic poem, or, more commonly, as comic parody.[9]

In these discussions much useful information has been brought to light, but the result has often been to make *Murphy* seem more like a pamphlet than a novel. Yet *Murphy* flaunts its autonomy as a work of fiction, and a more effective start to reading it as a novel can be made by examining the differing rhetorical or structural moves the narrative makes as it proceeds. It soon becomes clear that at the heart of *Murphy* (as well as in Murphy's heart) lies the by now familiar purgatorial logic of oxymoron and chiasmus, contradictory apposition and rhetorical inversion.

Murphy opens under the sign of dualism and paradox. (Even the sight of the 'poor old sun in the Virgin again' [5] is paradoxical.) The first chapter establishes two contrasted characters, Neary and Murphy, each endowed with his own idiosyncratic system for dealing with dualism, binary conflict and paradox. Murphy is characterised in terms of the opposition between freedom and constraint, on which is superimposed a further contrast of mind with body. As Murphy sits surrounded by the repetitive circularity of a world typified by barter and substitution (mirrored in the echoing street-cry of '*Quid pro quo! Quid pro quo!*' [5], which suggests not only 'one thing in return for another' but also, 'one thing mistaken for another'), he is put in a position of bodily constraint, enjoying (via a perverse chiasmus) the freedom of mind which his physical imprisonment makes possible. (But already the clarity of the situation is troubled by the problem of how many scarves are tying Murphy to his rocker – is it six, or seven? – and the difficulty of whether it makes sense to talk of imprisonment when it is both self-inflicted and relished by the victim.) The dualistic contrast of mental freedom versus bodily confinement is further complicated by the chiastic structure (in A:B::B:A) of Murphy's (misnamed) commerce with Celia, his prostitute *amour* (who is heaven-sent only to the extent that her name signifies the heavens and Murphy meets her while consulting the stars [13]): for 'the part of him that he hated craved for Celia, the part that he loved shrivelled up at the thought of her' (9). Celia, for her part, feels likewise.

From the outset, the unity of the character Murphy is disjointed, parcelled up according to a series of rhetorical as well as physical snares. Torn between his love for himself and his love for Celia, which seem mutually exclusive but turn out later to have rather a lot in common, harnessed to – that is to say: on, but, more plausibly, also: off – his rocker, Murphy is a character inhabited by many discordant oppositions. Body versus mind, desire versus apathy, alienation versus sanity, solipsism versus gregariousness are some of them. Moreover, as Murphy is introduced, he is contrasted with his guru manqué, Neary, in whom some critics have begun to recognise the figure of Beckett's psychoanalyst of the mid-1930s, W.R. Bion.[10] Neary is placed at the centre of a similar, if less elaborate, network of competing forces, but, unlike Murphy, is able to quell the discord in his heart by resolute exertion of mind over matter. He is able, as a result, to mediate between extremes of sexual desire or frustration by inducing in himself, and, theoretically, his acolytes, an hypnotic state of temporary cardiac arrest. This was how Murphy had come to consult Neary, in the hope that, in turn, he might learn from this failed guru – and guru of failure – how to achieve bliss, which goes here under a variety of different names, ranging from 'the Apmonia' to 'the Isonomy' or 'the Attunement' (6).

Neary's and Murphy's systems, though they seem to mirror each other, diverge on the key issue of mediation. Neary can harmonise his extremes by imposing on them, by superhuman means, some equilibrium or concordat with various fanciful labels. Murphy's case, however, admits no such mediation between the clash of contraries. Murphy is a living demonstration of the impossibility of unity, the perpetual instability of synthesis and the irredeemable admixture of the purgatorial circle. Murphy is a 'surd' (56) to Neary's Pythagoras. His heart is a protest at the dialectical equalisation of opposites.

Two antagonistic responses to dualism, then, are rehearsed in the opening pages, the one claiming the possibility, or the hope, of resolution, the other objecting the irreducible nature of fiasco. They announce two parallel sub-plots which mock and contradict each other. Their course is sketched in a characteristically gnomic snatch of repartee between Neary and Murphy, where it is never quite clear if the joke is on the reader, the characters, or the author:

Neary came out of one of his dead sleeps and said:
'Murphy, all life is figure and ground.'
'But a wandering to find home,' said Murphy.
'The face,' said Neary, 'or system of faces, against the big blooming, buzzing confusion. I think of Miss Dwyer.' (7)

One series of events follows Neary's quest for a face with which to harmonise the confusion around him. The other is kept in movement by Murphy's attempts to elude the antinomies of his heart by suppressing one or other of their causes. Their relationship is of both attraction and repulsion. While Neary transfers his affections to Miss Counihan and is forced into masterminding the quest for Murphy, Murphy, for his part, struggles to withdraw from the public world of desires and rewards. The relationship between the two intrigues is of ironic opposition, and at the end, rather than converging to a common denouement, they exchange places. The more Neary needs Murphy to further his ends, the less available Murphy becomes, and when Murphy is located, dead, at the end of the novel, the effect on Neary is the reverse of what was anticipated.

These chiastic twists in the tale are more than decorative or comic ploys. In their arabesques, they enact the purgatorial logic driving the novel. This takes the form of an elaborate rhetorical network of chiasmus and oxymoron, ironic reversal and disjunctive combination. As Neary, for instance, yearns for a face to harmonise the confusion, and fails in his quest, so Murphy, in reverse, though he possesses the heavenly face of Celia, struggles to elude it and yearns for the non-face of a Mr Endon. When he finds Mr Endon, he tries in vain to scramble back into the world he has already abandoned. This heterogeneity of structural and thematic relations becomes the novel's stock-in-trade and plotting the novel becomes an elaborate rhetorical game, not unlike the one Murphy plays with Mr Endon on – or over – the chess-board, in which the basic moves are chiasmus, oxymoron, parallelism and reversal.

Neary and Murphy, seemingly, embark on opposite quests. Neary wants for reciprocity, Murphy strives for relief from reciprocity. The contrast, however, turns out to be much less secure than it appears. The ironies and reversals of purgatorial rhetoric always have the last laugh, and if they mean that similars diverge, they also imply that dissimilars converge (and this is foreshadowed in the names of the pair, with Neary's echoing, in the shape of an anagram, Murphy's 'yearning' for home, and Murphy's, if it is taken, as Ruby Cohn suggests, to derive from the Greek *morph*, reflecting Neary's search for figure against ground).[11]

Neary's and Murphy's systems are both closed systems in which resources are finite but their permutations endless. Murphy considers his own mind one such 'closed system' (77) and it is to there he retreats. Neary does the opposite but achieves no more satisfactory solution. The desired face – Miss Dwyer at first – once possessed, fades into the chaotic background (37). Desire and possession are in inverse proportion: as the one increases, the other decreases, and it is to impose some equilibrium on this endless seesaw that Neary invents Apmonia in the first place. But the system is not stable. Neary admits that ' "Love requited [. . .] is a short circuit" ' (7) and his yearning takes the direction of that law of unrequited frustration by which A loves B who loves C who loves D. . . who loves A. In other words, no sooner is one opposition equalised by Neary than another appears to take its place (as one might expect in the world of '*Quid pro quo*'). As Wylie, whom Neary cites on the matter (137), archly portends:

the syndrome known as life is too diffuse to admit of palliation. For every symptom that is eased, another is made worse. The horse leech's daughter is a closed system. Her quantum of wantum cannot vary. (43)

' "Humanity" ', adds Wylie, ' "is a well with two buckets, one going down to be filled, the other coming up to be emptied" ' (44).

Neary's search for some mediation between extremes founders on its impossibility (he had achieved Apmonia before only by superhuman means). The desire for stability is undone by the perpetual motion and unresolved dualities of the closed system. Neary's pursuit of a face is a vicious circle. Instead of homogeneity Neary finds instability, instead of unity disintegration. His system refutes itself and turns into its own opposite. At the close, far from succeeding in stilling frustration, Neary sees his hair turn white and he wanders away, abandoning his quest, an inconsolate figure not of reciprocity, but stark loneliness. He joins that band of aged solipsists, like Celia's Mr Kelly, or the oxymoronic 'old boy' who commits suicide, or Murphy's own Mr Endon, who all inhabit something resembling the outer reaches of the purgatorial circle.

Ironic reversibility takes charge of the novel's meticulously drawn verbal and structural patterning. Celia suffers a similar reverse to Neary. Initially a partisan of the big world and commerce, she commits her time to love, marriage, and work (on the streets). But as she pines for her cherished Murphy, who, having done as he was asked by Celia and gone in search of a job, wants less than ever to return to her, she discovers that she is taking on many of the attributes of her absent love. Beckett's text makes the point by applying several of Murphy's catchphrases to Celia, who now discovers in herself the desire to be sitting naked in the rocker (49). Celia comes to mirror, by chiastic inversion, the fate of Murphy, who by now thinks he has found home in the M.M.M. mental home. Celia retreats into her own closed world just as Murphy begins to realise that M.M.M. ought to stand for 'music, MUSIC, *MUSIC*' (161).

If Murphy corrupts Celia's resolve from afar, slowly changing her into the reverse image of what she once was, then the same is also true of the effect of Murphy's death on Cooper. Cooper is a familiar Beckett grotesque, who is subject to a set of arbitrary and inexplicable constraints, never takes his hat off (unlike Murphy who abhors hats), and is unable to sit (unlike Murphy). Cooper's role is as a go-between and detective (and Suk's horoscope had prescribed these duties for Murphy). Again, a radical change comes over him towards the end, as Wylie had darkly predicted, and in chapter twelve Cooper is found seated in the taxi, only for him to celebrate, in Proustian fashion, by crushing his hat. There is here a sudden, comic reversal from one extreme to the other, which is not mitigated in the text by any attempt at plausible motivation. The reader is left with an unmediated transition which has no other cause than Beckett's purgatorial rhetoric.

Extremes meet, stable contrasts give way to discontinuity and paradox, and the novel plots a whole series of unreconciled, self-inverting dichotomies. It is in the character of Murphy that these techniques reach their apogee, or nadir. Unlike Neary's response to discord, Murphy's reaction is to endeavour to find peace in the motions of the little world rather than the large. This he achieves in the now celebrated manner:

Slowly he felt better, astir in his mind, in the freedom of that light and dark that did not clash, nor alternate, nor fade nor lighten except to their communion, as described in section six. The rock got faster and faster, shorter and shorter, the iridescence was gone, the cry in the mew was gone, soon his body would be quiet. Most things under the moon got slower and slower and then stopped, a rock got faster and faster and then stopped. Soon his body would be quiet, soon he would be free. (10)

These moments of hypnotic ecstasy become Murphy's hallmark. Unlike Neary's exercises in cardiac arrest, Murphy's bliss does not lie in immobilising the purgatorial round of desire and frustration in contemplative stasis. What Murphy experiences here, like a slowly effaced iridescence, is the mobile coalescing and merging of differences in his mind. Speed accelerates into a state of rest and the movement of the rocker, following the Bruno paradox, reveals the suspended indifference (lack of distinction as well as lack of desire) at the core of purgatorial chiasmus as the medium of its inversions, paradoxes, and oxymora, like the still centre at the hub of infinite motion. Prey to 'the freedom of indifference, the indifference of freedom' (73), as Beckett puts it in a neatly calculated chiasmus, Murphy frees himself from the big world around him only to lapse into a little world where freedom is annulled. Searching for the purity of unmediated apperception, Murphy finds (or: loses) himself in a zone where apperception dissolves into nothingness. In such moments of bliss, extremes are no longer mediated, as Neary intended, but give way to something else in which fixity and identity are no longer available and there is no longer any question of there existing any unification.

It is impossible to claim for Murphy's goal of solipsistic ecstasy any value that is philosophically stable. As Murphy wanders homeward into the microcosm of his own mind, he necessarily follows a purgatorial circuit which constantly has him facing two ways, spiralling back as he lurches forward, subject to uncontrollable paradoxes and chiastic inversions. When he reluctantly turns aside from the charms of the little world and opts for the music of Celia, to the extent of looking for work to please her (even if it is only pretence on his part), it is to find the refuge of the Magdalen Mental Mercyseat, which offers him the chance, paradoxically, of working in the little world, not the big. When he appears on the point of discovering his truly solipsistic fellows (to perpetrate another oxymoron) in the M.M.M., he discovers his freedom to indulge in recuperative trances drastically curtailed.

Finding asylum, Murphy is denied asylum. The word splits into two and squints sceptically at itself, since, in common with the inmates – if there is anything common to them at all, which the text seems to doubt – asylum is precisely what Murphy does not find in the asylum. The gulf between Murphy and the true inhabitants of the little world proves to be unbridgeable, and, the narrator reports, Murphy 'felt it was very likely with them that craved to cross it as with them that dreaded to – they never did' (161). Only vicariously does Murphy enjoy the 'microcosmopolitan' (163) society of the M.M.M. The reason for Murphy's exclusion is made clear in his night-time encounter with Mr Endon. The true inhabitant of the little world, Murphy discovers, is impenetrable to the outside onlooker. Murphy and Mr Endon relate only through the formal gambits of a chess-game played out according to a logic of non-engagement. No response is forthcoming from Mr Endon to Murphy's hope that he might reciprocate his lack of identity. The only encounter with Mr Endon is a radical absence of encounter, and nothing can mediate between two closed systems.

For Murphy to be free in mind, his body must be calm; when he finds a semblance of physical serenity, his mind finds retreat cut off. Only in the big world does Murphy find refuge; in the asylum he is left on its threshold. The paradoxes revolve with a vengeance and throw Murphy forwards into a last metamorphosis. As he stares into defeat at Endon's hands (and the defeat concerns the game of life as well as the game of chess), Murphy, 'with fool's mate in his soul, retires' (168). Acknowledging Endon's world is inaccessible, Murphy discovers that, paradoxically, the route to his own microcosm lies not in apperception but in being unperceived by the world around him. Once unperceived, as by Endon, Murphy regresses to that core of stillness which is the ground and limit of his existence. Under the exacting non-gaze of Endon, the reverse of a face seen against the confusion, Murphy both loses and finds himself, refinds and reloses himself, and he

began to see nothing, that colourlessness which is such a rare postnatal treat, being the absence (to abuse a nice distinction) not of *percipere* but of *percipi*. His other senses also found themselves at peace, an unexpected pleasure. Not the numb peace of their own suspension, but the positive peace that comes when the somethings give way, or perhaps simply add up, to the Nothing, than which in the guffaw of the Abderite naught is more real. (168)

Beyond the contemplative quietism ascribed to Neary, Murphy encounters the affirmative side of indifference. But the impact of his psychotic hiatus is rapid. Murphy's mind is no longer a refuge. It returns Murphy to the blankness of birth, without knowledge of who he is, unable to envision even his own father, only the sight of his own castration in the form of the 'rigid upturned face of the Child in a Giovanni Bellini Circumcision' (172). Mental images give way to 'scraps of bodies, of landscapes, hands, eyes, lines and colours evoking nothing' (172). Dimly resolving to quit the engulfing madness for Celia, Murphy returns to the rocker.

This final return to the rocker proves, of course, to be the death of him and Murphy ends up a truly burnt-out case. Murphy reaches his goal, and 'soon', this time, says the narrator, 'his body was quiet' (173). Exit Murphy, into the chaotic excellence of the gas-stove. Murphy achieves his end (but whether his end was his goal nobody can tell) only at the price of becoming dross, a package of ash, as prescribed by the Bible, scattered to the four corners of the bar-room floor. In this final extremity, there is no little world or big world any more for Murphy, only a purgatorial circle which recycles him into ordinary life just as he dies, and puts an end to him just as he was about to return. In death Murphy's existence (or non-existence, depending on how one looks at it) is the same as it was when he was born, he weighs four pounds, and is identified only by the angioma on his buttocks. Life turns full circle, and Murphy's bottom becomes his most prominent part.

For Murphy, life is an interval between two interpenetrating but opposed limits, birth and death. Between them is a purgatorial spiral, rising as it falls, falling as it rises. The spiral has no culminating conclusion or any fullness of origin, but is almost like a form of writing, a story, even, which, paradoxically, seems both freely adopted and yet without alternative. Its indeterminate status is mirrored in Suk's horoscope: does the star-chart determine Murphy's life or Murphy determine the meaning of the star-chart? In Murphy's story, the external fate of the stars and his own inner purpose converge, rendering the direction of causality undecidable. What remains is the enigma of something, Murphy's life, which cannot be redeemed or altered, only embodied by the character whose task it is to live it. That is the lesson of the horoscope, like the novel it prefigures. It becomes for Murphy a personal system that, at the last, he incorporates into his own life like a fictional script, 'the poem that he alone of all the born could have written' (126).

Living, for Murphy, is to read from a poem fashioned in advance of life by someone else but needing at every turn to be written by him, embodied and underwritten by him as the tale which is his own. Murphy's horoscope is both prior and posterior, cause and effect of his life, external to him and beyond his control, yet immanent in his life and belonging to no other. Murphy views prophecy as 'an out-and-out preterist' (127), believing that the end, like the apocalypse, has already taken place, but knowing that knowledge of the event still lies in the future. Beckett's novel, too, is an unredeemed and unalterable fiction which hangs enigmatically over the purgatorial mystery of its own birth. The meaning of Murphy's quest is a haphazard and unchangeable effect of a system which seems to have no prior cause. Murphy began his life with a double flat vagitus (52) and ends it with a bang that is just another name for a whimper. Whichever way one looks, the same logic of paradox, inversion, chiasmus and oxymoron undermines the foundations of meaning, stripping them of stability and coherence. Oppositions are set up to be subverted, convergences established only to diverge again.

In *Murphy*, Beckett radicalises the rhetoric explored in his preceding texts. He harnesses for his own purposes the purgatorial dynamic discovered in Proust and Joyce. Unlike them, however, he does not cover his tracks by adopting within his novel an epiphanic theory of art. Rather, what accompanies *Murphy* as an enabling framework, providing it with some provisional means of discursive legitimation, is more a piece of mock metaphysics, a hand-me-down philosophic patchwork used to hold *Murphy* together from within, but which, by so doing, has the effect of almost unravelling it. This is the much-glossed sixth chapter, the one giving a farcical topological exposition of Murphy's mind which is often taken as a summary view of the author's philosophical ideas and a conceptual key to the text. But what is less usually highlighted is how the chapter is organised as an analogue of the novel as a whole, indeed as a *mise en abyme* of its various levels of purgatorial movement.

The argument of the sixth chapter is aesthetic, not philosophic, figurative, not conceptual. The description of Murphy's mind is proposed as a fiction concerned not with 'this apparatus as it really was – that would be an extravagance and an impertinence – but solely with what it felt and pictured itself to be' (76). The comment sets the chapter up as a representation of a representation, and the chapter as a whole is strategically placed at the mid-point of the novel's thirteen chapters (it is this off-centre position which signals the chapter as a *mise en abyme*).[12]

As a pivotal model of the whole novel, the chapter has an explanatory function, with regard to what precedes, and a predictive one, in respect of what follows. The ternary structure of Murphy's mind, divided into the light, the half-light and the dark, recalls the limping dialectic of purgatorial rhetoric oscillating between extremes of contrast and finding resolution, or, more accurately, dissolution, in the third zone, characterised by indeterminate mingling, in which identity is lost and stability yields to uncontrollable motion. (The diagram is complicated only by the fact that Beckett poses the light and half-light as opposites, allowing the dark, appropriately enough in symbolic terms, to enact the demonic 'becoming and crumbling' [79] of forms.)

It is clear from the fact that Beckett draws his examples from his own fiction that what these three zones can be seen to identify are the three layers of the aesthetic process set out in the critical essays: first, the novel's rejection of the reality of social convention: Murphy toying with the vengeful idea of having Ticklepenny rape Miss Carridge; second, the autonomy of writing as a exploration of imaginary forms: the world of Murphy's 'Belacqua bliss' (78); and, finally, writing as exposure to the disintegration of meaning: dissolution as 'the ceaseless unconditioned generation and passing away of line' (79). *Murphy* ends with a strong sense of the precarious nature of writing as such. If Beckett set out, perhaps like Neary, with the hope of creating some order from the many dichotomies existing in his voice or of containing the pressure that was at the heart of life, it was to discover, like Murphy, that the circle of purgatory would always have the last laugh, but that if, as Murphy's law seems to suggest, everything that might go wrong always would go wrong, then the only solution was to erect that law into a rhetoric and, therefore, an aesthetic.

2

THE LOSS OF SPECIES

God is a witness that cannot be sworn.

Watt

The outbreak of the Second World War found Beckett hurrying back to France. As an expatriate, but also while in internal exile in Vichy France, Beckett, in English, wrote what was to be his second novel, *Watt*.[1] Like *Murphy*, it is a novel which probes the precarious foundations of meaning by showing clarity and stability to be provisional effects of a larger network of inconsequence, arbitrary coincidence and self-defeating discontinuity. But in *Watt*, these ironies are no longer held in place by the recourse to a series of meticulously organised plot events or by an allusive repertoire of pseudo-philosophical comic themes. Instead, mixing disjointed burlesque with mock allegory, pastiche *Bildungsroman* with nit-picking satire, *Watt* is held together more by stylistic excess than by the interests of story. The language of the novel, exhaustive, repetitive, and obsessional, but given to moments of wild intensity, cuts across the book's already half-hearted concessions to narrative continuity and turns it into a rhapsodic patchwork papering uneasily over the cracks of internal disorder.

The novel's dogged exposition of logical and linguistic puzzles and its seemingly endless permutations of terms and hypotheses have mobilised the attention of most readers of the text.[2] It quickly becomes clear that the book's pedantic, hair-splitting elucidation of the seemingly obvious is in the service of more than hyperbolic overstatement or the playing with conventions. *Watt* unfolds as an intricate cartography of language, a fictional inquiry into what constitutes the foundations of language and the real world, language and human subjectivity. In order to uncover what is at stake in the novel, the first task is to plot the impact and source of *Watt*'s obsessional energy and to attempt to retrace the affective drama which lurks behind or, more accurately, within the novel's turbulent surface rhetoric.

Fairly rapidly, in reading *Watt*, three events, all in the second chapter, take on paradigmatic significance. These are the episodes of the visit of the Gall family to Knott's house, the vexed question of Knott's pot, and the problem of the dog to whom Watt is instructed to feed Knott's leftovers (whenever there are leftovers to be left over). In these events, Watt is confronted with a number of logical and verbal conundrums, all of which reveal problematical aspects of the relationship between language and reality.

Each of the three puzzles that Watt attempts to tackle concerns a different axis of the relations between signs and objects. The first, the visit of the Galls, father and son, finds Watt playing at being a receiver of information in a communicational dyad. At issue is the capacity of Watt as a human subject to articulate, in the form of a stable memory trace, an event he has supposedly witnessed. The cornerstone of experience, however, with its reliance on memory and intelligibility, proves unequal to the task and the remembered event resists Watt's efforts to represent it for himself in his mind. He thus fails to acquire any mastery over it. But the coming of the Galls was not unique in Knott's house, the narrator informs the reader. It was typical of many other incidents

in the sense that it was not ended, when it was past, but continued to unfold, in Watt's head, from beginning to end, over and over again, the complex connexions of its lights and shadows, the passing from silence to sound and from sound to silence, the stillness before the movement and the stillness after, the quickenings and retardings, the approaches and the separations, all the shifting detail of its march and ordinance, according to the irrevocable caprice of its taking place. (69)

In terms of Watt's position in language, what has changed here is not so much the referential dimension of the visit, for Watt remains persuaded that something happened, even if that something is in fact 'a nothing' (77). Rather, the 'outer meaning' of the visit falls prey to 'fragility' (70), and Watt's memory dissolves into an abstract pattern. It loses its distinctness as a perceptual trace, as the passage quoted above describes. Whatever it was that took place is swallowed up into an incident 'of great formal brilliance and indeterminable purport' (71).

This figure of indifference or indeterminacy intervenes here to strategic effect. In *Murphy*, the structure it presents is one of contrasts collapsing and of apparently stable units dividing against themselves. In Watt's case, what is dramatised by indifference is

the confusion arising from the loss of difference, and the memory of
the visit, no longer relying on a secure memory trace, fogs in Watt's
mind. But paradoxically, this loss of distinctness comes not from a
lack of difference, but from the uncontrollable turbulence of
difference, from the disorientating interplay of light, dark, sound,
silence, movement and stasis. It is this mobility which defeats
Watt's attempts to 'exorcize' (75) the memory of the Galls. That
memory flickers in Watt's mind as though it were another of his
'meticulous phantoms' (74). The whole incident, says the narrator,
'seemed rather to belong to some story heard long before, an
instant in the life of another, ill-told, ill-heard, and more than half
forgotten' (71).

The last phrases recur regularly at important moments in
Beckett's work as a whole, and, suitably varied, turn up in the title
of a late work like *Mal vu mal dit* (*Ill Seen Ill Said*), in 1981. This is
why they require particular attention. What, then, is at stake here
in Beckett's text? Interestingly, the account of the visit of the Galls
is interwoven with a brief series of recollections which come to the
reader as though they, too, told of a rather different Watt from the
character struggling with the enigmas of Knott's house. There are
four of these memories. Watt, the novel says, at first

> could recall, not indeed with any satisfaction, but as ordinary occasions,
> the time when his dead father appeared to him in a wood, with his trousers
> rolled up over his knees and his shoes and socks in his hand; or the time
> when in his surprise at hearing a voice urging him, in terms of unusual
> coarseness, to do away with himself, he narrowly escaped being knocked
> down, by a dray; or the time when alone in a rowing boat, far from land, he
> suddenly smelt flowering currant; or the time when an old lady of delicate
> upbringing, and advantageous person, for she was amputated well above
> the knee, whom he had pursued with his assiduities on no fewer than three
> distinct occasions, unstrapped her wooden leg, and laid aside her crutch.
> (70)

What characterises each of these memories is that they seem
generally safe from the confusion of indeterminacy or indifference.
Here, there is no tendency for Watt's father's legs, say, to dissolve
into incoherence. On the contrary, his father's legs and trousers
remain quite distinctively those of his father (71).

What is to be made of this apparently free textual association
between Watt's dead father and the Galls, and of the narrator's
claim that Watt's father is 'quite different', and not therefore
subject to the 'farce' of indifference? One reason might be that the
contrast between Watt's fate now, in Knott's house, and his

recollections from earlier times, before he arrives, allows Beckett to underline the dramatic effect of Watt's memory loss. But something more seems to be at issue, and this is indicated by Beckett's use, twice over, of this motif of the father. Watt claims that, in his memory, his own father, though dead, retains his identity and difference, while in the case of the Galls, what seems to have happened is that a 'family and professional relation' (69) has lost its coherence for him.

The puzzle of the Galls is the puzzle created for Watt by their family relationship. Beckett writes: 'There was no family likeness between the two, as far as Watt could make out, and nevertheless he knew that he was in the presence of a father and son, for had he not just been told so. Or were they not perhaps merely stepfather and stepson' (67). The question, like many others here, has Biblical overtones (recalling some of the problems of Christ's paternity in the Gospels), and has little chance of being resolved, but this is enough for it to open a large gap in Beckett's fiction. The gap could be described, metaphorically, as the question of the father's name, the question of names as such, both family names and common names, of Watt's own gender identity and his symbolic relationship to the figure of the father (which is the reason for the covert reference to the New Testament).

At stake, then, is Watt's place in language as a subject of filiation, that is, a subject who, as his father's son or heir, is in the position of acceding to subjecthood by incorporating the body and language of his father. This theme of incorporation, like much else in the novel, is treated skittishly as well as solemnly. What is revealed is how incorporation in Beckett's text turns into a botched fiasco, a failed act in both symbolic and physical terms.[3] In *Watt*, the theme of incorporation occurs in many guises. It is the subject of a perplexing joke, for example, in MacKenzie's letter to Mr Spiro, as to whether or not a rat eating a consecrated wafer ingests 'the Real Body' (26). By way of a response Spiro offers a lengthy commentary based on ecclesiastic tradition but fails to provide an answer. The implication is that words merely serve to defer the question. They have no solution to what is an unanswerable conundrum. Via theology, incorporation is related to the eucharist and the motif of crucifixion, with Christ having to incorporate a non-human father and being rewarded on the cross by the offer not of bread, but sour wine. The motif of crucifixion is evoked in turn in Sam's depiction of Watt coming through the garden fence (157), or apropos of Watt's amorous dealings with Mrs Gorman for when

Watt does kiss her he lapses afterwards, the text says, 'into his post-crucified position' (139).

Despite their dispersion through the text, what is common to all these scenes involving themes of incorporation or crucifixion is a deep instability concerning binary contrast. It is not accidental that the canonic example of binary instability in Beckett's work relates to the crucifixion and is contained in Vladimir's account of the two thieves on the cross, one of whom (but which?) was damned and the other saved, according to whichever of the Gospels is believed.[4] In the case of the rat, the source of difficulty is the problematic question of the difference between human and non-human, holy and unholy, consecrated and desecrated. (The possibility of there being no intelligible difference between the holy family and families relying on – botched – sexual reproduction for their survival is floated in the winning answer to Spiro's competition for re-arranging the names of the holy family: the improper – and incorrect – answer: 'Has J. Jurms a po? Yes' [26] – to which there is more than a hint of the pot, or potty. In due course Watt, too, will have to face the conundrum of a pot, or potty.) When Watt turns up looking like 'the Christ believed by Bosch, then hanging in Trafalgar Square' (157), it is the difference between Watt and Sam which becomes blurred and uncertain. As for the scene between Watt and Mrs Gorman, what seems at issue there is the enigma of sexual attraction and the difficulty of determining sexual difference: 'What was this in Mrs Gorman, what this in Watt, that so appealed to Watt, so melted Mrs Gorman?', asks the novel, and it continues:

Between what deeps the call, the counter-call? Between Watt not a man's man and Mrs Gorman not a woman's woman? Between Watt not a woman's man and Mrs Gorman not a man's woman. Between Watt not a man's man and Mrs Gorman not a man's woman? Between Watt not a woman's man and Mrs Gorman not a woman's woman? Between Watt neither a man's nor a woman's man and Mrs Gorman neither a man's nor a woman's woman? In his own vitals, nucleant, he knew them clasped, the men that were not men's, that were not women's men. And Mrs Gorman was doubtless the theatre of a similar conglutination. But that meant nothing. (141)

If we return to the free association between Watt's memory of his father and the event of the Galls, similar stresses are at work, with the precarious character of difference fomenting panic and confusion in Watt's mind. The memory of the smell of flowering currant in the rowing-boat is a memory of disturbance, hallucination and personality loss (in *Krapp's Last Tape*, some ten years later, the reference is to a punt and gooseberries, the latter having scratched Krapp's girlfriend's thigh like a mark of sexual otherness and impending loss, while the narrator in *L'Innommable* counters to the effect that: 'l'amour je l'ai inventé, la musique, l'odeur du groseiller sauvage, pour m'éviter').[5] The memory of almost being run down by the dray leaves it unsaid whether the voice was Watt's or belonged to the driver; and Watt's memory of Mrs Watson, as she is later named (meaning: son of Watt, or, more likely, by inversion, mother of Watt?), places her as a sexual object who bears her difference as a comic repetition of Watt's own phallic anxiety, being amputated, or castrated, of her phantom member and supplied with an appropriate phallic prosthesis (that it is a 'crutch' leaves neatly suspended the question of what it is she really has where her crotch ought to be).

The contrast, then, between the memories the text claims to be stable and the memory of the Galls is, as one might expect, dubious, if not entirely a red herring. The memories are as uncertain in meaning as the visit of the Galls. The difference, if there is one, is of degree, or rather of attitude on Watt's part. If Watt, earlier, clings to the compromise belief that his father's legs and trousers were somehow 'quite different' (71) from other legs and trousers, he is quickly disabused once he arrives in Knott's house. The prospect Watt faces is that his own identity, however much he may wish it otherwise, cannot be derived from contemplation of his father's nether regions such as his legs and trousers and this lack of distinction or difference, located where his father ought to be, is at the heart of Watt's problems. It is as though from this point on his entire identity, his bodily autonomy, even, is engulfed by a loss of difference which expels him from himself. What the theme of incorporation denotes here is not the possibility of presence, but its removal, its obliteration by bodily fiasco.

(It is worth opening another parenthesis at this point to recall, though in this instance the information seems given only in passing, that, in addition to a 'block hat' [217] from his grandfather, Watt inherits from his father a greatcoat, 'still green here and there', which, having been purchased secondhand 'from a meritorious widow', is already the coat of a dead man, and 'was of such length, that Watt's trousers, which he wore very baggy, in order to conceal the shape of his legs, were hidden by it from view' [216]. Watt's father's coat serves precisely to obscure that part of himself Watt remembered earlier as his father's most distinctive personal trait. Were his father's legs and trousers also hidden? Why is the distinguishing factor of Watt's father annulled in this way?

This story of the paternal greatcoat is a long-running saga in Beckett's texts. It recurs throughout Beckett's writing as a coded memento of the father's death, some of the recurrences of which are worth plotting here, if only briefly. For if Beckett's text is a labyrinth, allusions like this serve as intricate threads allowing the reader to chart a course through the writing. After the passage from *Watt*, the next installment in the story occurs in 'Le Calmant': 'Je portais mon grand manteau vert avec col en velours, genre manteau d'automobiliste 1900, celui de mon père, mais il n'avait plus de manches ce jour-là, ce n'était plus qu'une vaste cape. Mais c'était toujours sur moi le même grand poids mort, sans chaleur, et les basques balayaient la terre, la râclaient plutôt, tant elles avaient raidi, tant j'avais rapetissé.' The symbolic implication of such a 'great dead weight', pressing down onto the son's body and encasing it in stiffness, hardly need spelling out. *Malone meurt* continues this tale of a coat apropos of Sapo–Macmann: 'c'est le manteau surtout qui est remarquable, en ce sens qu'il le recouvre et le soustrait aux regards. Car il est si bien boutonné, de haut en bas, au moyen d'une quinzaine de boutons au bas mot, éloignés les uns des autres de trois à quatre pouces au plus, qu'il ne laisse rien paraître de ce qui se passe à l'intérieur. [...] Maintenant pour ce qui est de la couleur, car la couleur est elle aussi une chose importante, on a beau le nier, tout ce qu'on peut en dire c'est que le vert y prédomine.' 'From an Abandoned Work' is the next episode to appear: 'I could never bear the long coat, flapping about my legs,' complains the narrator, 'or rather one day suddenly I turned against it, a sudden violent dislike.'

Some years later, *That Time* returns to the scene: 'was your mother ah for God's sake all gone long ago all dust the lot you the last huddled up on the slab in the old green greatcoat with your arms round you whose else hugging you for a bit of warmth'. *Company* joins in, with its memory of 'Father's shade [...] Topcoat once green stiff with age and grime from chin to insteps'. So, too, *Mal vu mal dit* with its description one of the text's twelve witnesses – or apostles – anthologising in the process the allusion to Memnon in the passage from *Malone meurt*: 'Les faits sont si anciens. Vers les douze donc l'œil veuf faute de mieux. N'importe lequel. Il se dresse au loin de face face au couchant. Manteau sombre jusqu'à terre. Chapeau bombé du temps jadis. Enfin le visage frappé de front par les derniers rayons. Grossir et dévorer vite avant qu'il fasse nuit.'[6])

Between the memory of Watt's dead father and the Galls, tipping

Watt into amnesic confusion, stands a fundamental event, Watt's arrival at Knott's house. What seems to be implied is that the figure of Knott has the effect on Watt of demolishing the already fragile structure of his identity as a subject of filiation. Knott, as it were, usurps and cancels out the memory of Watt's dead father. Readers of the novel have often referred to Knott, as Ruby Cohn puts it, as 'a vague deity figure', a patriarch, even, who functions as a mysterious legislator with total authority over Watt.[7] (In turn, Watt himself, who drinks only milk and walks with a characteristic 'funambulistic stagger' [29], is like a child, still learning to smile and make himself understood. His first mention in the novel, like some newborn thing with his umbilical cord still dangling from him, is as 'a parcel, a carpet for example, or a roll of tarpaulin, wrapped up in dark paper and tied about the middle with a cord' [14].) And if Knott does usurp the position of the dead father, the effect is not to provide Watt with a clearer identity. Rather Watt is engulfed by Knott's presence and denied his remaining bearings and semantic signposts.

If Knott is a figure of paternal indifference, engulfment and indeterminacy, apathy and invisibility, it follows that his pot is irreducible to the semantic inquiries of his servant. The naming of Knott's pot, the 'famous pot' (84), as a pot, and the impossibility of doing so, is the second conundrum of chapter two. Manifestly, if Knott's role is to engulf in indifference all stable differences on the linguistic and psychological level, then the pot is Knott's most fitting emblem. Its function is to hold the 'mess, or poss' (84), which is Knott's only food, made up of more than three dozen separate ingredients which, mixed together, lose all culinary identity.

If Watt's relationship to his father turns on a failure of incorporation, it becomes clear here how problematic that process has become. For ingesting Knott's foul brew would be more likely to act on Watt as an emetic and force him, regressively, as though he were proceeding backwards, to repeat over and over the act of expulsion that is birth and which already had him tumbling, unbidden and unasking, like a parcel, from the back of a tram. After all, as Arsene had warned him, in a memorable prophecy, 'when you cease to want, then life begins to ram her fish and chips down your gullet until you puke, then the puke down your gullet until you puke the puke, and then the puked puke until you begin to like it' (43). For Arsene, too, 'the poor old lousy old earth', alluded to in one of his most acerbic diatribes, culminates, having exhausted preceding generations, in 'an excrement' (45). As

Malone discovers later, incorporation has as its outcome in Beckett's work anal expulsion or vomiting more often than genuine embodiment, and it is no surprise to find that, in *Premier Amour*, the news of the father's death is met also with much vomiting – of eel soup as it happens – together with intimations of mortality on the narrator's part: 'C'était au mois de décembre, je n'ai jamais eu si froid, la soupe à l'anguille ne passait pas, j'avais peur de mourir, je me suis arrêté pour vomir'.[8] Well may Beckett remark, in his note to the appendix, that 'only fatigue and disgust prevented its incorporation' (247), for that is clearly what is at issue here: the possibility of a form or language in which the spectre of the father can be incorporated. *Watt*, as a novel, as the presence of the Addenda show, is marked in its very structure by this puzzle of failed incorporation.

The ingredients blended in Knott's pot survive, for their part, as a concoction in which differences are erased but whose identity remains, at best, hypothetical. Confusion is found at work at the centre of binary opposition and mixture. The same problem faces Watt as he attempts to name Knott's pot. At issue is the capacity of language to move from the singular to the general, the concrete to the abstract. For Watt the fundamental relation between sign and referent is found to be incommensurable. There seems no way of bridging the gap, and as a result the pot stands poised undecidably between distinctiveness and undistinctiveness, between its identity as a pot and its lack of identity as something which is not quite a pot (78).

The whole scene of the pot is very funny, but the humour is charged with real disquiet. For the gap revealed here between word and object has telling consequences for Watt when he tries to apply words to himself. Watt realises the impossible relationship between himself as an exemplar of the concept 'man' and his existence as a thing of flesh. His own identity suffers from the same indeterminacy as the pot and there begins the crisis described as Watt's 'loss of species' (82).[9] Watt soon realises that his own name is a casualty of indeterminacy. So when he asserts, 'Watt is a man' (79), the statement comes back to him as a question concerning the limits of his own humanity:

As for himself, though he could no longer call it a man, as he had used to do, with the intuition that he was perhaps not talking nonsense, yet he could not imagine what else to call it, if not a man. But Watt's imagination had never been a lively one. So he continued to think of himself as a man, as his mother had taught him, when she said, There's a good little man, or,

There's a bonny little man, or, There's a clever little man. But for all the relief that this afforded him, he might just as well have thought of himself as a box, or an urn. (80)

Watt's identity as a man is bordered and held in place by two things: first, his relation to his mother and the dialectic of recognition sustained by the figure of the mother, and, second, his relation to the non-human, in the shape of the box, or urn, that one day will contain his human remains. To be a man is to be articulated as a difference on the level of gender (in relation to the mother) and species (in relation to death and finitude), and it is when these differences are threatened, as they are here by the indifferent pot, that Watt undergoes a 'loss of species' which is a loss of gender identity as well as a loss of humanity.

Watt's reaction to this loss, however, is paradoxical. It launches him on a quest for the impossible difference which will secure or anchor language, self, or reality. The lesson of Knott's pot, however, is that there is no foundation to the round and rote of words. Words posit as the basis of their intelligibility the system of differences that articulates them as differences. When that system is no longer attached to any figure of stable paternity (and the implication of *Watt* is that no figure of paternity is stable, because it is itself already an effect of the system of language), then there is no longer any reliable term of reference. Watt loses all grasp of what or who he may be. For Watt there is no place, beyond death, where his flesh might coincide with his name or reality with his words. To assure himself of this, Watt undertakes an exhaustive census of Knott's world. To be engulfed by indifference, for Watt, is to be forever careering onwards in the search for some reliable difference, but the quest for difference is itself in turn haunted by the erasure of difference. Extremes meet once more. The endless surveying or production of differences in language converges with the paradoxical movement by which all qualification of meaning becomes a disqualification.

It is largely to chart the possible correspondences between verbal differences and the world outside that Watt sets out to try to establish the existence – or otherwise – of Knott's dog. If no respite is forthcoming on the side of words, perhaps objects will provide some adequate foundation. Accordingly, Watt embarks on an attempt to clarify Knott's instructions regarding the disposal of his leftovers to 'the dog' (87). There is no doubt in Watt's mind about the meaning of the word, nor about its reference to the animal known as dog. But, asks Watt, is 'a dog the same thing as the dog' (93)? Does dog include or exclude a plurality of possible dogs? Beckett's prose splits hairs and refines distinctions over some ten pages. But instead of arriving at a firm anchorage, the novel is forced, to maintain some token credibility, into the extravagantly implausible millenarian fiction of the Lynch family, whose business it is to look after 'the dog'. Knott's instructions, it seems, refer not to a given case, but to an hypothesis. Language and reality, for Watt, fail to coincide, and the clarity of the one reveals only the intractable obscurity of the other. Reality becomes a 'vermicular series' (254) of possibles, and any real object is simply the effect of intersecting series. The appearance of an actual dog, perversely named Kate (i.e. 'cat'), does little to resolve the situation. Rather it projects Watt, and with him Beckett's novel, onto another manic circuit of the logical possibilities. Reality, like language, becomes a closed system, capable of endless permutations, but sustained by no cause outside of its own gyrating movement.

In Knott's house it proves impossible, then, to provide meaning with any external foundation. Names fail, reality lurches into unfounded hypotheses and arbitrary coincidences, Knott's presence erases differences, and Watt loses his identity. Indeterminacy, aporia, indifference, self-defeating contradiction lie in wait for Knott's servant as though according to some obscure plan. Secure meanings are engulfed in a whirl of manic energy, and Knott is the still core of indifference at the centre of the novel, the figure in whom extremes meet and in whom quietism becomes a mode of perpetual motion. 'Nothing changed, in Mr Knott's establishment,' writes Beckett, 'because nothing remained, and nothing came or went, because all was a coming and going' (130).

Watt is more than an ironic vehicle in an epistemological comedy. This is clear from the third chapter. Watt is found living in some sort of institution. He undergoes a physical and linguistic transformation. The second is probably the more spectacular of the two and much attention has been paid to Watt's inverted language games. But the physical changes which come over him are no less critical. Considerable time is spent describing the arbitrary if systematic criteria which regulate the movements of Watt and Sam, the novel's intermittent narrator who is introduced at this point as though to alleviate the text's implausibility but only with the result that it is made even more outlandish.

Watt and Sam are enclosed in their respective gardens, share no common ground and never meet except by coincidence due to an unusual combination of climactic factors. Finally, something scandalous takes place within this world of carefully policed distinctions. A gap appears in the fence in Sam's garden, followed by a similar gap in Watt's garden. Watt turns up dressed back to front and 'advancing backwards' (157). As the fence between them is breached, Sam and Watt contemplate each other as though in a mirror, but the encounter between the narrator and his double is not a reassuring experience for Sam. The reason is in Sam's description of Watt:

His face was bloody, his hand also, and thorns were in his scalp. (His resemblance, at that moment, to the Christ believed by Bosch, then hanging in Trafalgar Square, was so striking, that I remarked it.) And at the same instant suddenly I felt as though I were standing before a great mirror, in which my garden was reflected, and my fence, and I, and the very birds tossing in the wind, so that I looked at my hands, and felt my face, and glossy skull, with an anxiety as real as unfounded. (For if anyone, at that time, could be truly said not to resemble the Christ supposed by Bosch, then hanging in Trafalgar Square, I flatter myself it was I.) (157)

Watt does not provide Sam with a stable image, nor even with a recognisable mirror image of himself. Rather, Watt's image functions as a distorting mirror, and what it reveals to Sam is an image potent enough to elicit from him the same double movement of recognition and refusal that had characterised Watt's own response to his 'loss of species'. What Sam, too, is confronted with (and it is difficult not to read this as a mode of cryptic autobiography on Beckett's part), is, like Watt before him, the margins and limits of his own identity.

What Sam sees is an image of the crucifixion. To this extent, what Watt's image portrays is the traumatic imprint of birth and embodiment. In Beckett's work, crucifixion often serves as a metaphor for birth (readers of Deirdre Bair's biography will recall Beckett himself was born on a Good Friday).[10] Crucifixion dramatises for Beckett the whole process of embodiment and nomination, the being-made-flesh and trying on of names on a recalcitrant body which, like Watt himself, has little alternative than to accept that name. Crucifixion, too, as I suggested earlier, alludes to the – precarious – incorporation of the father as a possible basis for identification. Christ, from Beckett's standpoint, is the son of an impossible father, an impossible son, therefore, who, like Watt at the station, carries only the stigmata of his birth and is stoned for his pains, seemingly without reason.

In close parallel with this metaphor of crucifixion, the crisis of

identity that spreads from one side of the mirror to the other, from
Watt to Sam, is the result of a crisis in filiation. Like Christ, and,
perhaps, Sam, too, Watt is the son of an impossible father. Watt
cannot integrate within himself the law of his descent and find a
home in names. As a result, it is perhaps Watt who, in the famous
phrase in the Addenda, has 'never been properly born' (248), and is
suspended on the threshold of birth, left to envisage it as an
impossible, catastrophic event. (Though if, as J. M. Coetzee
reports, in the MS the phrase originally referred to Knott, then this
explains why Watt fails to incorporate his father, or, when he tries,
why it has such a calamitous outcome.)[11] Birth, for Watt, as it was
for Murphy, is an act which is as unwilled as it is unaccountable, and
it is noticeable that the disjointed opening scenes of the novel,
which mingle the story of Larry's birth, amid much eating and
drinking, with the expulsion of Watt from the tram, dramatise birth
as an act of fantasmatic anal expulsion, engulfing Watt in the
turbulent ambivalence of a situation in which sexual difference is no
sooner articulated than effaced. As Watt is delivered by the tram,
Tetty, having just told of giving birth to Larry, is said to be 'not sure
whether it was a man or a woman' (14). To this extent, Watt, like
most of Beckett's protagonists, is born in an act of violent expulsion
and finds himself unable to accede to any identity as a man, unable
to assume his selfhood by reference either to name or gender.

Watt's bodily transformation is only one aspect of this crisis. Its
more eloquent symptom is Watt's inability, or refusal, to recount to
Sam his meeting with Knott by using a commonly accepted language. Instead, his language, like his body, is turned back to front,
arsy-versy, as Sam puts it. Watt's encounters with Knott turn on the
question of indifference. If Watt's role is to witness, what he must
witness is not Knott's identity and presence, but his elusiveness, his
lack of qualities or distinction. Beckett puts it as follows:

> But what kind of witness was Watt, weak now of eye, hard of hearing,
> and with even the more intimate senses greatly below par?
> A needy witness, an imperfect witness.
> The better to witness, the worse to witness.
> That with his need he might witness its absence.
> That imperfect he might witness it ill.
> That Mr Knott might never cease, but ever almost cease.
> Such appeared to be the arrangement. (202–3)

Knott, Watt had declared earlier, if his words are translated, is
'the source of nought' (164), hardly seen, hardly heard, desired but
absent, almost like a memory of Murphy's Mr Endon. Watt's

description of Knott at this stage, full of yearning and the sense of loss, is a reminder that indifference (in so far as it is the one or the other) is a thing or experience that is desired as much as it is feared. Indifference is a blurring of frontiers and a losing of identity and represents fusion as much as engulfment. It is thus a source of pleasure as well as terror, of the merging of identities as well as the impossibility of separation, and it is no doubt this very ambivalence which is responsible for some of the strangeness and difficulty of Beckett's writing, in particular, for its perverse endorsement of negative states. Indeed, as well as disorientation, a strong sense of underlying identification between Watt and Knott comes to the fore in Watt's cryptic pronouncements to Sam.

The last memory of Knott dictated to Sam by Watt illustrates this. Knott, when first seen by Watt, has his face downcast and 'head bowed down' (144). The motif of the bowed head is one Beckett uses extensively in relation to the figure of the dead father. It spins another thread through the labyrinth to connect with other writings, with *Assez*, for instance, with its enigmatic scenes of companionship between two characters with heads bowed. In 'Au loin un oiseau', Beckett writes: 'il est courbé sur son bâton, je suis dedans, c'est lui qui a crié, lui qui a vu le jour, moi je n'ai pas crié, je n'ai pas vu le jour, les deux mains l'une sur l'autre pèsent sur le bâton, le front pèse sur les mains, il a repris haleine, il peut écouter, le tronc à l'horizontale, les jambes écartées, les genoux fléchis, même vieux manteau, les basques raidies se dressent par derrière, le jour point'. Nowhere is it clear who the third person refers to here, but it seems to be some double who has usurped the narrator's place. The text ends with the narrator declaring: 'il confondra sa mère avec des grues, son père avec un cantonnier nommé Balfe'. Is Balfe a name for the father? In 'From an Abandoned Work' it refers to a gruesome 'roadman': 'the ragged old brute bent double down in the ditch leaning on his spade or whatever it was and leering round and up at me from under the brim of his slouch, the red mouth, how is it I wonder I saw him at all, that is more like it, the day I saw the look I got from Balfe, I went in terror of him as a child. Now he is dead and I resemble him.'[12] Across these compact and enigmatic texts a chain of associations is set up between a bowed figure, the dead father, a gravedigger, and a usurping double. There are here all the elements of a scene of great density and confusion, in which the borders between identification and jealous rivalry become impossible to determine. It is as though all these figures, whoever they are,

somehow have become equivalent to one another within the buried
world of unconscious fantasy that Beckett's text is exploring here.
No moment, no allusion in Beckett's writing is ever gratuitous.
Watt's final memory of Knott is in the form of a palindrome and
succeeds in capturing with both pathos and humour the strange
circularity and impenetrable darkness of indifference both as figure
and as object. It runs as follows and has to be read from right to left,
though spoken from left to right:

Dis yb dis, nem owt. Yad la, tin fo trap. Skin, skin, skin. Od su did ned
taw? On. Taw ot klat tonk? On. Tonk ot klat taw? On. Tonk ta kool taw?
On. Taw ta kool tonk? Nilb, mun, mud. Tin fo trap, yad la. Nem owt dis yb
dis. (166)

This recourse to cryptic language by Beckett to dramatise the
enigmatic content of Watt's meetings with Knott is comical and
disconcerting. Beckett is obviously mocking conventions of narrative structure, clarity of exposition and plausibility. But more
importantly, Watt's turn to cryptic language also raises the question
of Beckett's own writing. What Watt's peculiar idiom does is to
take up words and to invert them according to an arbitrary but
systematic scheme. His new-fangled mode of expression is an
exercise in articulating, cancelling out, and then reinscribing verbal
distinctions. And if they were not reinscribed, by virtue of the
systematic nature of Watt's permutations of ordinary language,
then he would be simply unintelligible for Sam and reader alike.

What is true of Watt is true of Beckett's own practice as a writer.
Beckett dramatises the threat of engulfment by indifference by
multiplying all manner of differences, contrasts, distinctions in his
own text. Indifference becomes an uncontrollable proliferation of
difference. This is a strategy that affects the novel's treatment of
sexual and bodily differences as well as its use of verbal or logical
distinctions which are continually propelled by the novel into
meaninglessness only to be retrieved by the novel as a means of
survival. But as they survive, they do so only in blurred, problematic and unstable fashion.

Watt's backwards language also has another important effect.
For it functions like any cryptic language, both to conceal what is
said and to protect it from the threat of exposure. In his early verse
in the 1930s Beckett was already using elliptical allusions as the
basis for a private, self-protective poetic idiom, and the situation
here is somewhat analogous. Watt's language clearly risks engulfment by the indeterminacy of Knott, and it is symptomatic that

Watt is at one point even mistaken for Knott. Cryptic language acts as a protection against this threat. Yet what Watt's cryptic words to Sam stress is the desire for fusion with Knott. Watt's cryptic language becomes the paradoxical site of profound ambivalence, serving to express the desire for fusion and defend against it as well as enacting the effects of engulfment while holding it at bay.

Watt's inverted words, then, dramatise a deep-seated division in identity, one which was already visible in his ambivalent attitude to his dead father, asserting the difference of his father's nether parts while unable to substantiate that difference. The use of cryptic language to enact this division of the self supposes that within one language various different treatments of language, different idioms, or different voices are able to coexist simultaneously. As a result, not only is the status of language as a common measure of experience severely compromised but language itself splits into a number of simultaneous, though distinct, even opposed, positions of enunciation, each existing independently of the others, while concealing, or encrypting, what cannot be incorporated in the other tongue.

With the recourse to cryptic language, then, *Watt* seems to envisage the possibility of the parallel existence of a plurality of languages, or at least of different layers of language, memory, or speech. Watt, as he speaks in riddles, seems to express the desire for another tongue in which it would be possible to speak something other than what is available in his original language. The self divides, with one idiom, or voice, playing the part of what Abraham and Torok, in their study of Freud's multilingual 'Wolfman', call a pseudo-unconscious, an artificial or alternative self in which words and memories can be preserved, concealed, and perhaps expressed in covert manner, and it is this division which is perhaps at issue in Beckett's preoccupation with the theme of the usurping twin or false brother dramatised in the second 'Foirade' ('J'ai renoncé avant de naître') and 'Au loin un oiseau'.[13]

This awareness of the plurality of language and languages is a critical one, because in 1945 Beckett's writing underwent a major shift in status. After completing, or abandoning *Watt*, Beckett began writing in French. It seems likely, in the first instance, that this shift into French was a result of a growing detachment from Ireland on Beckett's part and reflected a wish to experiment with the language of the country where, on and off, he had now been living for some ten years. It is possible, too, that French seemed a more hospitable cultural idiom for the type of novels Beckett wanted to write. But the adoption of French is not a single, contingent or isolated event in Beckett's work. Another ten years later, the move to French was doubled by a partial return to English, and since 1956, much of Beckett's work for the theatre has been composed in English, while most of his narrative prose has been in French.

The result of these complex interactions between French and English and English and French is twofold. Beckett, who is, after all, an Irish writer, ceases to belong to any single language or cultural tradition, be it English or French. Beckett's work comes, instead, to occupy a strange in-between world, a no man's land lying between languages and national identities, and fascinates rather more for what it does, across its various idioms, than for what it says by means of those idioms. Differences between languages as well as differences in language play a central role in the structure of Beckett's work.

The position is a strange, literally outlandish one. Beckett's literary bilingualism is unlike the conventional bilingualism of the Middle Ages or the Renaissance, when Latin or the vernacular had different hierarchical functions.[14] Similarly, his use of French and English seems to have little in common with the situation in many multilingual cultures where, largely for historical or political reasons, particular languages fulfil specific cultural or social roles. In Beckett's case, beyond the criterion of genre, the pertinence of which is at best intermittent, there is no hierarchical relationship regulating the use of French or English. Beckett writes original texts in both, theatre and prose, and translates into and from both.

In Beckett's case, the relation between languages seems to be more a matter of choice rather than historical necessity (though it might be argued that some of the factors which drove him, like other Irish writers, into exile enter into this second category). For that reason alone his bilingualism is a fundamental component of his writing and not mere accident. For one does not speak, or write, a foreign language with impunity. Language is not an implement that can be exchanged without further implications. As Vladimir Nabokov put it, 'a language is a live physical thing which cannot be so easily dismissed', and he glosses the phrase with the remark that *Lolita*, for him, was something akin to 'a love affair with the English language'. (His portrait of the English language as a voluble nymphet no doubt had something to do with the fact, revealed in *Speak, Memory!*, that Nabokov, in writing English, was reacquiring a language first learnt in early childhood from his English nurse.)[15] As for Beckett, the decision to write in French seems to have corresponded more to a wish, after *Watt*, to dispossess himself: 'A la libération,' he replied to Ludovic Janvier, decorously eschewing the *passé composé*, 'je pus conserver mon appartement, j'y revins, et me remis à écrire – en français – avec le désir de m'appauvrir davantage. C'était ça le vrai mobile.'[16]

The issue of Beckett's bilingualism is usually addressed in terms of Beckett's technical performance as a self-translator. Clearly, however, more is at stake than the question of how Beckett exploits the verbal resources of his two languages. Hugh Kenner identifies some of the problems involved when he remarks that 'between a native language and a language of adoption is a difference not merely of tools but of selves'.[17] As all students of languages know, speaking in a foreign language implies a changed relationship to language. The effect is often substantially to alter the speaker's sense of self. This may be intensely liberating or awkwardly inhibiting. For his part, Kenner, extrapolating from his Cartesian reading of Beckett, claims such modifications to be the result of increased linguistic self-awareness, but this is less convincing, if only because language, as *Watt* shows, affects much more than the surface of consciousness. It permeates the affective and unconscious roots of subjectivity. This is why it is common for students of languages, as Beckett's Belacqua Shuah had done in *More Pricks Than Kicks*, to dream in the foreign language and associate foreign words according to the unconscious logic of condensation and displacement.

There are clearly many differences between acquiring a non-native language and learning one's mother tongue, particularly when, as in Beckett's case, the second language is learnt as an object of academic study, at school and university, rather than as a result of direct immersion. The method of learning, the time taken learning the language, the age, and physical and psychological maturity of the person learning the language, his or her prior awareness of the world and cultural or personal identity, all these factors, and others, too, make the apprenticeship of a non-native language radically different from the primary acquisition of a mother tongue by an infant. The two languages are not symmetrical in status or position. The second language does not replace the first. Rather the second language, especially if learnt (as was most likely the case with Beckett) through the medium of the first, becomes grafted onto the mother tongue, which it supplements, displaces, extends, complicates, usually entangles. (And there is evidence in the Gallicisms dotted through *Watt* that some of the pressure on Beckett's English comes from interference from French.)

What is crucial is that, though the person speaking the two languages may be the same, the subject learning the second language is not identical to the subject who acquired the first. The position of the speaker changes, and the split between languages also becomes a split between positions of subjectivity. In other words, when a non-native speaker takes up the adopted language, his or her subjectivity is remodelled. The relation between the two positions of subjectivity is usually one of variation. While the deep-seated structures of the personality probably remain constant, they are usually dramatised in a different way, and verbal behaviour is often changed as a result. It may happen, as is suggested by Watt's recourse to cryptic language, that one language speaks more readily of matters to which the other tongue has little access. The self is released from the pressure for homogeneity or unity and bilingualism becomes an experience not just of the differences between languages and how they represent or construct the world differently, but also of the mobility within language as such.[18]

The non-native speaker, then, talks in the first person but speaks with a different voice. Beckett's position as a bilingual writer may be described in these terms. To begin writing in a non-native language is to abandon a whole repertoire of verbal strategies first elaborated in the mother tongue and thus almost to be faced with some of the difficulties experienced by Watt in the presence of Mr Knott. The problem is especially acute for a writer since, unlike the non-native speaker, he or she cannot rely on the pragmatic context of verbal interaction with the audience. (Beckett himself seems almost to have sought out this difficulty on purpose, and began writing *Molloy*, for instance, in French, while still in Ireland.) These are no doubt the reasons why, for Beckett, the move into French is usually thematised as dispossession.

But in contrast to Watt, except for his use of cryptic language in addressing Sam – and it is here that the parallel between Watt's back-to-front speech and Beckett's French becomes more interesting – Beckett's losses are harnessed to the production of language. This is why Beckett's abandonment of his mother tongue is as much a liberation as a renunciation. It is a discovery of a new language and of a new position in language. Dispossessed of the familial intimacy or security of his native language, Beckett is rewritten into a language to which he is no longer bound by filial obedience. Consequently, in French, areas of experience become potentially accessible to him which were not previously available in English.

Recently, some accounts of Beckett's work have sought to establish a link between his abandonment of English in 1945 and his ambivalent relationship with his mother.[19] This seems unduly reductive. What the shift into French achieves for Beckett is, more broadly, the creation of productive distance or difference between his writing and the stresses at work in *Watt*. Beckett's position in French is a purely verbal one. In French, Beckett is anonymous. He has no birth certificate in the language, no identity outside of the words themselves. He exists as an effect of words, as a fictitious entity, whose relationship to language is shifting or indeterminate. The link between himself and the difficult matrix of his own birth is secret, cryptic, known only to himself. French words create that distance, protecting and conserving Beckett's desire to write from the threat of engulfment.

But distance is only part of a more complex dialectic. As Beckett the bilingual writer is written into French as a displaced person, he is forced to confront there, once again, the event of birth. To wish to be reborn, into another language, into the words of others, as another, does not allow Beckett simply to annul his genealogy. Incorporating a foreign language does not resolve the enigma of birth. Rather, in the foreign tongue, Beckett is obliged to re-enact and repeat the process of birth itself and reinscribe, albeit from a different position, the confrontation with language and birth as such. Beckett's emancipation from English is a submission to French, and his self-expulsion from the mother tongue a re-enactment of birth itself.

Distance here becomes proximity, and it is no surprise that when Beckett turns to French he also turns unreservedly to the use of the first person. The French language functions here as a cryptic idiom which allows Beckett to articulate a new position in language and a new relation to fiction. There is clear evidence of this new turn in Beckett's work in the first texts written in his adopted language, his four *Nouvelles*, 'Premier Amour', 'L'Expulsé', 'Le Calmant' and 'La Fin'. What is immediately striking about all these stories is the reinvestment of narrative by a string of compelling subjective fantasies: from scenes of violent expulsion to descriptions of metaphoric spaces of confinement telling of both birth and death. Imaginary landscapes are constructed as though they were memories of Ireland, but made unreal, turned into landscapes of writing with no other existence than their precarious uncertainty as figments of alien words. In their enactment of Beckett's position in French as a writer born into otherness, they indicate the possibility of a new departure.

3

THE TRILOGY TRANSLATED

C'est pour l'ensemble qu'il ne semble pas exister de grimoire.
Peut-être qu'il n'y a pas d'ensemble, sinon posthume.

Molloy

Beckett's post-war trilogy – *Molloy*, *Malone meurt*, and *L'Innom-mable* – has its beginnings in a mode of writing akin to that first attempted in the *Nouvelles*.[1] But although written in French and in the first person, the novels do not rest unproblematically in Beckett's adopted language. There is an unmistakable sense of unbelonging, contained, for instance, in the trilogy's bog-filled landscapes and its occasional mentions of shillings and pence. But Beckett's status as a non-French author is perhaps most clearly marked in the Irish names used in the titles as well as elsewhere in the trilogy. Though composed in one language, French, the novels gesture towards another, Anglo-Irish, and it is far from evident, in the original text, even how some of the names of the characters are to be pronounced.

These references to Ireland are emblematic of the hybrid status of Beckett's trilogy as a whole. Though they function as a source of familiarity for the author or as referential clues for the English-speaking reader, they serve in the original French more as an indi-cation of the author's eccentric relationship to the language in which the trilogy was written. Though foreign in that it speaks a strange language, Beckett's text adopts that language to speak of something deeply familiar, as Eoin O'Brien's recent research into *The Beckett Country* has begun to show.[2] The paradox works according to the chiastic model of much of Beckett's earlier writing. It resembles the structure of what Freud identifies as that of the *unheimlich*, or 'uncanny', meaning something close to home, but which has been expelled or repressed, and returns like an alien ghost to haunt the present. Freud adds that there seems to be an almost privileged relationship between the *unheimlich* and the literary text.[3]

These disturbances in linguistic context are significant. They raise questions of what speech community Beckett's novels are addressing, to what idiom they belong, public and private, and what tradition they invoke. Certain crucial interpretative decisions must be deferred as a result. *Molloy*, on one reading, tells, in French, of an unnamed Irishman, a writer perhaps, who explains to his readers that 'da, dans ma région, veut dire papa' (I, 23), makes sardonic remarks about 'l'Irish Stew' (I, 151), and is compelled to narrate his life within words not his own. Alternatively and simultaneously, the novel is also an account of how an anonymous, French-speaking narrator struggles to come to terms with the pseudo-Irish world that haunts him even though it seems to belong to someone else.

The status of Beckett's trilogy as an object of reading is far from settled. But it is unusual in literature not only for being composed in a non-native language. Though written in French, seemingly more as a result of private deliberation than by pressure of circumstance, Beckett's three novels had, within ten years of their composition, acquired their own uncanny doubles or ghosts in the shape of the author's own English translations. The text of the trilogy exists not once, therefore, but twice. Reading the trilogy becomes doubly problematic. Not only can no stable national identity or idiom be attributed to its narrator (and author, too), but the work itself loses its unity as a single body of text. The trilogy divides into two, and readers are faced with two competing versions, each with equal claim to authenticity or legitimacy.

Translations of texts are usually accorded secondary status to the texts they translate. This is not always the case, and some translations, like, say, Hölderlin's versions of Sophocles, have in their own language earned the status of original works in their own right. Beckett's self-translations arguably fall into the same category. But, in Beckett's case, the fusing together of the roles of translator and author in the same person has curious consequences. As Brian Fitch points out, the conditions of reception of the trilogy are altered, and the usual hierarchical relationship between original and translation no longer holds.[4] There are no compelling reasons, for instance, why Beckett's English translations (or his French versions of English texts) should not be read as autonomous works in their own right (as they are by the vast majority of Beckett's monolingual readers). The chronological precedence of the French text of the trilogy is not, in itself, sufficient justification for treating the French as a more accurate or faithful version than its English

counterpart, just as the fact that the English translation was done
later does not constitute grounds for considering it as more defini-
tive than its predecessor. The existence of the later English translations does, however,
clearly change the status of the original French. From the moment
that the name Samuel Beckett signs two non-identical texts both
entitled *Molloy*, neither of those texts can claim to be unique. So it
is with the French *Molloy*. With the existence of the English
Molloy, the French original becomes incomplete, provisional. (The
incompletion is structural, and does not imply any judgement as to
the relative literary qualities of the two texts.) The English version,
in turn, is similarly affected. It is dependent, parasitic even, on the
earlier French text, and though it may incorporate what seem to be
textual changes, these have no direct relevance for the earlier text,
which is written in a different language. The changes made in the
English version (minor cuts, additions, apparent shifts in phrasing)
become variations on the text of the trilogy, not improvements.
Beckett's trilogy does not have a single verifiable text. That text is
plural, and the effect of this, as the work of recent critics has shown,
is to transform Beckett's writing as a whole into a complex fabric of
variations running backwards and forwards from French into
English and English into French.[5] Rather like a myth or legend, the
trilogy exists and survives as the sum of its own differences and
variants.

The question of translation is central to Beckett's work. It exists
not in isolation from Beckett's creative writing, however, but as a
constant component or circumstance of the writing. Already in the
early work, as the story 'Dante and the Lobster' shows, Beckett
was drawing on the linguistic and literary knowledge he had
acquired as a student of Romance languages. Later, too, Beckett's
French prose displays its own academic beginnings in a number of
humorous and self-conscious ways. When, for instance, in *Molloy*,
he writes: 'J'approchai un fauteuil d'une chaise, m'assis dans
celui-là, posai sur celle-ci ma jambe raide' (I, 56), what Beckett is
doing, amongst other things, is offering the reader a textbook
illustration of the different prepositions to be used with 'fauteuil'
('easy chair') and 'chaise' ('pouffe'). Similarly, when he jokes that
'ça fait du bien de changer de merde, d'aller dans une merde un peu
plus loin, de temps en temps, de papillonner quoi, comme si l'on
était éphémère' (I, 61), what Beckett's text evokes, by feigning to
ignore them, are the no doubt lengthy explanations once given in
the classroom as to the important distinctions to be made between

these two closely related terms, 'papillon' ('butterfly') and 'éphémère' ('mayfly').

In this way, it is difficult to see how one might separate Beckett's relationship with French from the question of translation. Trained as a linguist at school and university, no doubt by old-fashioned academic methods, Beckett most likely owed much of his initial expertise in French to learning the language by translation exercises. For Beckett, as for others of his generation, to learn French was first of all to learn to translate French. Throughout the 1930s, as a result, Beckett went on to work, intermittently, as a translator, undertaking, among other less memorable commissions (in collaboration with Alfred Péron) a French version of Joyce's 'Anna Livia Plurabelle' (from *Finnegans Wake*). In addition, when he began original work in French after the war, Beckett already had behind him, as a first experience or trial run, the French translation of *Murphy* (which was begun with Alfred Péron).[6]

In this way, when Beckett began writing in French in 1945, his proficiency in French was probably due as much to his experience as a translator, both academic and professional, as to his direct cohabitation with the language during his years of residence in France. This is reflected in the ludic awareness of rhetorical conventions and formal rules which characterises much of Beckett's French prose. The calculated shifts in register, the use of repetition, puns and esoteric allusions, the manipulation of standard word order, even the self-conscious demonstration of grammatical constructions, these are all aspects of Beckett's French which show the effects of approaching language from the perspective of translation. They are consistent with an experience of language in which making statements is less important that knowing how meaning changes when words change, and where the ability to express ideas is less crucial than observing the twists and turns of meaning which take place within a given language as well as in the move from one language to another. For a translator, language is not a vehicle for ideas, it is a fabric of verbal differences, a network of localities which does not embody a totalising or all-encompassing project but segments and articulates reality in discontinuous ways.

In Beckett's case, then, to begin writing in French was to begin writing against a background of translation. This does not just apply to the French text. For it was via translation that the trilogy also made its appearance in English, by Beckett's reworking of his own Anglo-Irish. It is impossible to distinguish in any reliable way between Beckett the translator and Beckett the original writer. The issue of translation inhabits the trilogy from the outset. The translation of the trilogy into English is not an unimportant accident, it is more a direct consequence of the writing of the trilogy. Beckett's trilogy shares with translation as such a fundamental condition of existence. That condition is the post-Babelian dilemma of the multiplicity of tongues. It is the multiplicity of tongues which makes it possible not only for Beckett to write in a language not his own but also to translate from that language into his own native language. Translation, like the trilogy itself, implies the knowledge that there is no universal idiom for speech, and that all language is multiple as well as provisional.

This is one reason why Beckett's practice as a translator merits particular consideration for what it reveals about the trilogy. It is sometimes suggested that Beckett's position as self-translator is different from that of other literary translators. To an extent this is true. Beckett has more apparent control over his text than a translator producing a version of a classic text. A lapse or error will be more readily construed by Beckett's readers as a revision or improvement. But the convention also works to Beckett's disadvantage. As his freedom is greater, so is his responsibility towards his text. For while there are numerous English versions of, say, *Madame Bovary*, one can safely assume there will be only one English translation of *Molloy*, the one done by Beckett himself (though, if for different reasons, the case is in fact much the same with the vast majority of contemporary translations). For all that, Beckett's actual position as translator is little different from that of any other translator. In principle, the task is the same, that of transposing, without perceptible loss, a set of meanings, rhythms, connotations, rhetorical effects, and much else besides, from one language system to another. Beckett may be thought to have more direct access to the original intentions of the author (i.e. himself), but it is debatable whether knowing these (if they exist, and in a form that can be adequately reconstructed) is much help in the matter. Translation is not an exercise in expressing thoughts but in handling words. To that extent, it is far from clear how Beckett enjoys any real advantages over any other conscientious translator.

Inevitably, though, Beckett's role as self-translator is to provide, in a different language, a reading of his own text, in the knowledge that that reading will be received by the audience as an authoritative one. Beckett's translating strategy needs to be examined in this light. To this end I reproduce here the two versions of the same passage, selected more or less at random from *Malone meurt*:

Mais j'ai tant senti de choses bizarres et sans fondement assurément qu'il vaudrait mieux peut-être les taire. Parler par exemple de ces périodes où je me liquéfie et passe à l'état de boue, à quoi cela servirait-il? Ou des autres où je me noierais dans le chas d'une aiguille, tellement je me suis durci et ramassé? Non, ce sont là d'aimables tentatives mais qui ne changent rien à l'affaire. Je parlais donc de mes petites distractions et allais dire je crois que je ferais mieux de m'en contenter au lieu de me lancer dans ces histoires à crever debout de vie et de mort, si c'est bien de cela qu'il est question, et je suppose que oui, car il n'a jamais été question d'autre chose, à mon souvenir. Mais dire de quoi il retourne exactement, j'en serais bien incapable, à présent. C'est vague, la vie et la mort. J'ai dû avoir ma petite idée, quand j'ai commencé, sinon je n'aurais pas commencé, je me serais tenu tranquille, j'aurais continué tranquillement à m'ennuyer ferme, en faisant joujou, avec les cônes et cylindres par exemple, avec les grains du millet des oiseaux et autres panics, en attendant qu'on veuille bien venir prendre mes mesures. Mais elle m'est sortie de la tête, ma petite idée. Qu'à cela ne tienne, je viens d'en avoir une autre. C'est peut-être la même, les idées se ressemblent tellement, quand on les connaît. Naître, voilà mon idée à présent, c'est-à-dire vivre le temps de savoir ce que c'est que le gaz carbonique libre, puis remercier. Ça a toujours été mon rêve au fond. Toutes les choses qui ont toujours été mon rêve au fond. Tant de cordes et jamais une flèche. Pas besoin de mémoire. Oui, voilà, je suis un vieux fœtus à présent, chenu et impotent, ma mère n'en peut plus, je l'ai pourrie, elle est morte, elle va accoucher par voie de gangrène, papa aussi peut-être est de la fête, je déboucherai vagissant en plein ossuaire, d'ailleurs je ne vagirai point, pas la peine. Que d'histoires je me suis racontées, accroché au moisi, en enflant, enflant. En me disant, Ça y est, je la tiens ma légende. (*Malone meurt*, 93–4)

Malone meurt was first published in Paris in 1951. Five years later Beckett's English version, *Malone Dies*, appeared. The passage cited above is given as follows:

But I have felt so many strange things, so many baseless things assuredly, that they are perhaps better left unsaid. To speak for example of the times when I go liquid and become like mud, what good would that do? Or of the others when I would be lost in the eye of a needle, I am so hard and contracted? No, those are well-meaning squirms that get me nowhere. I was speaking then was I not of my little pastimes and I think about to say that I ought to content myself with them, instead of launching forth on all this ballsaching poppycock about life and death, if that is what it is all about, and I suppose it is, for nothing was ever about anything else to the best of my recollection. But what it is all about exactly I could no more say, at the present moment, than take up my bed and walk. It's vague, life and death. I must have had my little private idea on the subject when I began, otherwise I would not have begun, I would have held my peace, I would have gone on peacefully being bored to howls, having my little fun and games with the cones and cylinders, the millet grains beloved of birds and other panics, until someone was kind enough to come and coffin me. But it is gone clean out of my head, my little private idea. No matter, I have just had another. Perhaps it is the same one back again, ideas are so alike, when you get to know them. Be born, that's the brainwave now, that is to say live long enough to get acquainted with free carbonic gas, then say thanks for the nice time and go. That has always been my dream at bottom, all the things that have always been my dream at bottom, so many strings and never a shaft. Yes, an old foetus, that's what I am now, hoar and impotent, mother is done for, I've rotted her, she'll drop me with the help of gangrene, perhaps papa is at the party too, I'll land head-foremost mewling in the charnel-house, not that I'll mewl, not worth it. All the stories I've told myself, clinging to the putrid mucus, and swelling, swelling, saying, Got it at last, my legend. (225–6)

There are dangers in generalising from any sample as brief as this. Translation is a perpetual testing out of linguistic possibilities, resistances and effects and it is far from self-evident that Beckett's practice as a self-translator can be reduced to a single uniform strategy. Beckett's practice does change from text to text, according to chance and circumstance. Notwithstanding these reservations, a number of observations can be made about the treatment of the passage from *Malone meurt* given above. The first relate to the divergences in the texts. Beckett makes two cuts from the French ('Pas besoin de mémoire' and, referring to the narrator's mother, the phrase, 'elle est morte'). The reasons for these excisions are unclear, though they may be rhetorical rather than to do with content, with the author, in the second instance, wanting to avoid repeating what is already implicit (in English) in the statement, 'mother is done for' ('ma mère n'en peut plus'). On the other hand, there are occasions when Beckett reworks his text. As critics have pointed out in the past, Beckett often does this in order to make ironically literal use of English idioms or to inject into the text a note of self-reflexive humour, or, at times, to reinvent forgotten words. Translation then becomes an exercise in disruption rather than transposition. Tone is something which often varies from one text to another. Thus, in *Malone Dies*, the sentence, 'what it is all about exactly I could no more say [. . .] than *take up my bed and walk*', or the reference to 'being bored *to howls*', neither of which is present as such in the French. In other instances, Beckett does something analogous and modifies, or interprets, his text in order to be more explicit. Thus, for 'tentatives' he offers 'squirms', and for 'accroché au moisi', the more emphatic and specific 'clinging to the putrid mucus'.

Against such gains as these last few must be set certain losses. Some of these are the result of inherent differences in the target language. Thus, while in French 'naître' is an active verb, to 'be born' is a passive one, and the narrator's phrase 'be born, that's the brainwave now' inevitably suffers as a result (and its awkwardness is increased, if anything, by the clumsiness – perhaps intended – of 'that's the brainwave now'). Similarly, 'until *someone* was kind enough to come' is more personalised, and arguably less effective, than the corresponding French, 'en attendant qu'on veuille bien venir'. In some instances Beckett's French text proves quite troublesome to translate and the author has to find a way of rendering the wordplay of 'ces histoires à crever debout' (a joke on the idiomatic 'à dormir debout') and comes up with the suitably punning, but less fluent solution, 'all this ballsaching poppycock'. Similarly, when Beckett does not find a direct equivalent for the ironically literal 'je déboucherai vagissant en plein ossuaire', he resorts to the evocative, but less precise and inelegant 'I'll land head-foremost mewling in the charnel-house'. In turn, the phrase 'she'll drop me with the help of gangrene' seems to lose the force of the original 'elle va accoucher par voie de gangrène', that might have been rendered more compactly, if more elliptically, as *'she'll give birth to me by gangrene' (on the model of 'by forceps', or 'by Caesarean section').

At other times, the translation is surprisingly literal in its account of French idioms. Thus Beckett renders 'papa aussi est peut-être de la fête' as 'perhaps papa is at the party, too', rather than, say, *'perhaps papa is joining in, too'. 'J'ai dû avoir ma petite idée' appears as 'I must have had my little private idea on the subject' instead of, say, *'I must have had something at the back of my mind'. This faithfulness to the French text occasionally extends to word order, and the sentence: 'Or of the others when I would be lost in the eye of a needle, I am so hard and contracted?', unless it be an Irishism, is quite untypical of standard usage. But this disregard for the norm can have creative rather than aberrant results, and one is reminded of Beckett's comic use of Gallicisms in English, as in the famous instance of Mr Nixon's 'facultative stop' in *Watt* (17).

There are numerous other divergences, of course, which have to
do with the differing rhetorical conventions, speech patterns, and
connotations of individual words in French and English. The
French 'impotent', for instance, meaning 'crippled' or 'helpless',
does not have the same immediate sexual implications as the
English 'impotent' (French reserves those for 'impuissant'), and
this difference is sufficient, one might argue, to change the emphasis of the passage. Translation, of course, is not an exact operation,
but a constant, never final, exploration of the similarities and
differences between languages, a testing out of cultural borders and
verbal margins which can never claim a position of truth or clarity
outside one or the other of the languages being used. Though, in
principle, translation is always possible between languages, untrans-
latability, as any practising translator knows, haunts the process
like a perpetual nightmare. And translation only succeeds, paradoxically, by effacing that upon which it depends as its condition of
existence: the otherness or difference of the source text.

   One complaint that is often levelled at a translation is that the
translator has clung too closely to the idioms and word forms of the
source language and that the result is nonsense. Conversely,
though perhaps more commonly, translations are often criticised
for departing from the original text, and substituting for it a
disrespectful copy which treats the source text more like a parasite
does its host than a faithful servant its master. Such excessive
freedom, charges Nabokov, often the result, as he puts it, of
'omissions and additions prompted by the exigencies of form, the
conventions attributed to the consumer, and the translator's ignorance',[7] can be the undoing of many foreign texts which, when
translated, are thus naturalised out of recognition. Translation,
then, is a hazardous undertaking, and any final version the result of
a compromise. There is no such thing as a canonic translation
beyond challenge. Even Beckett's translations, which are usually
viewed as authoritative (but more because of the translator's name
than his skill or proficiency), could always have been different from
what they are and it is always possible to conceive of alternative
translations of Beckett's texts. The act of translation needs therefore to be understood not as a process of unproblematic transmission, dedicated to the recovery of original, essential meanings,
but as a rewriting of the original, a regulated transformation which
recasts the original as a different text. In Beckett's case, translation
is a work which entertains a strangely chiastic relationship with the
original writing: same but different, different but same.

The question then is not: how does Beckett improve his text or clarify his meaning in translation? but rather: how does Beckett write differently across his other language of composition? The evidence of the extract from *Malone meurt* reproduced above suggests that Beckett's translation of the trilogy is a good deal less spectacular in its effects than is sometimes claimed by selective accounts of his English text. A proportion of what may be called revisions (the term is wrong here, interestingly, since Beckett does not go back over his original text) serve to compensate for effects lost elsewhere in the translation. The remainder, when they are not circuitous attempts to render the original text idiomatically, are disruptions rather than additions. Beckett does not embroider his text in his translation, though there must surely have been a temptation to do so, and cuts far more frequently than he adds. He avoids obscuring the original text by adding new material. And when he does rework the original, it is usually to undermine meaning rather than clarify or expand it.

For Beckett, then, translation is an exercise in understatement, and, in normal circumstances, in the trilogy, he rarely uses the more inventive when the more literal will do. (There are famous exceptions to this, of course, which are usually explained by the need to compensate for one kind of effect by the use of another. Beckett's English seems to make more use of implied quotations, dead metaphors, or ironic puns, while the French offends against rhetorical convention more readily by exploiting shifts in stylistic register, by repetition, or by the extensive use of parataxis. Occasionally, Beckett will use greater freedom, either to cut or to rework, when translating a text first written many years earlier.[8] This is notably the case with the English versions of *Premier Amour* and *Mercier et Camier*, or the French *Watt*.)

Beckett began translating *Molloy* in collaboration with Patrick Bowles, but finally assumed responsibility for translating it and the rest of the trilogy himself. Since that time, bar a few joint versions (such as *Tous ceux qui tombent*, *Cendres*, or the French *Watt*) done in conjunction with other translators,[9] Beckett himself has been responsible for all the translations of his own work to appear in English or French. It is not known what Beckett's reasons were for taking over the English version of the trilogy. The motive cannot have been to rewrite the trilogy in the sense of producing a revised, improved, or augmented version, because this is not what the English version does. Except for local, often minor, reworkings of the type quoted above, no material is included in the English trilogy which is not already in the French. Beckett's motive cannot have been to use the translation as a means of communicating his ideas to a larger audience (assuming, absurdly, for an instant, that it might be possible to abstract from the trilogy anything as reliable as a set of ideas). If that were the case, the most that would be needed would be a cursory rereading of the translation and there would be no justification for Beckett to undertake it himself. From the author's viewpoint, if the reason for the trilogy was to express ideas, then those ideas had already been expressed, as well as being published and in print, and there would be little need to write them over again by translating them oneself.

'The relationship of the translator to the original', comments Paul de Man, 'is the relationship between language and language, wherein the problem of meaning or the desire to say something, the need to make a statement, is entirely absent.'[10] In the same way, the task of translating the trilogy has, for Beckett, little to do with expressing ideas. Beckett's practice as a translator suggests more that the object of his English version of the trilogy, in so far as was possible, was to restate the original work, to replicate the French text and double it with an English text which resonates with the original as closely as possible. What Beckett seems to want is the same text, but with the difference that it is in a different language. This is at any rate the effect created by the restraint of much of Beckett's translation and his refusal to restructure his text or incorporate new material within it.

One is reminded here of Walter Benjamin's reflexions on the task of the translator. Like Beckett, Benjamin resists the idea of translation as a recovery of essential meanings from the foreign text. Translation, he argues, rather than domesticate the text being translated, should aim to transform the target language. For Benjamin, as for Beckett, the object of translation is not what Beckett, speaking of Joyce, once called the scant cream of sense. Its role is not to formulate ideas, but more nearly to dissolve them, to use them as pretexts for the silent motion of language itself. Translation, then, is not a turning loose of sense, but an escape from sense.

The situation of the translator is, by definition, post-Babelian, and for both Benjamin and Beckett, that situation gives rise to a paradoxical enterprise. Translation takes the form of an unending – but necessarily failed – quest for a definitive language but it is a quest for perfection which knows from the outset that the idea of a definitive language is a contradiction in terms. The act of translation presupposes the possibility of the passage across languages and the existence of universal units of meaning. But if meaning were universal, there would be no need for translation, and no text to translate either. The art of translation is thus an art of failure which is driven by the knowledge that if difference between languages is the condition of translation, it is also proof of the ultimate impossibility of translation. Translation can be understood here as an endless movement across the multiplicity of languages, a constant matching, as Benjamin puts it, of fragments of language with each other in the attempt to fashion not an ideal whole (implying the reduction of all languages to one) but rather another piece in a larger puzzle, a puzzle which is the multiplicity of languages themselves. And this, as the object of translation, is what Benjamin, in messianic vein, calls pure language, '*die reine Sprache*'.[11]

To the extent that both versions of the trilogy achieve equal status (and the critical reception of the French and English texts suggests this is the case), what they illustrate and dramatise, by virtue of the relationship between them, is this difference between tongues which is their condition of existence. The two trilogies repeat and differ from each other in equal degrees, repeating each other in their differences, and differing from each other in the way they repeat one another. They reflect (and reflect on) one another across a divide created by the post-Babelian multiplicity of languages. If neither can claim authority over the other, both texts, the French trilogy and the English trilogy, become like versions of something else, and it cannot be coincidental in this respect that one of the themes explored most consistently by the trilogy is that of identity as mask, and person as persona. Beneath one layer of fiction lies a further layer, behind one text stands another, and similarly on through the trilogy from start to finish.

What Beckett establishes, then, both in the relationship of English text to French text and within the many interrelated stories in the trilogy itself, is the notion of language as a palimpsest and fiction as an infinite spiral of further fictions. There is no original, truthful account which might serve as a foundation for the narrators' attempts to tell their respective stories, but a plethora of versions which, like Vladimir's Gospels in *En attendant Godot*, fail to agree on crucial issues. Beckett's work is a commentary on that post-Babelian predicament. Just as there is no universal tongue, merely competing fragmentary versions of it, so there is no true story but many possible accounts of what it might be if it were to exist. The fictional structure of the trilogy echoes and repeats, in its uncanny way, the question of translation inherent within Beckett's writing. There is no true narrative to be written, just as there is no perfect idiom.

At the same time, paradoxically, both language and fiction in Beckett's work remain haunted by the possibility of another language, another tale. The paradox is inherent in the post-Babelian predicament. The unavailability of any definitive language gives rise to the need, or desire, to repair that lack. The search is both necessary and fruitless. One version, in one language, is not enough, but two versions, in two languages, are no better and are not a solution to the multiplicity of tongues, since that crisis is inherent in Beckett's whole undertaking as a novelist, both as a writer in his 'own' language and as a writer in a foreign one. It is part of the post-Babelian predicament that Beckett's writing should hunt endlessly for another story, and that the author himself should turn, beyond French and English, to yet another language, notably to German, and to staging his own plays in the language and, in the process, revising the German texts of his work.[12]

The unity of the trilogy lies not in its discovery of a universal idiom which can be expressed indifferently in French or in English, but in the movement of difference across and within languages which makes Beckett's work and his translations possible. This flight forward through languages and fiction is revealing of a more general structure in Beckett's work, the constant moving through and across linguistic differences, differences articulated in language, in the search for that something else, neither an experience nor an object, which lies between or beyond those differences, in the shape of the figure of indifference. In this way the trilogy is a continuation, though also a displacement, of the process begun in *Watt* and *Murphy*.

There is a place in the trilogy where language differences are exacerbated to the point of silence, and Beckett's prose encounters the untranslatable. That place is marked out by the trilogy's strange array of proper names. Proper names, it is said, cannot be translated. The role of names is to designate, not to signify, and they therefore have no conceptual content. But proper names are not universal. It is clear, in the trilogy, for instance, that the names are Irish, though the linguistic context in which they appear may be French. Proper names cannot be translated partly because they are already their own translation (and Beckett, in his English text, does not transpose his fictional names and change them into French names, say, but renders them for the most part unchanged).

Proper names are like fragments of Benjamin's pure language. They are empty of meaning, but somehow inexhaustible in their potential for meaning and interpretation. They seem to move freely from one linguistic environment to another, like nomadic and protean agents. But as they do this, they imperceptibly forfeit their apparent identity. As names pass from one language to another, they change. The name Molloy (like the name Beckett) does not have the same status in French as in English, it does not name in French as it does in English, and it is the impossibility of translating into any other language the effect created in French by the use of the word Molloy as a name that makes the name ultimately untranslatable. The effect of the name as a title, as *Molloy*, on the first page of a text written in French is something no other language can render. It opens up, within French, a space of strangeness, a pocket of otherness, a borderline with Irish English, which suddenly begins to exist in 'French'.[13] This effect is rigorously untranslatable. While it may be approximated, perhaps, in other languages, it cannot be translated. Put into English, the relationship between the name, 'Molloy', and the novel, *Molloy*, changes again.

Names, then, have a paradoxical status. Though untranslatable, they pass from one language to another seemingly without loss. At the same time they are utterly distinctive, and move from one language to another only with the effect of transforming what it is they designate or connote. Proper names, in this way, seem to occupy a space on the edge of ordinary language. They are part of those languages, but also exist outside the dictionary (and are only found, say, in the phone book). They resist being incorporated within a given language, but have no independent life outside it. For this reason, names are privileged objects in fictional writing. They provide literature with a metaphor of its own status as an untranslatable idiom, and mirror literature's own contradictory relationship with language, which is one of servitude and autonomy. No literary text is conceivable without the language in which it is written, but it is always possible for that text to have been written in another language. That is one of the paradoxes of translation, and it is one of the strange lessons of Beckett's trilogy and its dual life on the borders of French and English.

There is one important sense in which Beckett's trilogy, as a work of fiction, functions as a commentary on its own names (and, as I shall argue later, Beckett's own name). The names of Molloy,

Malone, together with that of the nameless Unnamable (if it is a name) appear as titles in Beckett's three novels, and it is with them, together with the name of the author, that any reading of the trilogy in fact begins. This should alert readers to the complexities and discontinuities that lurk behind those familiar names and titles. Though they appear straightforward, imperceptibly they are also working to destabilise and undermine the reading process.

The relationship between Beckett's three novels is far from simple. The practice of referring to them as a trilogy is a convenient one, and, no doubt for that reason, has been adopted by virtually all Beckett's critics, though it is noticeable that it is only recently that publishers have followed the convention. Despite its success, however, the term is arguably quite misleading when applied to *Molloy*, *Malone meurt*, and *L'Innommable*. The difficulty is in the extent to which it implies a preformed, organic or homogeneous unit. It is important to stress, as does Ruby Cohn, that Beckett 'did not preconceive of the trilogy as a trilogy'.[14] The oft-noted discrepancy in the opening pages of *Molloy*, which, in French, refer to the narrator's 'sens de l'avant-dernier', while, in English, seemingly to evoke the two novels to come, they speak of his 'premonition of the last but one but one', shows, if anything, considerable hesitation on Beckett's part as to the underlying structure of the three novels. It is worth remembering that all three were already completed when the first, *Molloy*, initially appeared in Paris in 1951. Had Beckett wanted, the same change could have been made to the French text as to the English. Moreover, the modification to the English text is perhaps inexact, as some readers have claimed, for if proper account is taken of the two-part structure of *Molloy*, the correct total should be four, not three.

Importantly, however, the indecision surrounding this change is reflected in the discontinuity apparent in the three titles of the novels. At first sight, admittedly, they seem to follow an ordered isomorphic pattern, and each title is usually taken to refer to some narrator-protagonist figure. It is this probably more than anything else that has given rise to the view that the three novels are the product of a single narratorial consciousness embodied at various moments in a series of merging characters, or, alternatively, that a single voice, lurking behind various mask-like names, is responsible for the various narratives.[15] Yet if the titles are examined closely, a number of strange slippages may be noticed. In *Molloy*, for example, there is an underlying problem of reference. Conventional expectations require that the title, if it is a name, should refer to a stable, all-embracing element in the text. That is how titles such as *Emma*, *Madame Bovary*, *Lord Jim*, or *Mrs Dalloway* function, by identifying the major protagonists of those fictions. (Interestingly, such titles name heroes, but rarely, it seems, narrators. The use of names as titles also seems more widespread in realist texts of the eighteenth or nineteenth century than in modern novels, which seem to prefer figurative or thematic titles, such as *The Sound and the Fury*, or *A la recherche du temps perdu*.)[16]

The oddity of *Molloy*, in this context, is that, if one takes the referent of the name in the title to be that belonging to the narrator-protagonist of the first part of the novel and then to the quarry whom Moran tracks down in Part Two (and readers are invited to do this by the text), the name, Molloy, occupies two separate and opposing positions in the text: that of the first-person narrator, then that of a third-person character. If the name, Molloy, is to embrace the fiction as a whole, it does so in dissymmetrical manner. The name slips from subject to object. The uncertainty as to the name's referent is of course emphasised by the hesitant way the name is first introduced in the novel. Recalled – or invented – in a fit of enthusiasm by the narrator, with obvious ironic implications, it provides the occasion for further doubt when Moran, in turn, tries to remember what it was.

Possibly the name of one of the book's narrators, even a name for a figment of the narrator's imagination, supposedly the name of one of the book's missing persons, the name, Molloy, as a title, injects into the novel a movement of uncertainty and self-contradiction that seriously undermines its unity. Readers cannot say with any confidence to what language the name belongs or to whom it refers. And this mobility of the name, with its dissymmetrical position in the novel, is at least one important reason why many readers have been tempted to reassert the name's hold over the text by arguing that Molloy is the narrator of Part Two of the novel, and that he is thus somehow metamorphosed into Moran, or, alternatively, that a third consciousness, neither Molloy nor Moran, but their common ancestor, is responsible for the narrative and reveals himself in the novel's opening paragraph.[17]

If the title of *Molloy* leaves the first novel prey to doubts as to its unity, the title of the second, *Malone meurt*, proves no less problematic. Once again, though less comprehensively, the name is the subject of much referential uncertainty, and can plausibly be taken to be that of the narrator (who claims it at one point), or some provisional mask. What is more confusing, however, is the use of the verb in the title. Does the present tense ('meurt') denote an action which is complete or incomplete? In other words: does Malone die? Does 'Malone dies' mean that he is (still) dying, or that he is (at last) dead? Or is it a stage direction, like the end of *Hamlet*, where he, too, 'dies'? The typographic presentation of the book's last pages, sprinkled with interrupted sentences and fragmentary clauses, suggests that something happens ('Glouglous de vidange'), though the fact that the narrator's end is couched in terms of being born leaves the nature of that end indeterminate. Since a confirmatory assertion, such as *'Je suis mort', is referentially impossible (and as though to prove the point Beckett begins *Le Calmant* with the words, 'Je ne sais plus quand je suis mort'), the narrator, at the end, and with him the novel as a whole, is left on a perpetual threshold, 'neutre et inerte' (II, 8), never able to make clear whether he is coming or going. ('Je sens que ça vient', says the narrator at one point, only to realise that what is coming has in fact already gone.) The temporality of the novel, which already in the opening pages the narrator had closely linked to the cyclical recurrences of feast days, refuses to coincide with referential time, leaving the question open as to whether any goal-orientated, linear reading of the trilogy as a whole is possible.

The third title, *L'Innommable*, beneath its apparent simplicity, displays the same indeterminacy. In this case, the uncertainties hinge on the gender system in French (and the same is true of the English title, *The Unnamable*, though not of the title in German, given as *Der Namenlose*). From the form of the title it is not possible to decide whether the referent is animate or inanimate, masculine or feminine. Because of the isomorphism with the family names occurring in the titles to the preceding texts (including *Murphy* and *Watt*), the reader is tempted to take *L'Innommable* as the name (by default) of yet another narrator or protagonist like Molloy or Malone. But this interpretation is nowhere vouchsafed by the novel, and it is arguable, as Maurice Blanchot forcefully contends, that the title refers more plausibly to the impersonal process which expropriates the narrator of all identity and which is none other than the fundamental movement of writing and language itself.[18] In the title *L'Innommable*, distinctions between human and non-human, character and narrative voice are under threat of collapsing, leaving behind them an indeterminate flux of words in which all naming becomes impossible.

There is a good case, then, for handling the idea of a trilogy with some caution. It seems clear that Beckett's three novels do not possess the threefold unity of a trinity, of three-in-one, or one-in-three (and one could argue that what is at issue in Beckett's novels is the impossibility of such a theological construction of genealogy and identity). Rather, it would be more accurate to conceive of them as following a decentred pattern of $2 + 1 + 1$, where the sign $+$ represents a relation not of cumulative totality, but of limping supplementarity. Crucial here are the gaps and excesses, the shortfalls and overspills of narrative organisation which make of each additional narration both a necessary supplement and an inevitable overstatement.

In this view, the trilogy begins in asymmetrical duality, in the twin, self-mirroring stories of *Molloy*, and proceeds via its own uncanny logic of lacks and excesses, whereby no final term supervenes to round off the text as an ideal totality. In this respect it is characteristic that the final novel, as though to guard against the spectre of closure, redoubles the implications of the logic of incommensurability it explores elsewhere. At the end of the trilogy, there is no closure, for the good reason that there is nobody there to close the door. Instead, there is just another threshold.

In this way, the interrelations between the three novels give rise to a complex topology. But, though they do not add up to an integrated, organic whole, structured around a constant expressive centre, Beckett's three texts are closely interconnected. Proof of this is provided by the numerous intratextual allusions and echoes found in the novels, as well as the author's initial insistence that all three novels be published or not at all. But crucial decisions of reading hinge on how that continuity is articulated. One common response among early critics was to think of the novels as existing in teleological sequence, and plotting the gradual dissolution of a single narrating consciousness who appeared first, logically if not chronologically, as the relatively stolid figure of Moran, only to undergo progressive disintegration through the various stages represented, in sequence, by Molloy, Malone, Mahood, the character called 'the Unnamable', and various others.

The approach has obvious drawbacks. There is no satisfactory explanation for the supposed inversion of the sequence in *Molloy*. To claim Molloy's tale, logically, comes after Moran's, is, without much justification, to privilege a thematic argument of progressive decay over the plot structure, which clearly requires Moran's story both to take place after Molloy's journey and to be written down after Molloy's account. Further problems arise when this scheme is applied to the other novels. It demands, contrary to the indecision of the text itself, that Malone be pronounced dead at the end of *Malone meurt*, and that the persona now identified, problematically, as the 'Unnamable' be thought of as a disembodied, anonymous state of pure consciousness, one who survives, according to some critics, in a post-mortem state of unpredicated being.

There are alternatives. Some of the difficulties mentioned above can be resolved if one imagines the novels to be simultaneous, not sequential. In this version, the texts would be arranged in parallel series. True, the problem of the supposed inversion of the Molloy and Moran stories remains, but there would be four coextensive stories, each recounting the same events or experiences from differing levels of consciousness. This would account in more satisfactory ways for the trilogy's recurrent allusions, but serious difficulties arise if one tries to impose an hierarchical perspective which requires that *L'Innommable* be viewed as a culmination, or as a moment of revelation with regard to everything that precedes it.

There is little doubt that such teleological or hierarchical readings of the trilogy derive from a wish to project upon the plot or thematic structure of the trilogy the linearity of the reading process. To read the trilogy is usually to begin at the beginning of *Molloy* and to end with the end of *L'Innommable* (though there seem to be no compelling reasons why readers adopt this sequence). But to read is also to engage in a recursive act which is tabular as much as linear. Beckett reminds readers of this by his numerous allusions to events or statements which have either already taken place (even, sometimes, in earlier novels) or are still to come. The trilogy might be thought of more accurately as occupying a space which, to invert the scholastic definition of God, has its centre nowhere, and its circumference everywhere. It is this form of planetary motion, with intersecting orbits and flat ellipses, and extremities converging at either end, rather like a purgatorial spiral, that is evoked quite explicitly at the beginning of *L'Innommable* (III, 15–16). A more demanding idea of the trilogy's topology is suggested here than the linear, teleological schemes expounded in the work of many of Beckett's early critics.

Appearances are deceptive. Beckett's trilogy, with its double text, its complex topology, is not a simple sequence of novels, but a much stranger concoction. The next three chapters will look into some of its more remarkable oddities and excesses.

4

DUALITY, REPETITION, APORIA

Il passe des gens aussi, dont il n'est pas facile de se distinguer avec
netteté.

Molloy

Like *Murphy* and *Watt* before them, but in new, more insidious
ways, the novels that make up Beckett's trilogy are quick to draw
attention to their fictional uncertainties. From the outset, as the
initial pages of *Molloy* demonstrate, Beckett's writing refuses to
accept as assured either the mimetic credibility of the fictional
artifact or the competence and mastery, the humanity, even, of the
narrating voice. The narrative organisation of Beckett's novels is
not a calmly formal affair. Considerable verbal and emotional
turbulence takes hold of the texts as a result of the indecision,
indeterminacy and aporias with which writing has to contend
before long.

Like most of Beckett's novels, *Molloy* begins with the tale of a
journey. That journey is not a simple one. *Mercier et Camier*, the
manuscript Beckett started and then abandoned some time before,
also began with a journey and, like *Molloy*, with a pair of
characters, one of whom was busily coming while the other kept
steadfastly going. In *Mercier et Camier*, as in *Molloy*, this self-
mocking double itinerary is itself doubled by another journey, that
of the narrator, though in *Mercier et Camier* it remains unclear in
what sense, if at all, the narrator does accompany his two protagonists, and if so, whether by word or by deed.[1] Together with *En
attendant Godot*, which it largely prefigures, *Mercier et Camier*
provides something like the definitive paradigm for the technique
of doubling or binary repetition in Beckett's work. Working on the
novel seems to have given Beckett further opportunity to explore
the literary possibilities of disruptive asymmetrical alternation
(which *Murphy* and *Watt* had already examined at length). One
central concern in *Mercier et Camier* lies therefore in plotting the

rhetorical discontinuities by which opposites negate or defeat each other. The novel also dramatises how internal differences (as, for instance, those existing within – or between – the members of the 'pseudo-couple' [III, 19] of Mercier and Camier) undermine identity, to the extent that the text largely scotches the idea that there exists any prior unity to the joint – hence disjointed – existence of its twin protagonists.

Continually, in *Mercier et Camier*, the two characters behave according to a system of self-cancelling alternatives. No sooner is their departure decided, for instance, than, by a detour, their journey becomes a return to its beginning. Instead of carrying out their declared common project, the two protagonists adopt a contradictory pattern of behaviour with arbitrary alternation becoming the dominant motif of their interaction. At one point, the pair stop to examine the situation. 'S'ensuivit un long débat', writes Beckett,

entrecoupé de longs silences, pendant lesquels la méditation s'effectuait. Il arrivait alors, tantôt à Mercier, tantôt à Camier, de s'abîmer si avant dans ses pensées que la voix de l'autre, reprenant son argumentation, était impuissante à l'en tirer, ou ne se faisait pas entendre. Ou, arrivés simultanément à des conclusions souvent contraires, ils se mettaient simultanément à les exprimer. Il n'était pas rare non plus que l'un tombât en syncope avant que l'autre eût achevé son exposé. Et de temps en temps ils se regardaient, incapables de prononcer un mot, et l'esprit vide. C'est à l'issue d'une de ces torpeurs qu'ils renoncèrent à pousser leur enquête plus loin, pour l'instant. (25–6)

The initial pages of the novel offer a similar illustration of the effects created by these false symmetries, disruptive alternations and contradictory combinations in which no two things are ever in step together and one aspect of behaviour is immediately paralleled by its inverse counterpart. Instead of meeting, as arranged, at a predetermined place and time, Mercier and Camier turn out to be constantly missing each other. Each follows a regular pattern of arrival and departure but these two patterns only coincide at the fourth time of asking, with the result that 50 minutes have been wasted (or gained) from the time planned for their joint departure. That they meet at all is more a haphazard mathematical or rhetorical event than the outcome of any prior intentional project and this discrepancy between a predetermined goal and the fiasco of failed realisation is a characteristically comic touch on the writer's part, especially since the goal – of meeting – is ultimately achieved more because of the fiasco than in spite of it.

Journeying, for Beckett, as was shown in the early story, 'Ding-Dong',[2] is a contradictory process, an alternating movement of egress and regress, attraction and repulsion, desire and loathing, displacement and stasis. As a result, when Beckett's trilogy takes up all the canonic, archetypal issues of the quest narrative – who? what? when? where? and why? – it is to complicate them or collapse them into one another. The space of journeying, like writing, becomes a space of indifference, according to the particular inflexion given the word by Beckett's work, of movements made and then undone, advanced but annulled, of opposites set up and then abolished, of unity assumed but then divided.

At the start of *Molloy*, the situation is reminiscent of that described in the opening chapter of *Mercier et Camier*. The narrator, 'à la façon de Belacqua, ou de Sordello, je ne me rappelle plus' (I, 13), sits observing, from his in-between (or indifferent) position beneath his rock of sloth, the coming and going of two figures, diagrammatically (and derisively) named A and B, as they, in turn, leave or return to their native city. Of these two, one, it seems, repents, while the other does not, though readers are denied the privilege of knowing which one. Is it B, the man who, like the author of the book, leaves the city, thus repenting having stayed there so long, or A, the man who – like the author in 1945 – has left and then returns, perhaps thinking better of his decision? Moreover, does B continue on his road away from the city, and A finally decide to remain?

The schematic character of the contrast between A and B, like their anonymity, is deceptive. The effect is not literalism but perplexity, not a paucity of literature but an excess.[3] Words, Beckett's text contends, are always either too much or too little, and the narrator of Moran's tale, doubling, or reiterating, the words of the book's earlier narrator, confesses that, for him, too, there is no pre-established reason or measure, that 'tout langage est un écart de langage' (I, 179). Already advertised as literature (though also as something considerably less than literature) by the allusion to Dante and the narrator's self-conscious remarks relating to the production of his text, the tale of A and B elicits, from the fictional margins of Beckett's narrative, a whole range of possible literary echoes which are also possible contexts for interpretation.

A and B might, therefore, be the murderous brothers of numerous mythic narratives, Romulus and Remus, say, or Cain and Abel. By giving the initials as A and C, the English translation invites this last possibility, but the change might equally well reflect the median position taken up by the narrator playing at *B*elacqua, or the author at a man named *B*eckett. Alternatively, A and B might refer to the two anonymous thieves on their crosses, of whom much is made in *En attendant Godot*. Indeed, later, the narrator remembers them as his 'deux larrons' (I, 61). Other images, too, are evoked, like that of the wayfaring pilgrim, or the prodigal son, and lie in wait for readers like ready-made answers to half-formulated questions. If to interpret a text is to apply to it a series of different frames of reference, then Beckett's text positively invites such attention. The lack of contextual definition acts as a powerful stimulant, persuading the reader to attempt to decipher the writing as though it contained the solution to its own enigmas.

Repeatedly, however, the writing refuses to allow itself to be read as some form of coded message. It does this, in part, by denying its own binary logic any stability. What is presented by the narrator as his beginning, 'mon commencement à moi' (I, 8), as he puts it, is not, in reality, the beginning of the novel. That place is taken – usurped – by a preamble, itself part of the narrative, but written, in terms of the chronology of plot, at some point in time later than the end of Part One of the novel (and perhaps also after Part Two). The real beginning is already the end of the story and the apparent beginning a false beginning, already a repetition of something else, of a past viewed in retrospect. This inversion of terms is a recurring strategy in Beckett's writing. Paradox and chiastic inversion affect almost the entirety of the oppositions and contrasts with which Beckett litters his text. The treatment of the two travellers is a case in point. The reader is presented with a binary opposition between similar elements, but Beckett refuses to mark either of the poles as positive or negative. The outcome is that there is no hermeneutic orientation to the contrast. What is left is a binary opposition which invites or solicits interpretation, yet refuses any contextual framework for interpretation. The contrast becomes both crucial and indeterminate, significant yet devoid of meaning.

These moments of intellectual crisis, by which key distinctions are both maintained and efface themselves, the narrator of *Malone meurt* calls 'des apories', aporetics. The narrator uses the term as he sets about detailing his programme for future survival:

J'ai dû réfléchir pendant la nuit à mon emploi du temps. Je pense que je pourrai me raconter quatre histoires, chacune sur un thème différent. Une sur un homme, une autre sur une femme, une troisième sur une chose quelconque et une enfin sur un animal, un oiseau peut-être. Je crois que je n'oublie rien. Ce serait bien. Peut-être que je mettrai l'homme et la femme dans la même, il y a si peu de différence entre un homme et une femme, je veux dire entre les miens. Peut-être que je n'aurai pas le temps de finir. D'un autre côté, je finirai peut-être trop tôt. Me voilà à nouveau dans mes vieilles apories. Mais est-ce là des apories, des vraies? Je ne sais pas. Que je ne finisse pas, ça n'a pas d'importance. Mais si je devais finir trop tôt? Pas d'importance non plus. (II, 10–11)

Aporia is the name for a rhetorical impasse, a space of radical indeterminacy or doubt where no passage exists, from which there is no exit or issue.[4] By aporia, distinctions collapse and arguments defeat themselves by espousing their diametrical opposites. In Beckett, as here, aporia is usually signalled by devices such as the careful rhetorical balancing of contradictory periods, the repeated use of terms like 'd'un côté' or 'd'un autre côté', 'peut-être', and the fondness for unanswerable rhetorical questions. Here, as in the early stories, Beckett takes care to instantiate the rhetorical figure he is describing. The text claims no place of safety outside of aporia, and Beckett has the narrator speculate, therefore, unanswerably – aporetically – on the nature of true aporia. (In the only other occurrence of the term in the trilogy, in *L'Innommable*, the text has its narrator state, archly, in similar vein, that 'je dis aporie sans savoir ce que ça veut dire' [III, 8].)

Paradoxically, though, aporia functions in Beckett's text, on one level, as a rhetorical figure like any other, as a moment of discourse, as an easing of passage from one verbal site to another. In Beckett's text, as in its etymology, aporia comes to mean a peculiar kind of discontinuous or circular movement, a crossing of navigable verbal territory into uncharted and disorientating non-space. On this reading, aporia describes a moment of passage that is somehow both impossible and yet inescapable if the writing is to articulate itself and thus continue. In the passage from *Malone meurt* the narrator's comments on aporia both identify aporia – truthfully – as a figure within the text and yet fall victim to the radical indecision of aporia as an impasse. Aporia, in Beckett's text, is a rhetorical place that describes yet challenges the impossibility of passage. It becomes a paradoxical manifestation or confirmation of itself, even as it refuses, necessarily, to adhere to the criterion of truth.

In *Malone meurt*, Beckett's text first stages the theme (or figure) of aporia by recourse to the paradigm (or, better, anti-paradigm) of sexual difference. The textual aporia of *Malone meurt* adopts as its emblem the aporia of the sexual difference between male and

female, man and woman. No sooner is that difference set down by
the text than it is effaced or denied, denounced as non-essential.
By an ironic disclaimer, the effacement of difference is denied any
general or universal status. This is not an isolated occurrence.
Elsewhere, in *Molloy*, similar associations are at work, though the
author puns on them with greater venom than here, when the
narrator claims, of writing itself, that 'on ferait mieux, enfin aussi
bien, d'effacer les textes que de noircir les marges, de les boucher
jusqu'à ce que tout soit blanc et lisse et que la connerie prenne son
vrai visage, un non-sens cul et sans issue' (I, 17). Aporia, here,
runs riot, almost cancelling the meaning of the sentence as well as
telling of the abolition of sexual difference, front and back. It is as
though sexual identity itself constituted a kind of savage exemplum
of the abolition of sense and its dissolution into aporetic – constipa-
tory – paralysis. And later in *Molloy*, this same rear passage is
dignified with the role of 'le vrai portail de l'être' (I, 122). It is as
though the lack of passage or issue leads Beckett's narrator – rather
like Watt when he first arrives at Knott's house – back to the
rediscovery, or reinstatement, of this rear passage. And what holds
true here for the 'petit trou' (I, 122) is no doubt also valid for the
passage from *Malone meurt* as it too pushes bodily against its own
impasse in order to write itself.

   While the passage from *Malone meurt* that I have cited describes
the impossibility of passage and details the radical doubt attaching
to sexual difference, it survives as a dramatisation of aporia. The
only answer to aporia which the text has available is a movement of
profound scepticism, indeterminacy or irresolution, that is to say,
further aporia. Similarly, the difference between the narrator's
fear of not having the time to finish his stories and the risk of
finishing them too early is articulated only then to dissolve into an
uncontrollable conundrum. 'Je me demande', asks the narrator –
unanswerably – 'si je suis en train de perdre du temps en ce
moment ou d'en gagner' (II, 13). To write, or tell his stories, for
the narrator, is to hope the end comes before the stories run out,
but also to hope the end is delayed long enough so that all the
stories may be told. The hope is for the end to come but also for it
to be deferred. And since the length and content of the narrator's
stories cannot be determined in advance of the moment of their
telling, the relationship between those stories and the time available or needed for the telling remains fundamentally indeterminable. What remains, as the ground of storytelling itself, is a movement of temporisation, a relationship to time in which to linger is

already to hasten the conclusion and where to welcome the end is also to postpone it.

Aporia, in Beckett's writing, is a figure of indifference, of differences articulated and then suspended. To the extent that it creates not significance but further aporia, it is circular in its implications, returning its proponent, or victim, to the very space which he or she would wish to resolve. Its typical form is of a dualistic relation stated and then effaced or, conversely, of unity posed and then divided against itself. This is the strategy used in the sequence of the two travellers in *Molloy*, who are described as both same and different. 'Ils se ressemblaient,' we read, 'mais pas plus que les autres' (I, 10). At the very moment when the text describes their similarity, it dismisses it as random and insignificant. A statement is made only then to be withdrawn. The positing of unity, suggests the narrator, is an error of perspective, a unilateral and precarious assertion which can always be overturned. Viewing the landscape, he notes, is deceptive. While one may guess correctly at where the valleys are between the hills, there may in fact be two or more valleys but of which only the one is visible from where one is standing (I, 11).

There is, in the trilogy, a long list of dualistic contrasts put forward and then withdrawn in this way. These include recurrent motifs such as the condition of the narrator's legs, one of which (the right?) is stiff at the time of his journey, but both of which are ailing at the time of his writing down of the story, if it is possible to distinguish with any certainty between the narrator's 'irréel voyage' (I, 22) through town and country and his tracing of that journey in words. In these cases, important distinctions are made between one member of a class and another with the promise of there being some significance or symbolic import to the distinction. But then the contrast is either left unexplained, often with comic effect, or its significance annulled when it proves impossible to secure the initial distinction or mark it coherently. What does it matter, the narrator implies, which leg was stiff, since at present both have gone stiff? In any case, he adds, does anyone know which leg it was in the first place? (I, 123). And one must bear in mind that there are parts of his story in which neither leg was stiff.

On the larger scale, problematical binary relations govern the interrelationship between different parts or layers of Beckett's texts. One case in point is the treatment of the relationship between the narrator of *Malone meurt* and the character Sapo, or Macmann, whom the narrator appears to fashion in his own image (albeit an image for which there is no model). It is worth noting what contradictory cues the text offers its readers as to how that relationship is construed.

At the outset it seems the narrator wishes to hold his own story at bay by inventing the tale of Saposcat. 'Je me demande', he wonders later, rhetorically, and undecidably, 'si ce n'est pas encore de moi qu'il s'agit, malgré mes précautions. Vais-je être incapable, jusqu'à la fin, de mentir sur autre chose?' (II, 25–6). Ten pages further on, the doubts appear less acute and he declares accordingly that 'rien ne me ressemble moins que ce gamin raisonnable et patient, s'acharnant tout seul pendant des années à voir un peu clair en lui, avide de la moindre lueur, fermé à l'attrait de l'ombre' (II, 34). Some twenty pages more and the situation has changed again, the reference to light and dark loses its dualistic reliability, and Sapo is found 'brusquement à nouveau errant à travers la terre, passant de l'ombre à la clarté, de la clarté à l'ombre, avec indifférence' (II, 58).

Here the allusion to indifference takes on an almost programmatic flavour. What it indicates is the loss of distinction between Sapo and the narrator. The relationship is no longer one of stable contrast or similarity, but one in which the two characters are both same and different, different and same. The text blurs and effaces not only the clarity or distinctness of the relation of the one to the other but also, more worryingly, the clarity and distinctness of their own relationship with themselves. Telling the story of Sapo as if he were a creature totally unlike himself, the narrator of *Malone meurt* finds himself in the paradoxical position of becoming the same as another, and thus different from himself, while yet turning into what he had aimed to become earlier in life and yet was deeply opposed to becoming: 'Ainsi je touche', he writes, 'au but que je m'étais proposé dans mon jeune âge et qui m'a empêché de vivre. Et à la veille de ne plus être, j'arrive à être un autre. Ce qui ne manque pas de sel' (II, 35).

A major textual device as a basis for these ironic and aporetic doublings is the use of repetition.[5] It is clear that Beckett's writing derives much of its labyrinthine and allusive quality from the way it reworks elements of text, either repeating familiar (and often familial) memories from one text to another (like the paternal greatcoat referred to earlier), or recalling objects which echo from one context to another (like those elements of Part One of *Molloy* that are alluded to, often dimly, in Part Two), or anthologising or recycling, covertly or sarcastically, material from other literary, mythical, or philosophical texts. Such recurrences, in the trilogy, range from the catchphrase objects (the hats, or knife-rests, or pebbles, or crutches) with which characters are mysteriously endowed, to large-scale narrative sequences like the invocation scene ('Tant de feuilles, tant d'argent' [I, 7]) described on the first page of *Molloy* and varied and rehearsed later in the shape of Gaber's visit to Moran and, subsequently, in more diffuse ways, at the start of each of the two works that follow. In all these cases, repetition implies a sign of recognition and thus some stability. But at the same time, repetition multiplies difference and challenges identity by producing a series of objects where formerly there was only one. To this extent (and this was one of the demoralising, if manically charged discoveries of *Watt*), repetition works more as a factor of fragmentation and dispersion. In Beckett's work, virtually without exception, repetition dissociates or separates more insistently than it assembles or unifies. Its usual function is to split units of meaning, whether narrative structures, objects or language, into two similar, but asymmetrical parts which (rather like Watt and Sam in *Watt*) ghost each other like reflexions in a mirror but with the result that the asymmetry ruins the appearance of identity.

Repetition, in Beckett's text, becomes largely inseparable from the worrying problem of non-identical replication. Take for instance, in *Molloy*, the account of the narrator's two testicles, which he has 'le droit plus bas que le gauche, ou inversement, je ne sais plus, frères de cirque' (I, 52). One testicle, then, perhaps the right (unless it turns out to be the left), dangles lower than the other. The second testicle, though it may repeat the first, is not identical with it. Yet there seems no way of distinguishing which is the first and which is the second of these two part organs. If out of these twin jesters one is the comic straight-man and the other the stooge, we neither know which is which, nor, even if we did know, what measure of rationality to apply to this puzzling dichotomy. Neither of the testicles can claim any priority over the other. There is thus no single or identifiable origin to secure the repetition of testicles as being a repetition of some form of object or organ identical with itself. There is no Platonic idea of the testicle in itself. Moreover, the difference between the narrator's twin private parts seems incidental, unrelated to the essential nature or function of testicles in general.

Rather than expressing the narrator's masculine identity in any significant way, the testicles become non-essential as well as

non-functional copies of a fundamental lack of identity and therefore of virility. Two possible answers suggest themselves, depending on whether one sees the case as deriving from a lack or an
excess. The problem might be the result of the shortcomings of the
narrator's testicles, their failure to perform the function of true
testicles. Alternatively, it might simply reflect the fact that two
circus jesters, neither different nor the same, are one joker too
many. Either way, Beckett's text suggests, the outcome is the same:
a crisis which creates havoc at the core of the narrator's anthropolo-
gical and sexual identity and, into the bargain, provides the text
with a series of neatly balanced and comical rhetorical moves.
Aporia is not overcome, but enacted and somehow the text passes.
By a circular paradox, by which excess meets insufficiency and
superfluity encounters lack, the non-identical dichotomy of the
narrator's two testicles joins together with the poverty of their
performance. There is no common measure in Beckett's text, as the
narrator points out, words are always too much or too little and the
principle applied to words holds good here for reproductive organs
as well, and vice versa (I, 50).

The same argument could be made concerning the relationship
between Molloy and Moran. The motifs and objects that are
repeated from one story to another create as many differences as
they do areas of overlap. To this extent the relationship between
the two is a case not so much of merging identities but aporetic
doubling. Repetition from one story to another splits the narrative
structure of the novel into two non-identical parts and refuses any
one instance the privilege of being unique and thus identical with
itself. Moreover, Beckett's text does not signpost its repetitions,
leaving it up to the reader to spot them, and thus the recurrence of
objects tends not to accredit the first occurrence as a founding
moment. As we have seen, the start of the novel itself is not an
origin, but already an end, already a repetition of something which
has already come, or gone, before, and thus, by the trilogy's
circular logic, a repetition (or a rehearsal) of what is to follow.

The use of repetition, then, is a powerful textual strategy. To
read the trilogy is to be constantly compiling a list of recurrent
motifs and the transformations they undergo. By adding suspense,
they act as a powerful source of fascination. Much of the fascination
runs along genealogical lines, with readers having to struggle to
disentangle something which might be described as the trilogy's
extended family tree. Thus when the narrator of *L'Innommable*, in
the opening pages, speaks of Murphy and Mercier–Camier, Molloy

and Malone, this raises, as though in some half-demented Dicken-
sian novel, a host of questions about obscure familial connections
and relationships. The presence of these names, memorialised
from earlier texts, as though they belonged to the members of one
vast clan or family group, leaves the reader puzzling over their
relationship to each other and to the narrator. In some places, too,
Beckett cannibalises his own text, quoting from *Molloy* in *Malone
meurt* ('Je ne me rappelle pas comment j'y suis arrivé. Dans une
ambulance peut-être, un véhicule quelconque certainement' [II,
15]), or reproducing the first line of the story 'La Fin' in *L'Innommable* ('Ils me vêtirent et donnèrent de l'argent' [III, 50]), or
otherwise retreading allusions from earlier novels.

   Repetition in Beckett's text rapidly acquires an obsessive, even
obsessional energy. This is helped by the interconnections between
the three novels in the trilogy. Events or formulations found in
Molloy are never simply abandoned in the subsequent novels but
are constantly being invoked, at times directly (as in the instances
just cited), but, more usually, indirectly or allusively. *L'Innommable*, towards the end, tells of a complaining voice ringing in the
narrator's ears:

... c'est comme une confession, une dernière confession, on la croit finie,
puis elle rebondit, il y a eu tant de fautes, la mémoire est si mauvaise, les
mots ne viennent plus, les mots se font rares, le souffle se fait court, non,
c'est autre chose, c'est un réquisitoire, une mourante qui accuse, c'est moi
qu'elle accuse, il faut accuser quelqu'un, il faut trouver quelqu'un, il faut
un coupable, elle parle de mes méfaits, elle parle de ma tête, elle se dit à
moi, elle dit que je regrette, que je veux être puni ... (III, 255)

Reading these lines, it is difficult not to be reminded of the early
pages of *Molloy* with their account of the narrator's incapacities
and the story of his visit to his mother. By repeating a number of
terms from earlier, the description of the voice in *L'Innommable*
glosses and elaborates what had remained unspoken in *Molloy*.
(One must also add, of course, that *Molloy*, in turn, serves as an
indirect commentary on the later novel.) The voice in the feminine
('*la* voix') becomes like a ghostly reminder of the figure of the
mother in *Molloy*, who is declared dead by the first page of the
book and said later, like the voice in *L'Innommable*, to have very
poor memory and to speak little, only in a 'babil cliquetant' amidst
a 'fracas de râteliers' (I, 24). The feminine gender of the voice (in
the French original) serves as a verbal link between the mother and
the voice. The gender distinction becomes a means of separating
the (masculine) speaker from this voice which is not his own.

However, it also dramatises the dynamic of identification operating between the narrator and the voice. This is expressive of both a desire for non-separation and inclusion and a fear of non-separation and inclusion. There is a deep-seated ambivalence inherent in all identification, a doubleness which, in Beckett's text, emerges as a structure of gender mingling or indifference. Thus the passage ends with the feminine voice speaking, as it were, in the masculine: 'je veux être puni', it says, substituting itself for the narrator's own impossible answer. Gender difference is set up only for it to collapse in a fearful erasure of distinctions.

Constantly, then, Beckett's text is returning back over itself. At the end, as *L'Innommable* speaks of the possibility of there being a final threshold of the journey, it is impossible not to remember the first threshold crossed at the outset, in *Molloy*, that which led the narrator back into his mother's bedroom (where, like the protagonist of *Company*,[6] he might easily have been conceived and born). In the ever revolving world of the trilogy, objects or textual motifs are never lost. To lose an object in Beckett's fiction – whether a mother, a father, a stick, or bicycle horn – is to be always rediscovering it in the guise of something else as a strange, often inverted, double of itself. Thus Molloy's mother, transmogrified into Lousse or Moll, Macmann's friend, or Molloy's crutches into Malone's hooked stick, Malone's stick into Lemuel's club, Molloy's corncrakes into Malone's vultures, and so on.

The text of *Malone meurt* provides a metaphor for this process of recurrence and replication: it is the movement by which corpses, if buried in shallow graves, rise to the surface. 'Le gros Louis' ('Big Lambert'), the reader is told, during the burial of the mule, 'n'ignorait pas la tendance des enterrés à remonter, contre toute attente, vers le jour. En quoi ils ressemblent aux noyés' (II, 71). The point is echoed later by the narrator's remarks as to the fate of the objects kept in his pockets when he was young. Tiring of certain cherished objects, he gets rid of them by secretly burying them or tossing them in the sea, only for them to rot and return to the surface like dead things and be found once again (II, 139–40).

The logic of this process, as might be expected, is a logic of paradox. The narrator keeps his objects in order to hide them away; once hidden away, they become as good as lost; as soon as they are lost they are found again. The process involved here, as the context of the burial scene implies, is closely linked to the work of mourning. In mourning, the aim is to transform a real, often traumatic loss into a symbolic loss, one which can be assimilated, signified, and thus acknowledged by the grieving subject. The lost object needs to be introjected as a representation or symbol. In this way, the object may be both preserved and its loss comprehended. Then, perhaps, the object may be truly forgotten. In Beckett's version of mourning there seems not to be this positive outcome. Objects are not forgotten, but recur like ghosts. Mourning seems never completed and there appears to be a fundamental obstacle preventing a resolution of the ambivalence inherent in incorporation. Incorporation entails separation from the object as well as partial identification with it and it is this tension which is never put to rest in Beckett's text. Instead, the fantasy of incorporation is endlessly repeated – ad nauseam, one might say, to the extent that the theme of vomiting in Beckett's writing seems to work always in tandem with the idea of grieving, loss and death. (This, too, returns later. In *L'Innommable*, vomiting as a theme and as a rhetoric becomes a compulsive gesture, and the narrator responds, of course, with the hope that what is being vomited is in fact himself [III, 76–7].) Something of this lack of resolution to mourning is reflected in the grim joke that Beckett extracts in *Malone meurt* (II, 140) from the idea of giving up old affections for new, implying all new loves are coloured by guilt and all new object choices ultimately premissed on imminent loss.

The narrator of *Malone meurt* observes later that this loss of objects is inherent in his writing. 'Mes notes', he says, 'ont une fâcheuse tendance, je l'ai compris enfin, à faire disparaître tout ce qui est censé en faire l'objet' (II, 162). One consequence of this is the fact that objects in Beckett's text are repeatedly given uncertain or problematic status. *Molloy*, famously, speaks of a time when 'la condition de l'objet était d'être sans nom, et inversement' (I, 45–6). Earlier, the narrator had decided that 'ramener le silence, c'est le rôle des objets' (I, 17). If the role of objects is to challenge names and create silence, this seems to be because objects do not conform to the rules of clear and distinct identity which, if they existed, might found language as an act of essential naming. Human names in the trilogy do not deliver the essence of the subjects who claim them and they do not correspond to any verifiable identity. The same is true of the names of objects. In *Molloy*, a knife-rest is not a knife-rest, because it could be something else, whose function, or meaning, cannot be established. 'Je pouvais donc l'interroger sans fin et sans danger', the narrator explains. 'Car ne rien savoir, ce n'est rien, ne rien vouloir savoir non plus, mais ne rien pouvoir savoir, savoir ne rien pouvoir savoir, voilà par où passe la paix,

dans l'âme du chercheur incurieux' (I, 96). Objects are without
essence, which is why they act as conduits of peace, indifference, or
silence, but this is also why, once lost, they return everywhere as
doubles of themselves (like the knife-rest which duly returns, in
Malone meurt, mysteriously, as 'un petit porte-couteau en argent'
[II, 159]).

Indifference, as embodied in such objects, is both a threat and a
source of enjoyment. The ambivalence of the relation to objects in
Beckett's text is nowhere more marked than here. To take the case
of the sucking stones in *Molloy*, it seems that the narrator's initial
frustration is brought about by the fact that the stones have no
recognisable individuality and can therefore be mistaken for one
another. To overcome this lack of singular identity, the narrator
devises a set of ever more complex (and comic) arrangements
which are designed to label each stone according to its place within
a recognised sequence. By incorporating the stones into such a
structure, the narrator transforms indifferent things into toys, a
source of pleasure rather than dissatisfaction. But incorporation
fails to change them into symbolic objects. By the logic of indifference, they have no essential identity and continue all to taste
exactly the same ('elles avaient toutes le même goût exactement' [I,
113]). They become indistinguishable, entirely dispensable, and
the narrator finds no better fate for them than, like Malone, to
throw them away, bar one, which acts as an indifferent substitute
for all the others and which the narrator finally loses, or throws
away. Anal expulsion takes over here from oral incorporation as
though to imply that objects can never be properly incorporated
and that the status of objects is already to be lost and that, in any
case, the stone will inevitably always return as a double of itself.

Objects, then, are never stabilised in Beckett's text. They are
vehicles of pleasure and hostility, and things that provide enjoyment to some, as is the case, in *Molloy*, with, say, bicycles and
crutches, prove literally murderous to others, notably an old dog
called Teddy and an anonymous charcoal burner. This ambivalence
is not just playful, for it betrays a fundamental lack of unity, a
violence, even, within the narrator. Indeed, Beckett's novels do
not accord their narrator any unified place in the text. Thus while
Molloy begins with an unambiguous assertion of place and position
by way of the narrator's reference to his mother's bedroom, the
statement is also tinged with an overriding sense of ambivalence.
The ambivalence derives both from the indecision voiced immediately after in the comings and goings of the two travellers and from

the questions that arise as to the nature of the mother's death ('Etait-elle déjà morte à mon arrivée? Ou n'est-elle morte que plus tard?', asks the narrator [I, 7–8]. Later, as though to echo these words and perhaps rephrase them, the narrator of *L'Innommable*, for his part, puts it about that 'je cherche ma mère, pour la tuer, il fallait y penser plus tôt' [III, 215]).

It is not by coincidence that this ambivalent invocation of the figure of the mother, raising, as it does, the issue of the extent of the narrator's separation or non-separation from her, is used by the narrator to instantiate the limits of his power of words ('Je ne sais pas grand'chose, franchement', he writes. 'La mort de ma mère, par exemple' [I, 7]). Throughout the trilogy, it is words, including the narrator's own text, that are treated, off and on, like the mother, with the greatest hostility and affection. One might conclude that the most ambivalent object of all in Beckett's trilogy is language itself. But language is not an object like any other, for it constitutes the medium within which the narrator's identity is articulated. The lack of control over language which the narrator of *Molloy* evokes by way of beginning implies a slippage or crisis affecting the narrator's position in language. The crisis in the status of the object which one can retrace through Beckett's text reveals another crisis, of which it is a symptom, a crisis that is centred on the verbal and bodily foundations of the narrating subject. The damage created in Beckett's text by aporia cannot be limited to the narrator's objects or simply his words. The very place the narrator attempts to occupy in the text proves vulnerable to the critical effects of aporia and thus just as capable of being wrecked as the story he is attempting to tell.

Aporetic doubling in the trilogy is not confined to the treatment of themes or the development of narrative incidents. It is employed to fragment the dimension of speech and self-expression itself. Indeed, fairly rapidly, in the text of the trilogy, two counterposed attitudes or positions of speech emerge, as, for instance, in the story of the two travellers from *Molloy*. On the one hand, what the text writes is how the narrator accompanies the two figures of A and B in his mind, as though in some flight of the imagination. To B, for instance, at one point, the narrator is able to 'retourner en esprit' (I, 17), or, again, to shift tense from past to present (I, 11–12), as though to underline how, behind the story of the travellers, written in the literary preterite (the French '*passé simple*'), a present tense of continuous verbal elaboration is at work, inventing and fabricating what the narrator pretends (or pretends to pretend) are actual events. Half-echoing the tone of an inquiring bystander while also half-rehearsing the role of an author reflecting on his text, the narrator inquires as to the behaviour of the man, B, as follows:

Portait-il seulement une besace? Mais cette démarche, ces regards anxieux, cette massue, peut-on les concilier avec l'idée qu'on se fait de ce qu'on appelle un petit tour? Mais ce chapeau, c'était un chapeau de ville, suranné mais de ville, que le moindre vent emporterait au loin. A moins qu'il ne soit attaché sous le menton, au moyen d'un cordon ou d'un élastique. J'ôtai mon chapeau et le regardai. (I, 17–18)

The transition, like most breaks in continuity in *Molloy* (of which there are many), is brusque and disorientating. At the moment when B seems to be (roughly) established as a character, the narrator calls his existence into question. He does this first by querying B's plausibility, then by implying that B is no more than a travestied version of himself, who might – or might not – be wearing a hat exactly like his own. But the reader is faced, once more, with an aporia: do B and the narrator have similar hats or not? Are the pair the same or different, and, if so, in what proportions?

Two inverse dynamics of linguistic activity seem to be simultaneously at work here. One, which might be called projective, works by means of an identification between narrator and character, as when the story of A and B is recast as that of the narrator, who seemingly dons (or doffs) B's hat. On this level, one might accept that the narrator of *Molloy* is, initially, a man named Molloy and that the story is taken up by one Jacques Moran. But it is apparent, throughout Beckett's trilogy, that this regime of speech, which is broadly synonymous with the realm of storytelling as such, is constantly being qualified – and thus disqualified – by an opposing, rejective position of speech. This regime is manifested most commonly by self-conscious discursive comments on the story which challenge or modify the terms of the text or question the plausibility, truth, even the relevance or clarity of the fictional material being elaborated.

The result of the interweaving of these two oscillating regimes of speech, the one inventing stories and the other calling narrative into question, is to undo the unity of the narrating voice. It is possible to describe the speech patterns of the trilogy, as Dina Sherzer has done, according to an hierarchically organised repertoire of speech levels.[7] Following a Jakobsonian model, Sherzer identifies five such levels: story and discourse, in which the tale or its telling, respectively, are articulated, together with what Sherzer terms metanarrative and metanarration, in which, in turn, the tale itself or the manner of its telling are the object of metalinguistic commentary by the narrator. Sherzer adds a fifth level, under the heading 'audition', to refer to those moments in the text where the process of communication is displayed for its own sake.

What is striking, however, at the end of Sherzer's otherwise useful taxonomy of speech levels in the trilogy, is how Beckett's text refuses to conform to the hierarchical arborescence of this mode of analysis as it follows through its rhetorical programme from trunk to bough and bough to branch. The various levels of the text are necessarily interdependent. But most important of all is how the different registers, or thresholds, of speech at work in Beckett's three novels play disruptively and critically against one another. Thus the metanarrative commentary deployed in the passage just cited, though it puts the story being told at a distance, itself produces a further level of story, that of the narrator as writer, or author, or even as habitual nit-picker.

The second level of text interrupts the first, the story of the narrator as character or observer, but the effect is not that of an hierarchically superior metalinguistic speech level, which might be capable of some truthful statement about the veracity or otherwise of the text it is talking about, but of a differentiated position of speech which cuts across the first in a gesture of some antagonism. This breaking up of the narrative voice into two or more conflictual levels creates in the text a multiplicity of speech registers which dispose of any single, autonomous persona and replace it with a churning series of verbal disruptions.[8]

Rather than following an hierarchically ordered programme of rhetorical effects, Beckett's text demonstrates the heterogeneity of the speaking voice. The voice is driven by the forward movement of the text to exist more as a sequence of discontinuous breaks than as a unified idiom. Beckett's writing sets up a perpetual dialogue with itself, constantly shifting the terms of speech in order to create disjunctive effects. Those disjunctive effects are what contribute most to the specific tone of Beckett's writing, with its caustic puns, its periods that repeatedly tail off at the end, and its fondness for rubbing verbal registers the one against the other in dissonant fashion (this is particularly evident in the French text which makes a virtue of shifting abrasively from the literary to the colloquial, the fancy to the vulgar).

Faced with the discontinuity of speech and self-expression that the trilogy dramatises in this way, it is not surprising that readers have attempted to differentiate, within the text itself, between different layers of narrative according to how much truthfulness and authenticity, purity or impurity they can claim to possess. For Olga Bernal, for instance, the key to the trilogy is to be found in this attempt to grasp the authentic reality of the speaking self outside of alienating fabulation. She explains: 'l'entreprise difficile, impossible, qualifiée par lui-même de "supplice", cette entreprise du héros de Beckett consiste à saisir, à vouloir saisir l'homme en deçà de toute fiction'.[9] But, in a novel, what is it, what words or episodes, that can be said to exist beyond or prior to fiction, as Bernal suggests?

Curiously, as though in anticipation of the question, the narrator of Part Two of *Molloy*, the self-styled Jacques Moran, already offers a response of his own. It is contained within the famous final words of his narration:

J'ai parlé d'une voix qui me disait ceci ou cela. Je commençais à m'accorder avec elle à cette époque, à comprendre ce qu'elle voulait. Elle ne se servait pas des mots qu'on avait appris au petit Moran, que lui à son tour avait appris à son petit. De sorte que je ne savais pas d'abord ce qu'elle voulait. Mais j'ai fini par comprendre ce langage. Je l'ai compris, je le comprends, de travers peut-être. La question n'est pas là. C'est elle qui m'a dit de faire le rapport. Est-ce à dire que je suis plus libre maintenant? Je ne sais pas. J'apprendrai. Alors je rentrai dans la maison et j'écrivis, Il est minuit. La pluie fouette les vitres. Il n'était pas minuit. Il ne pleuvait pas. (I, 272)

In closing, Beckett's narrator is again in the realm of paradox, circularity and ignorance. But what is the truth value of these closing words? One can distinguish in it at least two layers of speech (and no less than five different tenses), one (in the narrative '*passé simple*' and imperfect) given over to telling a story in the past, and one (in the 'passé composé' and present) referring to the immediate past in which the story has just been (or is in the process of being) written. At first sight, the passage seems to reproduce the canonic distinction between the narrative past and the present, by which the latter is seen as more immediate, hence closer to the truth, than the former, and a powerful literary and philosophical tradition lies behind this decision to privilege discourse over narrative and present over past.[10]

The straightforwardness of the passage, however, is deceptive. For in the final lines, it is the present tense, in the form of a quotation from the now distant beginning of the narrator's account, which is treated by the text as though it were an abusive fiction. By a sudden inversion, the imperfect tense appears to become the hierarchically superior form and the present to be changed into the realm of story and fiction. Beckett's ending forms a perfect chiasmus. What is implied at the outset about the relative status of past and present is overturned by the text. The present ends up just as fictitious as the past, and the past is as immediate as the present. This chiasmus of tenses draws a conclusion to the text of *Molloy* only by presenting the reader with an aporia. The mention of the voice poses the question of who is in fact responsible for the narrative, while the contradiction of the end leaves each of its sentences open to radical doubt. The novel's end is an aporetical end which is neither open nor closed, both finished and unfinished. It is finally impossible to tell whether it was raining or not, impossible to apply any criterion of truth or falsity to the text. It is thus entirely misleading to attribute to the rejective or metanarrative position of language – or any other – any greater degree of truth or authenticity than any other threshold of speech in the trilogy.

Language, then, whatever its internal differences or divergent registers, is coextensive with fiction. *Molloy* puts the point with epigrammatic vigour:

Et que je dise ceci ou cela ou autre chose, peu importe vraiment. Dire c'est inventer. Faux comme de juste. On n'invente rien, on croit inventer, s'échapper, on ne fait que balbutier sa leçon, des bribes d'un pensum appris et oublié, la vie sans larmes, telle qu'on la pleure. Et puis merde. (I, 46)

As these words suggest, fiction is a realm in which all is 'rightly wrong' (as Beckett's translation has the phrase). It entertains no stable relationship with either truth or falsehood. Rather it displaces the meaning of both truth and falsity so that the one is the condition and consequence of the other. As such, fiction constitutes the ground and limit of the narrator's position. All speech becomes tautological in the sense that to fabulate is to do no more, or less, than to rework and vary endlessly the text of living inscribed in the repeated encounter with words. There is, for Beckett's narrator, no respite from fiction, and no redemption from its paradoxes or from the aporia to which it leads.

In the trilogy, all Beckett's protagonists set out on a journey which ends in an impasse. The most immediate reason for their loss of direction is that they themselves, together with the sense of the journey, have already changed before they have reached their chosen destination. Thus the man called Molloy, at the end of his travels, is left lying abandoned and largely forgotten in a ditch.

Thus, too, the man who calls himself Moran and who returns home to dust, having seemingly failed in his quest. In these cases, where to go on is to end up always going somewhere different than planned, what seems most subject to catastrophic change is the relationship in the text between subject and object, self and other, pursuer and pursued, searcher and quarry. Neither remains constant and neither enjoys any stable position.

In place of the ordered dialectical polarity of subject and object comes something else, moving to-and-fro across the text, in the words of *Molloy*, like an 'inexorable navette qui mange ma page avec l'indifférence d'un fléau' (I, 205). The narrator of *Malone meurt* describes it as a series of bodily motions, of ingestion and expulsion, the one counterbalancing, deferring, contradicting the other: 'Vase, gamelle, voilà les pôles' (II, 18). The narrator calls this a game. But this game is not a minor pastime, for what Beckett's text speaks of is an aporetic crisis in the whole articulation of subjective space. Beckett's rewriting of the quest narrative is not an attempt just to toy with the forms of the past, for it has genealogical, analytic implications. It represents an attempt to come to terms with the issue, the question or outcome of human genealogy. This will be the starting point of the next chapter.

5
FABLES OF GENEALOGY

il n'était qu'humain, que fils et petit-fils d'humains. Mais entre lui et
ces hommes sévères et graves, à barbe d'abord, ensuite à moustache,
il y avait cette différence, que sa semence à lui n'avait jamais fait de
mal à personne. Il ne tenait donc à son espèce que du côté de ses
ascendants, qui tous étaient morts, en croyant s'être perpétués.

Malone meurt

Buried within the fictional content of Beckett's trilogy one finds the
elements of something resembling a family drama. This may seem
surprising, but the evidence is explicit. Familial bonds and amorous
intrigues run together through the three novels to create a puzzling
and fascinating, though discontinuous, network of textual relations. The narrator of the first part of *Molloy* speaks of his love for
'une petite boniche', and of his true love 'dans une autre' (I, 8), and
speculates as to the possibility of having a son of his own somewhere. Later, the same text refers us to the narrator's 'désir d'un
frère' (I, 20) and recounts, memorably, his journey towards his
mother, whose image, in his dim recollection, is interwoven with a
series of other sexually ambivalent women figures as well as that
of his own father. The narrator named as Moran, but whose name
doubles up, enigmatically, as Jacques Moran, père and fils,
wonders, for his part, whether Molloy might not turn out to be a
friend, or a father (I, 251).

In *Malone meurt*, apparently in an attempt to realise himself by
way of a fantasy of self-parturition, the narrator plays only begetter
to an homunculus of his own, 'une petite créature, à mon image'
(II, 96), and gives birth, as an inventor of fables, to the family
romance of Sapo, whom he later renames Macmann (meaning, as
in the Christian Gospels, the 'son of man'), before embarking on
the more difficult but analogous task of giving birth to himself in
reverse, that is, 'dans la mort' (II, 208). Further on, in the last text,
L'Innommable, where the claims of story over the narration are at

their weakest, one finds Beckett's text giving vent to a whole
genealogical fantasia, in words ascribed to the figure of the 'diffa-
mateur' (III, 73) named as Mahood, according to which the
narrator is surrounded by a whole family circle: 'pépé, mémé,
maman et les huit ou neuf morveux' (III, 62). And at the end of
L'Innommable, within fifteen pages of the trilogy's conclusion, the
text digresses, in a kind of sarcastic 'rappel' (III, 246), to tell a
particularly sinister tale of love, marriage and death, involving a
husband who returns home after being reported killed in the war
and who dies from the emotional shock of seeing his wife again, at
which point, conversely, the woman's second husband hangs
himself at his thought of losing her.

It would be misleading, without doubt, to take any of these
references at face value. Most of them are surely ironic and
demonstrate Beckett's fondness for parody or pastiche. Some,
moreover, seem to function almost entirely as interpretative red
herrings. But it would be false to conclude that they are haphazard
inventions. 'Même les histoires de Mahood,' notes *L'Innommable*,
'ne sont pas n'importe quoi' (III, 55–6). After its own fashion, with
its lists of fictitious names, almost all of which are Irish family
names, from Molloy, Moran and Malone through to Macmann,
Mahood and Worm, the trilogy is constructed like a mock dynastic
novel, following its story through, as it were, from one generation
to the next. Different episodes and protagonists rhyme with each
other as in a vast recurrent sequence in which characteristics are
passed down from one individual to the next. The point is made in
L'Innommable apropos of Mahood: 'Mahood', announces the
narrator, scornfully: 'Avant lui il y en avait d'autres, se prenant
pour moi. Ça doit être une sinécure passant de père en fils, à en
juger par leur air de famille' (III, 56).

These familial allusions designate a level of the text which is
present only in cryptic, displaced fashion. Though it is never
available in any fully complete version, this hidden, other layer of
story takes the form of an obsessive genealogical fable. It has its
existence, as it were, between the lines of Beckett's text, and to
interpret it means reading the text of the trilogy symptomatically.
This entails paying close attention to some of the repetitive and
elliptical figures, on the level of narrative discourse and plot
invention, which Beckett's text is continually in the process of
reworking, as well as to the numerous throwaway remarks or
allusions with which Beckett embroiders the text. Special significance also attaches to the web of associations which Beckett's

writing forges between seemingly disconnected themes or concerns by contextual interference. The transitions that Beckett's prose makes – or often fails to make – from one subject to the next are rarely mediated by the appeal to logic or plausibility. The discontinuities that result betray significant, though often discordant, thematic links between different strands of the text. Such links, though, are not usually overt and Beckett's text seldom owns up to its displacements. Reading Beckett is a case of having to disinter cryptic, subterranean passageways. If Beckett's writing, in the trilogy, becomes a process of personal and cultural excavation, then, in much the same way, interpreting the trilogy becomes a question of plotting the underhand circulation of meaning across different texts or from context to context.

The genealogical fable, then, is not a confessional thematics. Rather it exists within the fabric of Beckett's text only to the extent that it is also full of omissions and indeterminacies, gaps and suppressions, repetitions and displacements. The status it enjoys is in this respect closely paralleled by that of the 'leçon' or 'pensum', measured out like a debt and imposed like a curse on the narrator of *L'Innommable*, and which, he alleges, he must decipher and reinscribe in order to reach his end:

Oui, j'ai un pensum à faire, avant d'être libre, libre de ma bave, libre de me taire, de ne plus écouter, et je ne sais plus lequel. Voilà enfin qui donne une idée de ma situation. On m'a donné un pensum, à ma naissance peut-être, pour me punir d'être né peut-être, ou sans raison spéciale, parce qu'on ne m'aime pas, et j'ai oublié en quoi il consiste. (III, 46–7)

The goal which the narrator pursues sometimes seems as though it were an object beyond or outside language. This is not how the narrator describes it here. Rather, the object towards which the narrator appears to be struggling seems already to be a form of words, a magic formula, even, which, once spoken, would bring an end to speech and allow the narrator to remain in silence and peace ('Curieuse tâche,' says *L'Innommable*, 'que d'avoir à parler de soi. Etrange espoir, tourné vers le silence et la paix' [III, 48]). But this magic word, if it exists, proves unavailable, and the notion of a quest, together with the object of that quest, whether it be a final truth, an accurate story, a moment of silence or a state of peace, becomes itself nothing short of a fiction or a textual conceit:

Toute cette histoire de tâche à accomplir, pour pouvoir m'arrêter, de mots à dire, de vérité à retrouver, pour pouvoir la dire, pour pouvoir m'arrêter, de tâche imposée, sue, négligée, oubliée, à retrouver, à acquitter, pour ne

plus avoir à parler, plus avoir à entendre, je l'ai inventée, dans l'espoir de
me consoler, de m'aider à continuer, de me croire quelque part, mouvant,
entre un commencement et une fin, tantôt avançant, tantôt reculant, mais
en fin de compte grignotant toujours du terrain. (III, 54)

As far as the narrator is concerned, then, the notion of there being a
determinable goal giving rise to the quest for a final story or correct
formula proves untenable. Speech is a turmoil of language which
settles only provisionally, only for the duration of an unstable
fiction, into the linear simplicity of a relationship between a
speaking self and a non-speaking object. At bottom, it is that
relationship itself that is in crisis. In Beckett's writing, the end of
speech, that is to say, both the object of speech and the falling silent
of speech, cannot be separated from the movement of speech itself.
The moment of truth which *L'Innommable* evokes as corresponding to the 'souci de vérité dans la rage de dire' (III, 25) has its
existence, as a fictional moment, within the confines of speech, not
beyond them. The end of speaking, in the shape of that strange
figure of truth and silence promulgated by the narrator of *L'Innommable*, is somehow already located within the process of speaking
itself.

The end of speech, as *L'Innommable* displays it – as an ultimate
story, as silence, as the peace of indifference – is not an object, and
it is not something that can therefore be embodied fully in the act of
speaking. There remains, to speech, an excess, a supplement, a
waste which cannot be pronounced or incorporated within words,
though it seems to be inherent within the act of speaking. This is
one reason why the goal pursued by *L'Innommable* is never
reached and why the language deployed to attain that goal seems,
in principle, to extend to infinity.

In Beckett's text, the end of speech, one could say, stands at the
beginning of speech as what makes speech possible (and this is
made clear by the preamble to *Molloy* with its insistence on the
poverty of language of the narrator). At the same time, the end of
speech is also the final extremity of speech in the shape of the
silence to which all language inevitably returns. There is a circularity here, the outcome of which is a sequence of narratives which,
because of the gaps, paradoxes and rhetorical instabilities that they
contain, approach that true story which *L'Innommable* describes as
the object of the quest, and which, as the final lines of the book
illustrate, is not a story or an end or a truth at all, but more a
threshold, a mythological gateway back to the beginning. Paradoxically, and with the aporetic twist one now expects of the text, the

quest becomes its own end and a means of suspending its own end. 'La recherche du moyen de faire cesser les choses, taire sa voix', announces *L'Innommable*, 'est ce qui permet au discours de se poursuivre' (III, 25).

In this way, the end of speech, towards which Beckett's trilogy tends, and which *L'Innommable* dramatises as an ultimate, impossible story, or as a moment of final silence or peace, is not a revelation of truth. There is no truth, Beckett's text argues, and there are no vehicles for truth. The end of speech, both the object and the effacement of speaking, takes the form, however, of an anamnesis, a disinterring of the past as that which makes possible the writing of the present. In Beckett's trilogy, the process of anamnesis is a remembering which does not resurrect the past in its identity with itself but rediscovers what it was that was forgotten in order for Beckett's narrators to become who they are. And Beckett's writing responds by shifting back and forth via affirmation and negation in an oscillating rhythm of inscription and effacement: 'D'abord salir, ensuite nettoyer' (III, 25).

For Beckett's narrators, in a characteristic paradox, to speak is to submit to a compelling force which has no end, in the sense both of a terminus and a goal, because the act of speech already contains that end within itself as what makes it possible in the first place. That the end of speech has already taken place is what makes speaking endless. In turn, the endlessness of speech makes it impossible for that end to have taken place. 'La fin est dans le commencement, et cependant on continue', states Hamm in *Fin de partie*,[1] and the paradox holds for the trilogy as well. The narrator of Part One of *Molloy* makes a similar point: 'Ma vie, ma vie,' he laments, 'tantôt j'en parle comme d'une chose finie, tantôt comme d'une plaisanterie qui dure encore, et j'ai tort, car elle est finie et dure à la fois, mais par quel temps du verbe exprimer cela?' (I, 53).

Time, in Beckett's trilogy, seems to be both suspended and yet remorselessly continuous. Beckett largely eliminates temporal notations except those which relate to cyclical time. (The only exceptions seem mainly to fall in the opening pages of Part Two of *Molloy*, where the narrator makes a series of manically precise references to time, which have the effect of highlighting the confusing lack of any prior established time plan to the story.) Indications of time are often in the form of references to the seasons or to months in the seasonal cycle (I, 271). In other cases, the reader is given times in the day or week that have symbolic or religious significance (like the recurrent motif of the sabbath in

Molloy, or, in the same novel, the ironically appropriate reference
to the 'angélus, rappelant l'incarnation' [I, 20], made as the
narrator makes ready to visit his mother). And at the start of
Malone meurt Beckett makes similar humorous use of some of the
feast days in the French religious and secular calendar.
Time in the trilogy is not progressive but circular. As a result,
certain episodes become difficult to situate in time. The narrator's
visit to his mother in *Molloy* is a case in point. 'Je résolus d'aller voir
ma mère' (I, 20), the narrator tells us, before proceeding to digress
on the subject of bicycles. Two pages later, the narrator writes that
'ma mère me voyait volontiers' (I, 22–3) and goes on to describe a
visit to his mother. The description is concluded by the narrator
recalling how 'une fois' (I, 26) he kissed his mother's cheek ('j'y
posai mes lèvres [. . .] sur cette petite poire grisâtre et ratatinée').
He then pursues his narration by telling how he continued his
journey ('Je fis néanmoins quelques milles sans accroc . . .' [I, 27])'
Usually, according to conventional expectations, readers whould
construe these events as following on from each other in logical or
chronological succession. On first reading, the sequence seems to
be quite linear: first the narrator decides to visit his mother, then he
makes the visit and finally continues on his way.

Four pages later, however, when the man who gives his name as
Molloy is called by the police to render an account of himself, he
reveals that he is still planning to visit his mother ('je me rendais
chez ma mère' [I, 31]). The narrator somehow seems to have
moved on while managing to come full circle. The time sequence of
the story appears strangely incoherent, with the narrator going to
visit his mother when he would seem to have just finished visiting
her. Two solutions suggest themselves to explain this break in
continuity. One is that the narrator is misleading the police when he
asserts he is still on his way to visit his mother (and the text hardly
disallows this kind of suspicion). The other is that the visit to the
mother is more a memory of a visit, a kind of unannounced
flashback which is located in some unspecified, almost mythic time
prior to the narrator setting out on his journey.

Beckett is careful, however, not to introduce any hierarchical
distinctions between the different parts of the whole episode. The
only clue the reader is given as to the time plan of the sequence as a
whole is a change in tense. In his account Beckett shifts from the
passé simple ('je résolus') to the imperfect tense ('ma mère me
voyait'), then back to the *passé simple* ('j'y posai'). (But in the
English translation all these tenses are given without distinction as

simple pasts: 'I resolved . . . My mother never refused to see me . . . Once I touched with my lips . . . Nevertheless I covered several miles.') The change in tense (in the French text) gives a different temporal status to the visit, which takes on the air of a repeated or unfinished occurrence, unlike the other events which are treated as single, completed actions. Beckett's text does not explain the move to the imperfect, which can be justified referentially (because the verbs describe continuous states or habitual actions), nor does it label the episode of the visit as a flashback or situate it at any identifiable moment of time. The effect is to introduce into the novel a degree of temporal confusion which, over and above the question of narrative plausibility, throws into doubt the diegetic coherence of *Molloy*, and it is no surprise to find the narrator referring to his journey as an 'irréel voyage, pénultième d'une forme pâlissante entre formes pâlissantes' (I, 22).

Largely as a consequence of this strategy of both maintaining and blurring temporal marks, it is sometimes argued that time in the trilogy has much in common with the circular recurrence of myth. It is true that *Molloy* refers the reader at one point to something that is described as 'le présent mythologique', which is a present tense, the narrator contends, which is not present but in fact past: 'Je parle au présent, il est si facile de parler au présent, quand il s'agit du passé' (I, 37). This phrase, together with the numerous literary or mythological allusions that have been discovered in the trilogy, has sent many critics in search of elaborate sets of mythological concordances to account for the interpretative density of Beckett's writing.[2] But the reasons why Beckett's prose has this potential to fascinate its readers, both in *Molloy* and elsewhere, lie arguably much closer to home.

The case is clearer if one considers an example, like, in *Molloy*, the relationship between the narrator and his mother. The treatment of the mother, as many readers have noted, is remarkably ambivalent. This is particularly evident if one follows the discursive sequence of the text, as opposed to its diegetic construction, i.e. the order in which events appear in the text rather than that in which they are supposed to take place. From the very first paragraph, then, the mother is pronounced dead, even though, scarcely a dozen pages later, what is put forward as the nub of the plot, the narrator's decision to visit her, presupposes her being alive. While the narrator starts his story in her room, it is ambiguous whether this occupancy, at the outset, represents a moment of identificatory fusion between mother and son, or marks the fact that, in a kind of inverted reprise of his own birth, the narrator has himself expelled his mother from her room and is somehow responsible for her death. The subsequent course of the text is far from straightforward. If the narration leaves the mother's room behind, it is to tell the story of how the narrator goes about visiting his mother. Her house seems to be near the town slaughterhouse. But once he sets off, the only visit reported in the text is the chronologically incoherent episode already mentioned. For most of the novel, though the claim, diegetically, must be that he is still on his way to see her, the narrator travels ever further away from her and his mother's presence diminishes in the text. Attraction and repulsion match one another in a movement of reciprocal deferral and the end of the plot is reached only by the narrator abandoning it.

As I have suggested, this contradictory journeying is typical of Beckett's narratives. Perhaps the most useful understanding of the ambivalent relation to the mother in *Molloy* is provided by the logic of what Freud sets out under the heading of the uncanny.[3] The uncanny, Freud suggests, is a name for something close to home (or '*heimlich*') which was once put at a – seemingly safe – distance and ought to have remained secret. Instead of that, it stages a return, and comes back, as a lifelike but grotesque ghost, to haunt the subject. The uncanny is an affect which has no immediately identifiable origin but nonetheless is a source of compulsive fascination. It is more disturbing than any particular object which might be said to provoke it, since what it dramatises is a split or division in the subjectivity of the speaker. One persistent emblem of the uncanny, which has immediate relevance for Beckett's trilogy, is the idea of the usurping double, the other who steals the subject's place and becomes a substitute for him or her. It points to unresolved (and unresolvable) difficulties with frontiers and limits, like those existing between the human and the non-human, between life and death, or between male and female. The uncanny also has the dramatic capacity to appear most perplexing and unintelligible at the very moment when it seems to be about to deliver an enigmatic message that demands to be deciphered or translated.

The uncanny as a literary mode has a number of effects which closely resemble those described by readers of Beckett's trilogy: there is the same sense of impenetrable mystery but cryptic significance, the same impression of verbal concepts being over-powered by non-verbal affects or narrative clarity by intangible complications. Moreover, the uncanny would seem to speak of the same sort of cryptic genealogical fable as that running through the hidden passageways of Beckett's text. To this extent, then, what is encoded in Beckett's text has the recurrent structure of a scenario which details an unconscious fantasy. The references to myth, one can conclude, when they do occur, function less as an end in themselves than as a means of mediating the unconscious material which the uncanny brings to the surface.

In the course of the story of his decision to visit his mother, the narrator breaks off to deliver a disquisition on the theme of bicycles. The hiatus is comical, and the text moves with a jolt from the sublime to the ridiculous. But the association between the narrator's mother and bicycles, though abrupt, is hardly gratuitous. For the bicycle, too, like his mother, is an object of enjoyment and of mischievous, childish pleasures. The narrator's favourite part of his bicycle was its horn, which he took delight in squeezing. The passage is worth citing at some length:

Actionner cette corne était pour moi un vrai plaisir, une volupté presque. J'irai plus loin, je dirai que si je devais dresser le palmarès des choses qui ne m'ont pas fait trop chier au cours de mon interminable existence, l'acte de corner y occuperait une place honorable. Et quand je dus me séparer de ma bicyclette j'en enlevai la corne et la gardai par devers moi. Je l'ai toujours, je crois, quelque part, et si je ne m'en sers plus, c'est qu'elle est devenue muette. Même les automobiles d'aujourd'hui n'ont pas de corne, dans le sens où je l'entends, ou rarement. Quand j'en repère une, dans la rue, par la vitre baissée d'une automobile en stationnement, souvent je m'arrête et l'actionne. Il faudrait récrire tout cela au plus-que-parfait. Parler de bicyclettes et de cornes, quel repos. Malheureusement ce n'est pas de cela qu'il s'agit mais de celle qui me donna le jour, par le trou de son cul si j'ai bonne mémoire. Premier emmerdement. (I, 21–2)

Bicycles, amidst the vast repertoire of human artifacts, have an unusual characteristic in that they are sexually differentiated. Men and women, at any rate by gendered custom, ride different sorts of bicycles.[4] Bicycles are like an – uncanny – mechanical extension of the human body, and cycling enjoys as a result a kind of lewd vernacular association with sexual activity. Some fifteen years earlier, Beckett had made a joke about this, in the poem 'Sanies I', where he refers to his bicycle as 'her whom alone in the accusative / I have dismounted to love'.[5] But in that early poem, the chief pleasure in cycling was located in a different part of the anatomy, the seat or saddle: 'all heaven in the sphincter', the poem puts it, '*the* sphincter'. As in the poem, so too in *Molloy*, where something of an anal obsession permeates the language of the passage. In the context, squeezing bicycle horns comes to resemble, by analogy, the movements of the anal sphincter, and the whole chain of associations culminates in the recurrent figure of the narrator's anal birth as the event that gave him, as the English has it, his 'first taste of the shit'. Symptomatically, in 'Sanies I', as well, cycling home is also linked with being born and the poem has its rider ('like a Ritter with pommelled scrotum') yearning: 'ah to be back in the caul now'.

Across these two texts, the passage from *Molloy* and 'Sanies I', a complex chain of verbal motifs draws in a strange collection of items: the tooting of horns, the pleasures of the saddle, of coming and going, memories of birth, of larches, of Easter Week, of mother in labour and of father far away (in the poem, as much later in *Company*, he is portrayed as having spent the day out walking), and other things besides. More texts, in turn, could be adduced here, as , for instance, in *Malone meurt*, the references to Madame Pédale, in whose name women and machines, male homosexuality and cycling are linked together in cryptic shorthand, or the encounters with other women in the trilogy, Lousse, Moll, or Madeleine–Marguerite with her job of anointing the narrator as after crucifixion. In all these places the contextual associations, insistently and obsessively, turn on the event of the narrator's birth, one he presents as something botched or failed in the past or somehow still to be achieved in the future.

The theme of anal birth is common enough in the trilogy. In the first instance, it operates as a barring of sexual difference in terms which are now familiar. One of the main objects of the fantasy of anal birth is to deny or displace sexual difference and construe the female as an enigmatically crippled male (and there are in *Molloy* plenty of illustrations of the precarious and hypothetical character of sexual difference, ranging from the mother herself to the figures of Lousse, and Ruth or Edith). Elsewhere in the novel, however, the rear passage is made the subject of much mock lyrical enthusiasm by the narrator:

Je m'excuse de revenir encore sur ce honteux orifice, c'est ma muse qui le veut. Peut-être faut-il y voir moins la tare qui est nommée que le symbole de celles que je tais, dignité due peut-être à sa centralité et à ses allures de trait d'union entre moi et l'autre merde. On le méconnaît, à mon avis, ce petit trou, on l'appelle celui du cul et on affecte de le mépriser. Mais ne serait-il pas plutôt le vrai portail de l'être, dont la célèbre bouche ne serait que l'entrée de service? Rien n'y pénètre, ou si peu, qui ne soit rejeté sur le champ, ou peu s'en faut. Presque tout lui répugne qui lui vient du dehors et pour ce qui lui arrive du dedans on ne peut pas dire qu'il se mette particulièrement en frais non plus. Ne sont-ce pas là des choses significatives? (I, 122)

This panegyric to the rear passage is delivered with visible relish. This rhetorical flourish illustrates another dimension to the theme of anal birth. What the anal charge in Beckett's writing does is to inject into his text a specific energy, the energy of bodily and verbal expulsion. There is nothing, the narrator tells us, that the anal sphincter does not expel, and this is true of words as well as waste matter, and there are several places in the trilogy where that equation is made explicit, notably in *L'Innommable*, where the narrator enjoins: 'achevons notre pensée, avant de chier dessus. Car si je suis Mahood, je suis Worm aussi. Plof. Ou si je ne suis pas encore Worm, je le serai, en n'étant plus Mahood. Plof' (III, 104).

The anal impetus within Beckett's writing functions here as an aggressive, at times even sadistic force. There is, for instance, no filial piety evident in *Molloy* in the narrator's portrait of his mother. In the place of devotion comes the violence of a series of rhetorical reversals which, by substituting back for front, arse-hole for vagina, invert the riddle of birth, shifting it from an event undergone into a process continually being repeated. The squeezing of bicycle horns changes from a symbol for ingestion from the maternal breast into a gesture mimicking, joyfully, the expulsion of matter from the body's other extremity. Instead of incorporation, what the text enacts is a rhythm of evacuation and dispersion. Sucking as a metaphor for speech is supplanted by anal flatus, and as though to symbolise this recasting of literature by bodily motions, the text has the narrator farting scornfully through the pages of the *TLS*. In *Molloy*, farting becomes, in both senses, a fundamental body language ('a matter of fundamental sounds', Beckett wrote to Alan Schneider in 1957),[6] rhythmic as well as discontinuous: 'Que voulez-vous,' the narrator rejoins, 'le gaz me sort du fondement à propos de tout et de rien, je suis donc bien obligé d'y faire allusion de temps en temps, malgré la répugnance que cela m'inspire. Un jour je les comptai. Trois cent quinze pets en dix-neuf heures, soit une moyenne de plus de seize pets l'heure' (I, 43–4).

Beckett's texts derive some of their most comic moments from this interest in bodily functions. Beckett's humour is always a humour of abrupt disjunctions and is largely fuelled, as in the description of the mother in *Molloy*, by the discordance between oral pleasure and anal aggression, the enjoyment of words and the vituperations which they convey, between the imagined wholeness of the body and its dispersion into a collection of incongruous and mutually incompatible elements or affects. Anal aggression in turn often acts as a mobilising force for laughter in Beckett's text, at

least for that type of laughter which the appropriately named figure
of Arsene, in *Watt*, describes as

the dianoetic laugh, down the snout – haw! – so. It is the laugh of laughs,
the *risus purus*, the laugh laughing at the laugh, the beholding, the saluting
of the highest joke, in a word the laugh that laughs – silence please – at that
which is unhappy. (47)

What is invested here is not so much the anal as the nasal sphincter.
Arsene's diatribe ('an ordure, from beginning to end' [44]) derives
its energy from a thrusting snort of aggression which, though it
takes vengeance on the world, deprives the body of any intellectual
dominance over the object of mockery and brings to the text a sense
that what is being laughed at is the body itself as an anal excretum
which has no purity or wholeness. The effect is much the same,
towards the end of *Molloy*, when the narrator remembers his
superior Youdi, and shakes with uncontrollable laughter at the
thought that, after all, his own situation is more nearly, as he
describes it, 'celle de la merde qui attend la chasse d'eau' (I, 252)
than that of a man in search of himself or of another.

Anal aggression, then, in Beckett's case, forms the basis of a
textual idiom, an argot or 'sabir' (III, 78) even, a language, in any
case, the effect of which is to enable the narrator to reinvent or
rewrite the enigmatic scenario of his birth. This is what is finally at
issue in *Molloy* in the episode of the narrator's visit to his mother.
The major part of the visit is taken up with the description of how
the narrator enters into communication with his mother. This is
done by way of a regular series of violent blows or thumps on the
mother's skull. The narrator endeavours to impose on his mother a
rudimentary language system in which 'un coup signifiait oui, deux
non, trois je ne sais pas, quatre argent, cinq adieu ' (I, 24). But
since the mother cannot count beyond two, the code is in effect
reduced to two positions, either yes or no, depending on whether
the number of blows is odd or even. The result is something
approaching a grotesque analogue of the rhetoric of confusion
practised in much of the trilogy, as *L'Innommable* puts it, 'par pure
aporie ou bien par affirmations et négations infirmées au fur et à
mesure, ou tôt ou tard' (III, 8). In both cases, statements become
less important than the gestures of assertion or negation which
traverse them and meanings themselves become subject to mind-
boggling displacements and reversals, like the transformation – in
the ruined understanding of the mother – of the one blow meaning
'yes' into the one blow – for her – also meaning 'farewell'.

This idiom of reversal is also, clearly, a language of revenge. The association seems explicit between the narrator's thumps on the mother's skull and her attempts to shake him from the womb before term. The narrator forgives his mother for attempting to abort him, but he does so in order to harness for his own cause the thrusting, rejective violence which joins him and his mother together and maintains their identification. In turn, when the narrator finds himself by the sea and assembles his collection of sucking stones, what he discovers in sucking is not the mother-oriented delight of babbling nor, like a latter-day Demosthenes, the oral pliability of words, but the resistance to meaning of a group of solid stones that are shunted around his body like so many inert objects until the moment comes to discard them all. Sucking, in *Molloy*, like eating, is a constant encounter with the indigestible. It is no surprise to find the narrator react with a convulsion of anxious aggression when handed a cup of tea and a slice of bread by the social worker and send them both crashing to the ground with all his strength (I, 34).

In the narrator's relation to his mother, however, there are evident remnants of an Œdipal scenario. But the myth is reprised jokingly, in inverted fashion, for it is the mother who sees her son as a replica of his father. She calls her son Dan, and 'Dan', the narrator continues, 'était peut-être le nom de mon père, oui, elle me prenait peut-être pour mon père. Moi je la prenais pour ma mère et elle elle me prenait pour mon père' (I, 23). At this moment of greatest intimacy, the narrator denounces the familial bond between mother and son as being founded on an error: if the mother mistakes him for his father, then, equally, he mistakes her for his mother. The Œdipal scene is inscribed only to be disqualified. The agent of that disqualification, the narrator explains, is the letter g, which he describes, as it were, as the anal letter par excellence:

Moi je l'appelais Mag, quand je devais lui donner un nom. Et si je l'appelais Mag c'était qu'à mon idée, non que j'eusse su dire pourquoi, la lettre g abolissait la syllabe ma, et pour ainsi dire crachait dessus, mieux que toute autre lettre ne l'aurait fait. (I, 23)

As though to drive home this anal repudiation of the mother, the narrator glosses these words in turn with a closing reference to her double incontinence and her nickname, which turns out to be: 'la comtesse Caca' (I, 23–4).[7]

By the language of anal reversal, then, the narrator fends off the image of his mother. But while the mother is left behind by the text, the narrator constantly comes across her again as the reverse of what she is. The narrator's dependence on his mother for money is symbolic of other debts. The narrator refers to his mother at one point as 'cette pauvre putain unipare' (I, 26), which suggests the narrator's father was also little more than a passing client and the narrator's conception and birth something like the settling of an unwanted debt. The writing of the novel, as staged fictionally in the opening pages of the book, is itself a re-enactment of that unwelcome debt, and as though to balance the account, the narrator sits in his mother's room, giving up his text to the man who collects the pages in return for money.

The relationship to the mother, then, is not so much repudiated as displaced and transformed. In *Molloy* and the following novels, there are numerous examples of female figures who are also linked to the image of the mother. At times the link is textually explicit. For example, when the narrator details his anatomical doubts as to the true gender of the women whose names he gives as Lousse and Ruth (or Edith) he confesses that 'pour vous livrer le fond de mon effroi, l'image de ma mère vient quelquefois se joindre aux leurs, ce qui est proprement insupportable, de quoi se croire en pleine crucifixion' (I, 89).

In other instances, it is solely the recurrence of the motif of anal ambivalence that suggests a link, as in the case of Madame Pédale in *Malone meurt*. Towards the end of *Molloy*, too, the narrator declares that, for his part, he is engaged on a pilgrimage to 'la madone de Shit' (I, 268). Only in *Malone meurt*, on the part of Macmann's girlfriend, Moll, is there an apparent conversion from the anal to the oral. But Moll is an oral grotesque one of whose most repugnant characteristics, the narrator tells us, are her lips, which were 'si larges et grasses qu'elles semblaient manger la moitié du visage' (II, 157). Macmann kisses her with enjoyment only when he discovers the crucifix-shaped tooth that Moll wears like a prosthesis in her mouth. Finally, she, too, is killed off, but not before a scene in which an apparently phantom pregnancy terminates in an attack of uncontrollable vomiting (II, 170). Here, too, birth becomes a botched expulsion of undigested matter.

There is one episode in *Molloy* that may be read as a condensed commentary, or interlinear gloss on this whole fantasy scenario. This is the episode of the encounter with Sophie Loy, or Lousse (as she is later named). The narrator fails in his quest for his mother and the meeting with this other woman stands in for the anticipated visit to the mother. The names, Sophie Loy, or Lousse, have several possible resonances. The first is a partial repetition of the name, Molloy, and also draws attention to the law of naming (and the name, Molloy, is only offered, in the story, in response to the inquiry of the police). A loy is also, one might add, a peculiar kind of Irish spade, which in time has its own part to play in the story.

The name, Lousse, on the other hand, seems to echo the name, Lulu (pronounced: Loulou), used for the narrator's pregnant girl-friend in *Premier Amour*, which, in addition to its meanings in English, is also a term of affection in French and anticipates (in French) the arrival on the scene of a small doggie, or: 'loulou'. Lousse has overtones, too, of: 'loose' in English (as in 'loose woman') or 'louche' in French (meaning: 'cross-eyed', or 'shifty').

The story of the narrator's meeting with Lousse begins with his ungainly arrival in town astride his bicycle. He accidentally runs down Lousse's dog (name: Teddy) who, she says, she was taking to be put down anyway. After narrowly escaping being lynched, he is taken in by Lousse and helps bury the dead dog (or 'chien écrasé' in this novelistic foray into the world of weddings and fêtes). Next, after an interlude with an obscene parrot, the narrator wakes up as though prepared for his own burial (I, 57).

Two things here are immediately compelling. The first is the lengthy sequence of substitutions which the episode involves. Teddy, who is on his way to be put to sleep, but whom Lousse 'avait aimé comme un enfant' (I, 54), seems to be a substitute not only for this absent child, but also for Lousse's husband, who is already dead. The narrator, who kills Teddy, is adopted by Lousse as a replacement for her non-existent child, but also as a potentially cuddly partner (usually only bears are called Teddy). This second possibility, bearing in mind that Lousse (of whom the narrator asks, later, 'si elle n'était pas plutôt un homme ou tout du moins un androgyne' [I, 84]) is necessarily in the text something of a mother substitute, gives Beckett the opportunity of some crude sexual innuendo in the burial scene: it is the narrator who, 'quoique le monsieur' (I, 51–2), allows Lousse to do the appropriate digging.

The scene ends with the burial of Teddy under a larch tree. The narrator plays the part of an onlooker, but not a passive one:

Ce fut elle qui fit le trou, qui mit le chien dedans, qui combla le trou. Je ne faisais en somme qu'y assister. J'y contribuais de ma présence. Comme si ç'avait été mon enterrement à moi. Et il l'était. C'était un mélèze. C'est le seul arbre que je puisse identifier avec certitude. (I, 54)

Teddy's death is somehow changed into the narrator's own. Positions and identities within the scenario are exchanged with disconcerting ease, with child, pet, mother and lover all displacing each
other as in a game of fictional musical chairs. And at the same time,
with the nudging allusion to the larch tree, for instance, the scene of
the burial resonates cryptically, across this and other Beckett texts,
with the autobiographical theme of the writer's birth (as in the
poem 'Sanies I', where the phrase is: 'oh the larches the pain drawn
like a cork').

This echo of other texts within *Molloy* is the second remarkable
feature of this episode. For the sequence is far from isolated in
Beckett's work. In the story, *L'Expulsé*, the narrator, walking in
ungainly fashion, is stopped by the police and just misses knocking
down a child, but his own fall 'entraîna celle d'une vieille dame
couverte de paillettes et de dentelles et qui devait peser dans les
deux cents livres'.[8] (Interesting questions arise as to the secret
motivation of Beckett's writing here. The English version of the
passage renders this last item as 'sixteen stone'. This is correct only
if the 'livres' are metric, not imperial pounds. But if this is the case,
why does Beckett's text not give the weight in kilos, as one would
usually expect in standard French? Is there perhaps not some
connection here between the 'sixteen stone' of *The Expelled* and
the 'seize pierres' the narrator is fond of sucking in *Molloy* – and
which he insists are 'pierres' and not 'cailloux' [I, 105]? But, despite
these clues, the sequence remains enigmatic, lapidary and opaque,
an emblem of Beckett's labyrinthine text.) Making his escape from
the accident in *L'Expulsé*, the narrator runs into another policeman
and a funeral procession. There follows a brief discussion on the
subject of the sign of the cross:

Personnellement si j'en étais réduit à me signer j'aurais à cœur de le faire
comme il faut, racine du nez, nombril, téton gauche, téton droit. Mais eux,
avec leurs frôlements précipités et imprécis, ils vous font une espèce de
crucifié en boule, sans la moindre tenue, les genoux sous le menton et les
mains n'importe comment. (25)

Towards the end of chapter two in *Mercier et Camier*, a similar
incident takes place. 'Prends-moi par la main', says Mercier to his
friend. 'Je trottinerai bien sagement à tes côtés, comme un petit
chiot ou un enfant en bas âge' (51). Not only does the phrase
anticipate, in the figure of Teddy, the merging together of dog and
child, pet and offspring, but it also echoes the words *Molloy* uses to
describe Teddy, before he was run down, 'sagement se traînant aux

côtés de sa maîtresse' (I, 47). In *Mercier et Camier*, a moment later, a squeal of brakes reveals 'une grosse femme, d'un âge qui paraissait avancé,' lying in the street. 'Son sang,' the text adds, 'issu d'une ou de plusieurs blessures, gagnait déjà la rigole' (51). She, too, as in *L'Expulsé*, is fancily dressed and, we are told, 'le désordre de ses vêtements laissait voir des dessous blanchâtres et moutonnants d'une densité extraordinaire' (51).

One explanation for this curious but insistent recurrence of textual motifs might be that, in *L'Expulsé* and *Mercier et Camier*, both early texts in French, Beckett was exploring possibilities, and went on to give full treatment to the episode only in *Molloy* (which was written later). To the extent that *Molloy* provides the most detailed version of the episode, there is no doubt some truth in the argument. But in 1957, with clockwork regularity, the scene began again, this time in English.[9] Indeed, at the start of *All That Fall*, Mrs Rooney, who, according to her husband, weighs 'two hundred pounds of unhealthy fat' (31) – 'cent kilos de cellulite' in Pinget's French version – is tempted to 'flop down flat on the road like a big fat jelly out of a bowl and never move again!' (14), and narrowly misses being run down by Mr Tyler – on his bicycle. And the play ends with the report of a child being killed 'under the wheels' (39) of the train, as well as with a mention of the young girl (from Jung's Tavistock Lecture) 'who had never really been born' (36), followed by a reference to 'a dead dog' (36) lying in the ditch and a passing allusion to Christ's arrival in Jerusalem 'on a hinny' (37).

These recurring motifs seem to be hardly coincidental. But they work like so many cryptic clues which remain out of reach of the text and the reader. What they do establish, though, from text to text, is a disturbing law of mutually contaminating equivalences, according to which, at differing moments, a woman, a child, or a dog are all run down with mysterious, and often deadly consequences. Beckett produces four accounts which, though they seem to tell a similar story, rather like Vladimir's Gospels, fail to agree on significant points. Thus, one might ask, who was it that was run over? An old woman (*Mercier et Camier*, *L'Expulsé*), a dog (*Molloy*, *All That Fall*) or a child (*All That Fall*)? And who, like Watt earlier, narrowly escaped being knocked down? A child (*L'Expulsé*) or an old woman (*All That Fall*)? Why are these women fat (*All That Fall*) with frilly or lace underwear (*Mercier et Camier*, *L'Expulsé*)? And who was it that was buried? A stranger of indeterminate sex (*L'Expulsé*), a dog (*Molloy*), perhaps even the narrator (*Molloy*)? And what is the connection here with Christ, who is gestured at, as though still at the unborn or foetal stage, and a mere 'crucifié en boule', by the incompetent mourners of *L'Expulsé*? Christ is also remembered by Mrs Rooney entering Jerusalem in ungainly fashion on a 'hinny' ('aren't they barren or sterile, or whatever it is?' [37], she asks). So the reference to Christ is also reminiscent of the arrival in town of the narrators both of *Molloy* and *L'Expulsé*.

Of the four versions (and it is possible, as in the case of the Gospels, that there are others elsewhere) the most elaborate is the one given in *Molloy*. This is due in some measure to the motif of the animal, Teddy. The only other mentions of a dog are, in passing, in *Mercier et Camier* and *All That Fall*. Teddy, though, in *Molloy*, is at the crux of the many substitutions enacted by the story. He mediates not only between the child he is not and the mother figure to whom he belongs, but also between the narrator who shares his funeral and the dead father figure he has supplanted. It is not for nothing, perhaps, that his name, an odd one for a dog, is a contraction of Theodore, meaning 'God's gift' (and he is not the only one in the text, as the next chapter will suggest, to bear the name of God in this way). Despite, even because of that name, he functions in the text as a kind of general equivalent, even a supernumerary supplement, one who stands in for a dead child or a bleeding woman, whose ears (because of ticks) are covered in red specks, like budding larches, and whose own death, under the bicycle wheels of the narrator, like a farcical replay of the Œdipal myth, repeats that of Lousse's late husband 'mort pour une patrie qui se disait la sienne et dont de son vivant il ne retira jamais le moindre avantage, mais seulement des affronts et des bâtons dans les roues' (I, 48). And this very last spanner in the works (but which Beckett, disappointingly, translates, in Shakespearian manner, as 'vexations') leaves open the issue of how Lousse's husband actually died: is it possible, outlandish though it might seem, that the wheels in question were bicycle wheels?

The mention of Lousse's husband draws attention to the fact that, in this whole genealogical fable, there is a singular absentee. This is the figure of the father. His absence is symptomatic, but more apparent than real. In Beckett's work (and the poem 'Sanies I' or the later *Company* are notable instances of this), elements of the Easter story are used as an ironic frame for staging the painful and unreconciled event of birth. The reference to Christ, as I have noted, forms an integral part of the accident scenario in *L'Expulsé*, *All That Fall* and *Molloy*, and it would seem that, in that story, the figure of the father is displaced into the theme of crucifixion.

Christ's crime, and the reason for his execution, was to declare himself or be declared – aporetically, as it turns out, according to *En attendant Godot* – the King of the Jews and the Son of God. Christ's claim to be born of a divine father founders, however, on the cross, when it is realised that Christ's 'it is finished' (in John 19:30), which Beckett describes in *Murphy* as a back-handed 'parthian shaft' (52) and went on to use later as an insistent leitmotif in *Fin de partie*, is only a beginning of mourning, and that no dialectical resolution to that end is possible. In Beckett's text loss cannot be converted into symbolic presence. The only visible relation between the narrator of *Molloy* and his father is in the reverse Œdipal error or fantasy perpetrated by his mother in her naming of him as 'Dan'. In this confusion, there is identification without filiation or derivation, a panic of equivalence which denies the narrator the possibility of inheritance. Like Macmann (whose name is also a joke at Christ's expense), the narrator stands at the end of the line, in more ways than one.

In this way, the image of the father is not incorporated by the narrator and redemption thus made possible, but, instead, the body hangs suspended from the cross like a disembodied mass of flesh still awaiting birth. Crucifixion in Beckett's texts does not end, for the paradoxical reason that, like birth, it is not an event that has ever taken place. But the effect of this is to make matters worse, and the narrator of *Molloy*, in his journey to Golgotha, does not aspire even to the aporetic divinity of Christ (I, 120). This unreconciled suspension of crucifixion is a state of mourning for an impossible and absent father whom language is unable to make present. What remains, like a remnant expelled from the process of birth, is a body left in limbo, uncertain whether it is alive or dead, whether it is a human child or a dog. It is a flesh which, though nailed to the cross, somehow remains still to be born, like the 'crucifié en boule' of *L'Expulsé* ('crucified all of a heap', says Beckett's translation), and which asks itself the question, unremittingly, of what it is that lies beyond the mysterious inaccessibility of the womb, that strangely impaired or defective organ that Mr Tyler, speaking in *All That Fall* of the hysterectomy undergone by his 'poor daughter', describes hesitatingly as her 'bag of tricks' (14), and which in *Mercier et Camier* or *L'Expulsé* can only be guessed at through trickles of blood and swathes of lace and fancy underwear.

At the beginning of *Molloy*, there is a man who calls to collect the narrator's manuscript and gives him money in return. In Part Two of the novel, the other narrator also receives a visit, this time from the 'agent' Gaber, who, in due course, will demand of him some written account of his actions. Oddly, perhaps, both visits take place on Sunday. The narrator of Part Two suggests that, from his point of view, 'le sabbat, du moment qu'on va à la messe et qu'on verse sa dîme, peut être considéré un jour comme les autres, sous certains rapports' (I, 143). But is Sunday a day like any other? By stressing the day, Beckett's text plainly distances itself from its narrator, for it is evident that the mention of Sunday brings with it a string of religious associations. Allusions to these are frequent in Part Two of the text. These turn, for the most part, on issues of authority and of religious observance, and take the form, for instance, of the relations between Moran père and Moran fils, or the narrator's grudging confidence in his spiritual father, 'le bon père Ambroise' (I, 147)

Within the weekly round of secular, working days, the Sabbath day is given over to the paternal law. What Beckett's text suggests, by staging its own writing within the frame of the Sabbath day, is that there exists a relationship of identification or of reciprocity between the act of writing and the law of the Holy Father. To write, in this respect, would seem to be to enter into dialogue with this paternal, religious law. Indeed, the orders that Gaber delivers to the narrator are said to originate with a strange patriarchal figure called Youdi. The word, Youdi, in anti-semitic French slang, is a name for a Jew,[10] and with this glancing reference what Beckett puts into play in *Molloy* is the idea of a religious community which is not whole and does not possess its own law within itself but one which has fallen subject to its own diaspora. The community of the Jews (and Beckett names it from the perspective of the Holocaust) is synonymous here with its dispersion. The founding religious texts are not one (as they are in Christianity), but multiple, and constitute, not a single authoritative book of faith, but a palimpsest overlaid with successive commentaries and glosses.

The name, Youdi, therefore, names no centralised community that somehow embodies its own identity or essence. On the contrary, the only community Youdi sanctions is a community of difference and of enigmatic disconnections. This is made clear by the narrator when he explains his relations with Youdi and Gaber. Though there seems to be a distinction between himself, who is an 'agent', and Gaber, who is a 'messenger', there is much doubt in his mind about the very existence of the network of relations these titles imply. Each of them, paradoxically, is the only known example of the class of persons they are said by the text to exemplify. It is impossible to describe any common traits of all the members of that class except for the fact that they are presumed to be members of that class. The class, therefore, becomes an entirely fictitious construct, though not necessarily a false one. The authority ascribed to Youdi suggests the existence of a community and a code of communication, but the collective has no foundation outside of the words used to call it into – fitful and hypothetical – existence (I, 165–6).

The relationship between the narrator and paternal law figured by Youdi does not give rise to any dialectical synthesis, but to a situation of confusion where the only message available is the one addressed specifically and exclusively to the hearer and which he cannot verify or disprove by comparing it with another. The text to be read and to be written is irredeemably singular. And it is not even homogeneous with itself. The word, sabbath, does not just refer to Sundays. A sabbath (and Beckett uses it in this sense in describing Lousse's garden) is also a midnight meeting of demons, sorcerers and witches, a devilish hiatus wreaking havoc at the very heart of the law. The word, like the law of which it is an emblem, divides against itself. As it does so, another side to the act of writing is revealed. Writing, in the trilogy, is not reducible to a failed attempt on Beckett's part to subscribe to the law of genealogy and filiation. On the contrary, to confront the law, in *Molloy* and the other novels, is not only to encounter, as an aporetic disaster, the impossibility of birth or redemption, it is also, crucially, to have the chance of usurping that law by means of the act of writing itself. The narrator's lot, in *Molloy*, might be poverty, but, as the text puts it at one point, 'dans ce peu quelle puissance il y avait, d'amarres tendues à péter' (I, 29). The question for Beckett is whether it is possible, having renounced his filiation and abandoned his mother tongue, for him to mobilise this anal enthusiasm in order to reinvent his name by the act of writing itself. It is to that issue of the name, as developed in *Malone meurt* and *L'Innommable*, that I now turn.

6

NAMING THE BODY

Je vais le leur arranger, leur charabia. Auquel je n'ai jamais rien compris, du reste, pas plus qu'aux histoires qu'il charrie, comme des chiens crevés. Mon incapacité d'absorption, ma faculté d'oubli, ils les ont sous-estimées. Chère incompréhension, c'est à toi que je devrai d'être moi, à la fin. Il ne restera bientôt plus rien de leurs bourrages. C'est moi alors que je vomirai enfin, dans des rots retentissants et inodores de famélique, s'achevant dans le coma, un long coma délicieux.

L'Innommable

Towards the end of *Malone meurt*, Beckett's writing stages a crisis. A deep-seated shift or slippage seems to take place. This has the effect, reports the narrator, of suspending the obligation that he account for himself by means of a story, but also denying him the possibility of doing so. A distance, or gap, we are told (Beckett's English text calls it a 'lag'), opens up between the narrative and the position of the first-person pronoun. This separation, or delay, although – or because – it is a symptom of the narrator's expulsion from the realm of story, nevertheless holds out some ambiguous and paradoxical promise of survival.

This moment of survival is the second, more spectacular, aspect of the crisis. At the end of *Malone meurt*, the narrator's slow and unfinished fictional exploration of the question of his filiation and genealogy is brought to an apparent close with the strange and convoluted occurrence that the narrator describes as his own birth into death. It remains unsaid, however, whether this act of being born represents an emancipation from the compulsive fiasco of birth, or whether it ultimately underwrites or repeats that fiasco once more, thus denying birth any coherence as an origin or even a beginning.

Together, however, these two motifs add up to a fittingly dramatic finale:

100

Grandiose souffrance. J'enfle. Si j'éclatais? Le plafond s'approche, s'é-
loigne, en cadence, comme lorsque j'étais fœtus. Egalement à signaler un
grand bruit d'eaux, phénomène *mutatis mutandis* analogue peut-être au
mirage, dans le désert. Fenêtre. Je ne la verrai plus, me trouvant à regret
dans l'impossibilité de tourner la tête. Lumière à nouveau saturnienne,
bien tassée, traversée de remous, se creusant en entonnoirs profonds à
fond clair, ou devrais-je dire l'air, lumière aspirante. Tout est prêt. Sauf
moi. Je nais dans la mort, si j'ose dire. Telle est mon impression. Drôle de
gestation. Les pieds sont sortis déjà, du grand con de l'existence. Présen-
tation favorable j'espère. Ma tête mourra en dernier. Ramène tes mains.
Je ne peux pas. La déchirante déchirée. Mon histoire arrêtée je vivrai
encore. Décalage qui promet. C'est fini sur moi. Je ne dirai plus je. (II,
207–8)

Living and dying, like extremes, converge to erase all that may have
taken place between their confines (as had already been the case in
Murphy). By approaching death as a kind of rebirth, and describing
birth, in turn, as a passage into death, the narrator of *Malone meurt*
enters what might be seen as a final moment of self-possession. This
is what is implied by his account of birth as a reversal of normal
labour and the authoritative, if contradictory assertion that he will
henceforth abandon all use of the first-person pronoun. But this
moment of possession is also a moment of dispossession, and it is far
from evident, under these circumstances, what the value of the narrator's statements and assertions might be. Is it possible, for
instance, to accept a promise made by a man who is also, on his own
admission, in the process of dying? There seem to be no grounds for
putting any trust in the narrator, even in diegetic terms, and there is,
as I have suggested, no real proof that he actually dies.

This ambiguity can be perhaps better understood if the ending is
read in the context of the larger network of references to birth,
death and storytelling which occur in *Malone meurt*. Prior to this
finale, storytelling is consciously articulated by the narrator via the
themes of paternity, parturition and play. Thus, for instance, the
narrator's opening story. This deals with the painful adolescence of
the boy, Saposcat, who, as the text makes clear, bears that name by
patriarchal convention ('L'homme s'appelle Saposcat. Comme son
père' [II, 21]), and in view of Beckett's fondness for the association
of birth with anality it seems hardly coincidental that the name is in
part reminiscent of the Greek word for 'dung' ('-scat'). The boy's
father, for his part, considers spending his spare time working,
working, that is, 'à des écritures' (II, 22), rather like the teller of the
tale, who thus in turn, in his own way, becomes a paternal figure.

Shortly after, the narrator scornfully describes his own writing as little more than a game ('j'appelle ça jouer' [II, 25]), and what is perceptible in this allusion to playing, or play-acting (as the word 'jouer' does not discriminate between these two senses) is the link it suggests between fictional creation and procreation. To invent stories is to play at being master in a game of one's own devising and, like an author, to play at being the omnipotent father to one's own literary offspring. But playing is also, for Beckett's narrator, a regressive activity having for him the same function as it has perhaps for children. Playing with language and fiction becomes a means of exploring the limits between the fictional and the real, self and other, order and disorder, identity and difference. To play with stories is thus, as Beckett's text expresses it, to play at being the child again and to repeat the moment of birth by restaging, as though in a game, the process by which already, in earlier childhood games, the self was first constituted. To play with fiction is therefore to seek to occupy, simultaneously, the position both of the procreative father and the procreated child. In *Malone meurt*, by reasserting the paternal relationship between the author and his creation, the theme of playing is an attempt by the narrator to compensate for the non-event of birth and give birth to himself: 'Naître, voilà mon idée à présent' (II, 94).

Playing, of course, implies not real mastery but the appearance of it, not a true origin but a simulation. When the term, 'jouer', is introduced by Beckett in *Malone meurt*, it is more to describe the movement of the text as a series of uncontrollable slippages than a sequence of discernible, regulated moves. If writing is a game, it is a game in which, disturbingly, the limits can never be fixed between presence and absence, story and discourse, self and other. In *Malone meurt*, none of these oppositions necessary for coherent gaming possesses any verifiable structural consistency. Aporia is at work, unsettling and unbalancing these oppositional pairs. A precarious situation results which threatens the narrator's attempts at play by denying the game of writing any rules which the author of the game can pretend to claim as his own. There is no mastery to be achieved in the mirror of playing, rather dizziness and demoralisation.

Instead of overcoming it, playing repeats the aporia of birth. Birth, in the trilogy, is an event without issue and an act that happens in reverse, either by anal expulsion, or, as at the end of *Malone meurt*, as a slow death, from the feet up. Being born and playing with words come to share the same fate. Both culminate in failure and fiasco. Though he begins again and again, after every defeat, the narrator is only too aware of the fact that a fundamental lack of passage, rhetorical as well as bodily, has already denied his game any success: 'je ne réussirai peut-être pas mieux qu'autrefois', he writes. 'Je vais peut-être me trouver abandonné comme autrefois, sans jouets, sans lumière. Alors je jouerai tout seul, je ferai comme si je me voyais' (II, 10). As these last words suggest, play, ultimately, rests on a desire for recognition, an attempt to find in words a place of security which is sanctioned by another, either fictional or real.

When the narrator plays at storytelling, there seems to be no law to guarantee the relationship between his fictional offspring and himself in the role of author or father. Playing, in Beckett's text, is treated as the act of a child bereft of paternal love, and as a result no dialectic of separation and mutual acknowledgement is available to mediate between father and son, author and homunculus. The narrator devours his creature, like a jealous parent gobbling up its young, or as a child would a plaything, and this act of oral incorporation likens him to a mythic divinity ruling by whim rather than authority and whose aggression is itself the expression of an unsatisfied demand for love:

Non, disons-le, je ne naîtrai ni par conséquent ne mourrai jamais, c'est mieux ainsi. Et si je me raconte, et puis l'autre qui est mon petit, et que je mangerai comme j'ai mangé les autres, c'est comme toujours, par besoin d'amour, merde alors, je ne m'attendais pas à ça, d'homuncule, je ne peux m'arrêter. (II, 95)

As the narrator points out, in his shaping of the fictional lives of others, what is at stake is his own birth, rather than theirs, or, more exactly, theirs is a mirror image, a re-enactment of his own, and language itself is more revealing of the gaps and failures in the process than it is of the successful execution of the project of playful mastery.

Playing at being an authorial father in this way, then, reveals an absence of foundation and the breakdown of any dialectic of law and paternal naming. In the relation between father and son in Beckett's work, as *Malone meurt* bears out, there is no interaction, but rather a static mirroring of the one in the other which reveals the painful absence of mutual acknowledgement. The scene is one that is repeated throughout Beckett's work, in situations as different as, say, that of Murphy meditating blankly with Mr Endon, or Watt finally encountering Mr Knott, or the replication of Moran père in Moran fils. In the same way that the authorial narrator in *Malone meurt* swallows up his homunculus, so, elsewhere, the son fails in the attempt to separate from his invisible parent and thus encounter the parent as an autonomous other. Reciprocity is engulfed in the gloom of indifference (in both senses of the term). Witness 'gros Louis' and his son Edmond in conversation: 'ils étaient là, en face l'un de l'autre, dans l'obscurité, l'un parlant, l'autre écoutant, et loin, l'un de ce qu'il disait, l'autre de ce qu'il entendait, et loin l'un de l'autre' (II, 70).

The narrator in *Malone meurt* tries to be father to his fictional creations and thus give birth to himself by adopting a role in which he can be acknowledged and recognised as both father and son. In both endeavours he fails, and has to confront, in the place of the father and of the son, the same disconcerting blankness or lack. In *Malone meurt*, as in *Watt* and other texts, the predicament is dramatised by recourse to the theme of the crucifixion. In Beckett's counter-version of the Easter story (which reworks an influential anti-Christian literary tradition) Christ is abandoned on the cross by his impossible and unreal father, and in the place of salvation discovers instead merely the emptiness of the heavens and the puzzle of his own dereliction. When, some time later, it comes to the narrator's birth into death in *Malone meurt* it is naturally that same story of Christ's crucifixion and resurrection which is evoked. But the crucifixion is not present here, in Beckett's text, as an article of religious faith, however grudging, but more as the sign of an unsolved conundrum, as a paradigm for the strange impossibility of joining word and flesh together in such a way as to give birth to a speaking human subject in whom name and body share a common bond of identity.

As the theme of the crucifixion develops in the novel, the name Sapo is exchanged for that of Macmann ('son of man'), who first appears wearing a 'houppelande' (II, 102) (a 'surtout' in the translation). This greatcoat, as one might have expected by now, is a ghostly colour of green. Under cover of this paternal greatcoat, within the story of the crucifixion, another story of greater auto-biographical tenor is being told, which, though recounted only in fragments, runs like a cryptic trail from one text to another. Beckett is careful to bury his allusions within his writing as though to conceal them in some private vault, but, once hidden, like the narrator's 'amis en bois' (II, 140), they have a habit of returning to the surface of the text like litter, there to be read and deciphered like so many tell-tale traces. And what they tell is a story relating to the figure of the dead father and the crisis which affects the paternal name in Beckett's writing.

Birth and death have in common that, at bottom, they are both acts of naming. Both events are marked by the inscription of a name on a register or a gravestone and by the fact that in both cases the name is written by an agent other than the new-born or the newly dead. The failure to be born and therefore to die, to which the narrator of *Malone meurt* ascribes his predicament, is consequently a failure attributable in part to the function of the name. It is as though, in the absence of any law of filiation relating the narrator to the father, there no longer exists any name for him to embody as his own as proof of his singularity or personal identity.

It can be argued that, for Beckett the writer, in abandoning the maternal – and paternal – tongue of Anglo-Irish, what was really at stake for him was the possibility of writing something resembling his own epitaph in a cryptic, foreign language, therefore an idiom or tongue that might be known not to others but to himself alone. That is what is suggested, perhaps, by the passage in the story, *Premier Amour*, where the narrator, composing an abstruse text for his own gravestone, in a gesture perhaps only a student of foreign languages would appreciate, gives it pride of place in his œuvre, noting fondly that 'mes autres écrits, ils n'ont pas le temps de sécher qu'ils me dégoûtent déjà, mais mon épitaphe me plaît toujours. Elle illustre un point de grammaire' (9–10). And it is not without its subtle irony that the epitaph should have to do with the grammatical niceties surrounding the possibilities of escape: 'Ci-gît qui y échappa tant / Qu'il n'en échappe que maintenant' (10).

Instead of suffering death in silence as a process which would leave him at the mercy of an epitaph written by others, the narrator at the end of *Malone meurt* tries to transform the dispossession of death into a willed act of verbal presence. His demise is an attempt (as in *Premier Amour*) to escape the imposition of an alien name, or at least to elude the rule of pronouns. This is what is implied by his assertion: 'Je ne dirai plus je.' But at the same time, as he is being given birth into death, the narrator also declares that beyond story and beyond the given pronoun there is something else still to be named. The active refusal of names or pronouns is doubled by an undiminished desire to reinscribe them. The contradiction rests on a paradox which implies that to assume the name prescribed by others at birth, or death, is either to have no name at all, or else to suffer the alienation of a name which does not belong to whoever is obliged to bear it, or which fails to represent, or misrepresents the

flesh on which it is written. To accept the name inscribed by others
is to be born under an assumed name, and therefore not to live but
die, just as to be buried under a false name is not to die at all, but to
live on as a restless ghost.

The name may be false, or, at best, conjectural, as it is for most
of Beckett's characters, but there exists beyond the name a surplus,
an excess, something more, which has still to be named for it to be
witnessed in Beckett's writing. To embody that excess and to mark
its fragile existence, another name must be produced. That name, if
it exists, is not available in advance. It must first be discovered or
invented. Only then can it be written, as though for the first time,
by the body that will bear it. This new, additional, or fundamental
name does not belong to any previous language, even though it is
hardly possible for it to exist otherwise. It is rather a cryptic or
private name, like a 'surnom', or nickname, an idiomatic cypher
existing at the edge of language as though it were the object and
purpose of writing itself but which, like many nicknames, may turn
out not to be recognisable as a proper name at all, but rather as a
mark or a thing, a mere trace or phoneme. But it is no exaggeration
to say that the project of Beckett's writing, throughout the trilogy
and beyond, is an attempt to spell this cryptic other name.[1]

At the end of *Malone meurt*, the narrator's final moments, by
joining together in one encompassing circle the beginning and the
end of the narrator's genealogical itinerary, provide him with the
opportunity for a last farewell performance. The narrator, in
ending, rounds up, as though for a last curtain call, a number of the
characters who had appeared in Beckett's previous books or
stories:

C'est ma vie, ce cahier, ce gros cahier d'enfant, j'ai mis du temps à m'y
résigner. Pourtant je ne le jetterai pas. Car je veux y mettre une dernière
fois ceux que j'ai appelés à mon secours, mais mal, de sorte qu'ils n'ont pas
compris, afin qu'ils meurent avec moi. (II, 191)

As the narrator absents himself from his text, his place is marked,
as by an epitaph, by a sequence of comical, but also briskly
aggressive scenes of carnage. The tone is that of 'guignol', or a
Punch-and-Judy show. Though none of the narrator's special
guests are introduced by name, it is possible – as critics have argued
– to identify, in the party of inmates from Saint-Jean-de-Dieu, by
their catchphrases or other distinguishing marks, the figure of
Murphy ('un homme jeune, mort jeune, assis dans un vieux
rocking-chair' [II, 204]), Watt ('What! s'exclama-t-il' [II, 206]),

Moran ('un petit maigre allait et venait avec vivacité, sa cape pliée
sur le bras, un parapluie à la main' [II, 206]), and Molloy ('un
énorme barbu informe dont la seule occupation, intermittente,
était de se gratter' [II, 207]). Macmann is also present, disguised as
himself.

None of these characters from earlier texts is named. Conversely, however, a new, unfamiliar name is introduced for the
purposes of this last trip into obscurity. This is the name of Lemuel.
Lemuel is given the job of killing off all these characters, and he
does so with a strange assortment of weapons: a hatchet, a
hammer, a stick, a fist, and a pencil. These, it would seem, are the
tools not so much of a prison warder or psychiatric nurse as of an
author, or at any rate an author for whom the act of writing is a
process of self-inflicted injury (Lemuel's first victim is himself) or of
controlled belligerence directed against the world and language
and for whom, as at various points for the narrator of *Malone
meurt*, a protruding stick or pencil (code name: 'Vénus' [II, 89]
after a common brand of pencil) is the chief means of inscription or
apprehension of the world.

The name, Lemuel, is also a name from the Old Testament, from
Proverbs (31:8), where it is prophesied by king Lemuel's mother,
for instance (appropriately enough in the context) that Lemuel
should 'open [his] mouth for the dumb in the cause of all such as are
appointed to destruction'. In the Bible, the name is said to mean, in
Hebrew, 'devoted to God'.[2] The Biblical connotations of the name,
Lemuel, are important. For the character presents himself to
Macmann with the words: 'Je m'appelle Lemuel [. . .], quoique de
parents probablement aryens' (II, 174). There is here an oblique
allusion to Judaism, and to the Jewish origin of the name, Lemuel,
which resonates significantly with Youdi, the name of the Jew in
Molloy. In turn, the reference to Judaism brings to the margin of
the text another name, which the name, Lemuel, recalls and half
repeats and which, similarly, is a Biblical, therefore Jewish name
(particularly in anti-semitic, Catholic France), though (as in the
case of the author of *Malone meurt*) it may name someone baptised
as a protestant, especially a foreigner. That other name is the
name: Samuel.

Some six or so years earlier in Beckett's career as a novelist,
while first writing in France, he had used the name, Sam, as the
name for a narrator. That was in *Watt*. The same novel had also
made passing reference to a character called Mr Hackett. Interestingly, at the end of *Malone meurt*, one of Lemuel's chief imple-

ments of execution is what Beckett calls 'sa hache' (II, 216). In *Malone Dies*, Beckett takes care to translate the word as 'hatchet', rather than, say, as *'axe', or *'chopper'. Already in *Molloy*, Moran's son had spent his time reading from the bowdlerised versions of the classics published by 'les éditions Hatchet' (I, 203). The phrase is evidently a joke at the expense of the over-prudish French publisher Hachette. But, by substituting an English pronunciation for a French word, and thus making a bilingual pun, it also works as a secret clue, a nudging reminder of the eccentric position of Beckett, the native speaker of Anglo-Irish, writing here in French. The effect is cryptic, but considerable. For, as *Malone meurt* reaches its end, in the place of the author (whose job it is, like Lemuel, to be the one to kill off the superfluous characters), in the place of the name of the author, then, in the place of a certain Samuel Beckett, what the text inscribes, or encodes, is a cryptic other name for that author, one which might be read as: Lemuel Hatchet.

But if Lemuel's hatchet refers back, obliquely, to the unspoken name of Samuel Beckett, this name, too, is caught in a further chain of allusions. As all the names in the trilogy amply demonstrate, names are not points of fixity in language, but moments of passage or crossing which exist within an endless circulation of language or languages. No essence is ever named by the name, for what makes names possible and necessary is, paradoxically, the prior absence of names. It is that absence of names which creates the obligation for names, even though, in response to the fundamental absence, all names are necessarily insufficient. Names, as a result, do not reflect essential being, but bear witness to the absence of name.

Like Lemuel, the name, Samuel, is a name from the Bible, where, notably, it names two books, which follow the Book of Ruth (and she, too, has her role in *Molloy*). While the name, Lemuel, means 'devoted to God', the name, Samuel, on the other hand, means something more portentous, for it is, in Hebrew, the 'name of God' itself. In the Bible, in the first Book of Samuel, the name is inscribed for the child, Samuel, by his mother, Hannah (who also has a walk-on part in *Molloy*, as 'Hanna, la vieille cuisinière des sœurs Elsner' [I, 162]). The Biblical Hannah, unlike her counterpart in *Molloy*, prays to God so that he might lift the curse of sterility that has left her childless. In the King James version, the Book of Samuel carries on the story as follows:

And they rose up in the morning early, and worshipped before the Lord, and returned, and came to their house to Ramah; and Elkanah knew Hannah his wife; and the Lord remembered her. Wherefore it came to pass, when the time was come about after Hannah had conceived, that she bare a son, and called his name Samuel, saying, Because I have asked him of the Lord. (Samuel I, 1:19–20)

By the agency of his uniparous mother, the child Samuel is given to bear the name of God. Like the dog, Theodore, in *Molloy*, Samuel is God's gift to a barren woman, and comes to bear, as a consequence, as though it were his own, the name of this impossible parent.

After a proverbial observation on the subject of providential interference, the narrator of *Molloy* makes the acerbic comment that 'je n'avais pas étudié l'ancien testament pour des prunes' (I, 183). The phrase, immediately followed as it is by an allusion to Moran's son's constipation ('As-tu chié, mon enfant? dis-je tendrement'), is another bilingual pun, confusing French plums with English prunes. But the acidity of the narrator's remark should not divert attention from the Old Testament. For in Beckett's work, despite the numerous references to the Gospels and the crucifixion, the Old Testament, in some ways, looms larger than the New Testament, which it doubles and challenges by contesting, for instance, one of the vital premises of the New Testament: the status of Christ as the embodiment of God the father.

Through this motif of the impasse of divine embodiment, what Beckett's work explores, in a necessarily paradoxical manner, is the fundamental impossibility of foundations. The theme inevitably throws into question the possibility of its own thematic stability. It can only be dealt with ironically. There is a need for some minimal ironic frame which will serve as a temporary guarantee of legitimacy to enable the literary text to occupy and problematise its own particular space. Texts, like families, are not conceived in a void, they begin from other texts, and in Beckett's case, that other text, like a genealogical forebear, is provided, in part, by the text of the Bible. The Bible, of course, is not alone in having this role within Beckett's writing. Other founding texts, including notably Dante's *Divina Commedia*, work in much the same manner.

By way of some of its names, Beckett's text functions as a marginal gloss on the Bible. This does not imply that Beckett, in rereading – or rewriting – the Bible in this way, is necessarily giving voice to any personal religious convictions. Rather, Beckett uses the Bible in the same way as he does Dante, that is, as a contextual writing which sets out, in mythic and fictional form, and thus in some kind of anagogic or analytic shorthand, the cultural pressures which Beckett's own text, in its own way, is busy working through.[3] The Bible, it could be said, treats of many of the same questions as do Beckett's novels: of mythic genealogies and of the incorporation of names, of the body, sexuality and language, of debt and revelation, of mourning and ecstasy, of living and dying. Like the Bible, Beckett's text is also a multiple script, an act of inscription rather than a sum of determinable meanings and one which takes as one of its starting points Holy Scripture itself. The narrators of *Molloy*, as noted earlier, both start their stories on the Sabbath day, the day of the scriptures.

Beckett begins writing, then, so to speak, in the endpapers of a family Bible. The Bible mediates between private autobiography and public myth. And the family Bible, like the Old Testament that no doubt inspired the practice, is the place where family trees and genealogies are inscribed. In that Bible, the young Beckett might have found the story of the prophet Samuel. But he might also have found the name of another Samuel, his own mother's father, after whom, as by age-old custom, he had been named.[4] (This, too, leaves its mark on Beckett's texts and many a Beckett character seems to be old enough not only to be his own father, as in *Molloy*, but his own grandfather as well: 'moi qui suis en route, de paroles plein les voiles', says *L'Innommable*, 'je suis aussi cet impensable ancêtre dont on ne peut rien dire' [III, 134].) A strange repetition, then, affects the name, Samuel. What it names, doubly, in the case of the prophet and the future author, is the son as the product of a contract of naming between a mother and her father, holy in the one case, earthly in the other.

Understood in this way, what the tale of the birth of Samuel in the Old Testament renders, in condensed fashion, is the problematic position of a male subject caught between the mother's desire and the paternal name. Via the name of the child, but over the head of the child (who receives the name, but cannot contest it), the desire for a child passes from the mother to the divine father, but that father is never made present by the desire. In the Book of Samuel, the child's real father, Elkanah, already has other children, but by his other wife, Penninah. In a very real sense, then, the child, Samuel, is the child of Hannah and of God, and bears the mark of his conception and birth in his name, the 'name of God'. The Biblical Samuel is in this respect a forerunner of Christ, one whose story reveals, as though in advance, the dilemma that Christ

confronts on the cross, and which Beckett himself rewrites or
re-enacts in the light of an almost Judaic sense of the eternal wait
for the Messiah and the endless postponement of his coming.
Contrary to the evidence of the Gospels, whose incoherence
Vladimir is keen to stress, a more fundamental absence lives on in
the name, Samuel, to haunt Beckett's text, just as the name of
Godot resounds through the play to which he gives his name like an
indeterminable and perplexing enigma, a name that has no referent. This absence of a referent functions here as something rather
like the absence of the father himself and, beyond the name, of the
father's body.

The Biblical Samuel becomes a prophet, who answers God,
three times over, with the resounding words: 'Here am I' (Samuel
I, 3: 4–8). Beckett, for his part, is denied the simplicity of such
devotion, and becomes a writer of fiction instead. But like Lemuel,
who doubles as both, prophets and writers share a common
medium, which is language, and a common interest in the possibility of finding names for that which is irreducible to theoretical
understanding. The logic of naming, however, is not simple. Within
language, names are the locus of a complex double bind, and exist
at the limit of established categories, between translatable and
untranslatable, meaningful and meaningless, singular and iterative.
The name that is inscribed by others makes me into a body other
than what I am, but only my name denotes my existence within
language as a body able to speak. In the words of *L'Innommable*,
if, on the one hand, paradoxically, 'il n'y a pas de nom pour moi,
pas de pronom pour moi' (III, 240), at the same time it seems that
there is 'sans noms propres, pas de salut' (III, 103). The name
eludes the binary alternatives of private or public, authentic or
inauthentic, true or assumed. Any name simultaneously occupies
both sides of these oppositions, and this doubling generates a string
of contradictory possibilities. Foisted on me by others, the name is
an imposition and a falsehood; spelt or written by myself alone, it
names me with radical singularity. A name, being a proper noun,
brings with it no concept of identity or essence; but a name, being a
word like any other, can always turn into an object. The word,
'murphy', for example, in colloquial British usage means a potato.
The paradox is the same for a name like Samuel. Naming the name
of God, it cannot name a human being; but by naming a human
being, it changes the name of God into just another part of the
dictionary.

The trilogy explores these paradoxes and enigmas with great

persistence. Indeed, rather like the Old Testament, the trilogy, in the end, if somewhat perversely, could be seen essentially as a list of names, an anthology of Irish words which somehow seem to have been incorporated into the French language. In effect, Beckett rewrites the names of Molloy and Moran, Malone, Macmann, Mahood and the others into a foreign language. The names do not lose their strangeness, nor is the fact obscured that they all belong to Anglo-Irish, but they are, in French, names which have become utterly singular, singular by dint of being alien and alien by dint of being singular. There is, as it were, only one Molloy in the French language, and he is the one (but which?) whose name appears on the cover of Beckett's text as the name of the novel.

What is true of the name, Molloy, is also true of the name, Beckett. By using Irish names in the trilogy, Beckett marks his own Anglo-Irish origins as well as the fact that he is writing from somewhere outside the French language. To write in French is, for Beckett, to underline the singularity of his name and, in reality, to reinvent or rewrite it as a name that, like the French name, Molloy, has become unique. Instead of identifiable labels, names become moments of transformation, dispersion and dissemination, and the name, Beckett, need not just appear on the covers of books. Already in *More Pricks Than Kicks* it appears like a reverse monogram in the initials of Belacqua Shuah and it is not by chance, perhaps, that the name of Beckett's first protagonist is derived from a conflation of the tutelar texts of Dante and the Bible. The name Belacqua survives into *Murphy* and *Molloy* where it figures as a partial anagram or homophone of the authorial name it half echoes and invokes. On one occasion in French, Beckett explicitly incorporates his name into the text. This occurs in the unpublished play, *Eleuthéria*, written roughly at the same time as *Molloy*, and comprising various instances of self-conscious, spoof-like humour. What is the name of the incompetent author of this piece? asks one character. Someone called Beckett, comes the answer, and, the text reads, according to Ruby Cohn: 'il dit Bécquet'.[5] The formulation is an interesting one. It shows the author experimenting, if only skittishly, or from linguistic insecurity, with how French might rewrite or mispronounce his name and how, in turn, his name might be embodied into French.

The status of names with respect to the texts they surround is not fixed. Like Beckett's 'Bécquet', they can be contaminated by those texts, changed and rewritten by the language into which they are assimilated. Traditionally, it has often been the case for names, especially the names of Gods, artists, patrons or loved ones, to be incorporated by cryptic means, anagram or anamorphosis, into a work of art, almost as though, in themselves, they constituted secret messages, or clues to the origin and meaning of the work itself. As a result, there are always more ways than one of writing a name, and any proper noun can always turn out to be more common than it seems. As it happens, in French the word 'béquet', or 'becquet', as it more usually is, does exist, and has three different senses. In typography, it is something pasted on to a proof, an overlay, or the flimsy paper used for doing this. It can also mean the middle sole in a boot, or the hobnail boot itself. Alternatively, it is a male salmon, or a pike. There also exists the near homophone, 'becquée', which is a 'beakful' of food, as given, for instance, by a mother bird to her young. It would be fanciful to claim that, in playing with his name in *Eleuthéria*, Beckett was punning on any one or other of these meanings. But in their strange impertinence, what these possible alternative meanings of 'Bécquet' all demonstrate is the extravagant dispersion of the name itself, which ceases to be expressive of any identity or essence at all.

The randomness of the senses of 'Bécquet' and their apparent irrelevance for the reading of Beckett's text (though it might be possible to make something of the 'hob-nail boot' or the 'paste-on') also acts as a warning against taking the name too literally. Any crudely nominalist approach expecting Beckett's name to go into French as if there were already a word-for-word translation waiting for it would find it difficult to make sense of the relationship between Beckett and the three senses of 'bécquet'. No doubt, if there were such a translation, the whole meaning of Beckett's enterprise as a bilingual author would be changed, for it would efface the very possibility of the author rewriting his name. But the translation of the name into French by means of phonetic similarity is far from being the only way in which Beckett's name is encrypted in his work. His own writing draws sufficient attention to at least one of them. This is the obsessive presence in the trilogy of the letter 'm'.

In Beckett's three novels, the recurrent letter 'm', the thirteenth in the alphabet, operates as much as a stigmatum as a signature. Like a family monogram, it attaches itself to the given and conjectural names of all the major characters, from Molloy to Mahood, passing through all the intermediary points of Moran, Malone, Lemuel and Macmann. Only Saposcat is spared the mark, though in his case this is only for him to forfeit the name and have it replaced by Macmann. Only Worm, like Watt, escapes the initial 'm', and it is to succumb to its inverted mirror image, 'w', and to end on 'm', after all. The titles, too, of Beckett's novels carry the sign, including the last, *L'Innommable*. It is in *L'Innommable*, on Worm's baptism, that the letter is given the additional status of a pictogram, as a three-pronged trident which, according to the narrator, serves almost as a call-sign or password: 'Worm', he writes. 'Je n'aime pas ça, mais je n'ai guère le choix. Ce sera mon nom aussi, au moment voulu, quand je n'aurai plus à m'appeler Mahood, si jamais j'y arrive. Avant Mahood il y eut d'autres comme lui, de la même race et croyance, armés du même trident. Mais Worm c'est le premier de son espèce' (III, 103).

Despite the narrator's assertion to the contrary, Worm is little different from his predecessors. He sports the same letter 'm', though in reverse. The 'm' is an undeniable source of continuity. But what Beckett's text repeats is not identity but the constant displacement of the letter or phoneme as a trace. First of all, the trace is a bodily mark. It will be remembered that in *Molloy* the narrator contrasts the letter 'm' of 'mag' with the glottal sound which follows, and suggests that 'la lettre g abolissait la syllabe ma, et pour ainsi dire crachait dessus' (I, 23). In contrast to the spitting /g/, or /k/ (as in 'crachait' or 'comtesse Caca'), the phoneme /m/ seems to mark a desire for fusion or inclusion. The comparison with the three-pronged trident stresses this, for it represents the unification of three-in-one (as manifested, notably, in the Holy Trinity and in the fact, of undecidable purport, that the letter 'm' is the only consonant shared between the Christian names of Beckett's mother, father and himself). It is symptomatic to find /m/ already linked with triplicity and fusion in *Murphy* in the form of the celebrated 'Magdalen Mental Mercyseat', or 'music, MUSIC, *MUSIC*' in Murphy's personal argot. And it is curious to discover that even the erotic character of Murphy's music is somehow recollected in *L'Innommable*. This is done by courtesy of the solitary 'prong' by which Beckett translates the three-pronged fork of his French 'trident' in *The Unnamable*.

In this exploration of phonemes and letters, Beckett privileges two counterbalanced sounds or positions, the one a sucking motion with the lips, and said to imitate the sound of the infant at the breast, the other an expulsion of air animated by the sphincters at the rear of the throat, and echoing a coughing movement of expectoration. In the narrator's dimly unreal account of his visit to his mother in *Molloy*, the sounds /m/ and /g/ or /k/ are described as corresponding to his ambivalent feelings towards his mother. The difference between /m/ and /g/ or /k/ is the difference between attraction and repulsion, between embracing the mother and rejecting her, between the mother's kiss and her violence, between oral inclusion and anal expulsion, fusion and separation. Many of the fundamental moves of Beckett's writing are sketched out in the unresolved coming-and-going between the terms of this ambivalent relation, and they are echoed in turn in the phonetic structure of the name, Samuel Beckett. In that name, in strategically stressed positions, are found the same or similar letters or phonemes. As the lips make /m/ and /b/, the back of the throat says /g/ and /k/. Like a dramatic inscription of the body itself, what these sounds enact, in the form of the name, is a pattern of bodily traces, forcing their way through words to make a mark in the text and sign it with the author's name.

In many cases, then, Beckett's name does not function as a mention of authorial presence but rather as an integral part of the writing of the text. Writing, in turn, becomes a commentary on the name and an exploration or enactment of the message which Beckett's text finds written in the name. That message is not a statement of identity, but more nearly a rhythmic programme. The dilemma Beckett's text faces is captured in the ceaseless oscillation between the positions, /m/ and /g/ or /k/. Beckett's writing drama-tises the impossibility of resolving the differences or gap between these two letters or phonemes, between front and back, lips and sphincter, inclusion and expulsion. Of the two names, the one a Christian name and the other a family name, it is as though the first is in conflict with the second, and it seems no unified body can be posited as the point of junction of the two. In the trilogy as a whole, with the exception of the two figures named as Jacques Moran (thus proving the point by reversing it), few, if any, characters enjoy both first names and family names and this asymmetry is symptomatic of a general failure to embody both names simultaneously as a basis for any full identity.

In much the same way, bodies in the trilogy are rarely expressive of any organic wholeness or presence. They, too, are marked by the same disruptive lack of unity as the name. This reciprocity between name and body manifests itself in a number of curious ways. In *Molloy*, for instance, the narrator is provided with a number of bodily prostheses in the shape of his crutches and bicycle. Why does the narrator insist, when fondly addressing his bicycle, that he cannot call it 'bike', only 'bicycle', and thus declare, as the original

French (more coherently) has it: 'Chère bicyclette, je ne t'appel-
lerai pas vélo' (I, 21)? And what is the purport of the recurrent
allusions to crutches in that novel and those that follow? Is it
possible that these references to the narrator's 'bicyclette' (defi-
nitely not 'vélo') and to his 'béquilles' serve as secret allusions to
the author's name, as covert repetitions of the consonantal arma-
ture of that name (/b/k/t/), and thus as fictional reinscriptions of the
name that has become the very material of which the writing is
made?

If one reads Beckett's novel in this way, it becomes in principle
possible to interpret the whole trilogy as a vast encrypted text
endlessly glossing the author's own secret personal name. What
gets written in the trilogy, the stories it tells or the characters and
places it describes, could be seen as pretexts for a far more eccentric
and subversive enterprise. More than meaning or intention what
begins to count in Beckett's work is the body and letter of the text,
the fabric of the writing as it weaves the name of the author like a
filigree through the text as though it constituted an irreducible and
singular signature. The text of *L'Innommable* dramatises the
possibilities rather well at one point:

Ce ramassis de conneries, c'est bien d'eux que je le tiens, et ce murmure
qui m'étrangle, c'est eux qui m'en ont farci. Et ça sort tel quel, je n'ai qu'à
bâiller, c'est eux que j'entends, de vieilles assurances suries, où je ne peux
rien changer. Un perroquet, ils sont tombés sur un bec de perroquet. S'ils
m'avaient dit ce qu'il faut que je dise, pour être approuvé, je le dirais
forcément, tôt ou tard. (III, 99)

As the narrator, diligently but sarcastically, parrots everything that
the voices in his head keep whispering in his place, something else
becomes audible. It is a kind of belated response to the obscene
bilingual parrot that in *Molloy*, like Teddy the dog, once belonged
to Lousse. But instead of invective, though perhaps no less provocative than the vulgar four-letter words of Lousse's parrot, what lies
inscribed here, in *L'Innommable*'s 'bec de perroquet', as though in
code or a rebus, by way of assonance and pun, just out of reach of
the text, is something more resembling a name. That name could be
pronounced: Bécquet.

In cases such as this, the text behaves more like a material surface
of inscription than as a sequence of intentional statements, more as
body than as spirit. The equation between text and body is one
Beckett exploits at length. Throughout the trilogy, speaking and
writing are referred to insistently in terms of ingestion, excretion,

vomiting, or spitting. Assimilation and expulsion are the terms of this corporeal production of language. *Malone meurt* had announced it clearly: 'Vase, gamelle, voilà les pôles' (II, 18). These, too, are the bodily movements that Beckett's writing retraces as it treats the name as a series of affects, as a cryptic programme of letters and phonemes constantly being transformed as they pass through the body of speech. The distinctive rhetoric of indifference which Beckett explores in his work is itself an elaboration of these shifting bodily rhythms and routines. Patterns are created which are repeated and reworked at almost every level of Beckett's text. What Beckett rewrites endlessly in this way, as though it were his own name or signature (which in a cryptic sense it is), is the unceasing movement of a speaking self forced to oscillate back and forth, undecidably and perpetually, between maternal body and paternal name, between fusion and separation, absorption and expulsion, engulfment and abandonment, incorporation and rejection.

Words and names imply a body, but, as *L'Innommable* points out, that body is not necessarily identifiable as the narrator's own: 'ce sont des mots, c'est un corps, ce n'est pas moi, je savais que ce ne serait pas moi' (III, 253). But the dynamic of the body in Beckett's fiction is more persistent and more contradictory than this momentary denial allows. It is unfortunate that the theme of the body in Beckett's work should have been taken so often as simply illustrative of ontological decay or of the subordination of body to mind. Nothing could be further from the truth. For Beckett reinvents the idea of the body in much the same way as he does when dealing with the problematic of the name. Name and body in Beckett's text become inseparable. The body becomes, as a result, something like the referent of the cryptic name Beckett's text reinvents for itself.

What the cryptic name names, then, is a body. But this body is not the human body as an expressive presence, centred around the mental fact of consciousness or awareness. If, in *Molloy*, the narrator's 'bicyclette' or 'béquilles' can be read as cryptic rewritings of the author's name, it is symptomatic that both words refer to prosthetic devices. The human body, therefore, ceases to be purely human in Beckett's text, and loses its organic unity. Though it returns throughout Beckett's work as an insistent object of figuration, it does so to invent a new idea of the body, one which is less image than gestural rhythm, more flickering energy than calm appendage, not a support for apperception but more a flesh in process of disintegration.

Thus, for example, in *Molloy*, the narrator, seeing his shadow on a wall, is not so much struck by the likeness as moved, in familiar manner, to begin gesticulating to and fro with his bicycle, dissolving the image into a frenzied movement, a coming-and-going of forms: 'Une ombre complexe s'y dessinait. C'était moi et ma bicyclette. Je me mis à jouer, en gesticulant, en agitant mon chapeau, en faisant aller et venir la bicyclette devant moi, en avant, en arrière, en cornant' (I, 36–7). In the same vein, too, is the image glimpsed by the man called Moran, as he plumbs the depths of his mind in the search for Molloy or himself:

ce que je voyais ressemblait plutôt à un émiettement, à un effondrement rageur de tout ce qui depuis toujours me protégeait de ce que depuis toujours j'étais condamné à être [. . .] Et je voyais alors une petite boule montant lentement des profondeurs, à travers des eaux calmes, unie d'abord, à peine plus claire que les remous qui l'escortent, puis peu à peu visage, avec les trous des yeux et de la bouche et les autres stigmates, sans qu'on puisse savoir si c'est un visage d'homme et de femme, jeune ou vieux, ni si son calme aussi n'est pas un effet de l'eau qui le sépare du jour. (I, 230)

A lengthy anthology of portraits of bodies could be assembled from the trilogy. The effect throughout is of a body which has no longer any identity or distinctness, which bears the stigmatic marks of subjecthood like a mysterious inscription. The body becomes inseparable from a grotesque assemblage of prostheses and lop-sided missing parts. By the beginning of *L'Innommable*, the body, in the narrator's case, has been shorn of all organic individuation and he is depicted as a half-liquid Humpty-Dumpty, a 'grande boule parlante, parlant de choses qui n'existent pas ou qui existent peut-être' (III, 37). As for his limbs or other parts of his body, these have fallen off:

Pourquoi aurais-je un sexe, moi qui n'ai plus de nez? Tout cela est tombé, toutes les choses qui dépassent, avec mes yeux mes cheveux, sans laisser de trace, tombé si bas si loin que je n'ai rien entendu, que ça tombe encore peut-être, mes cheveux lentement comme de la suie toujours, de la chute de mes oreilles rien entendu. (III, 36)

In these descriptions, the body in Beckett's text begins to figure as what one might call a body of indifference, a body lacking in desire or distinctness, but subject still to the endless churning of language, under the effects of which the body is pummelled into shape, ever different from itself, 'matière, matière, tripotée sans cesse en vain' (III, 124). In *L'Innommable*, most markedly, the narrator's body undergoes a string of transformations according to the different relationships posited by the text between the narrator and the words he hears, reads, writes, imagines, invents or repeats. As a result, as is already clear from *Molloy* and *Malone meurt*, the body cannot claim any existence prior to the motions of language. In all these texts, the body is granted no stable or determinable interiority. Rather, when characters do turn, as does the narrator in *Molloy*, from the outside to the inside, it is to discover the ruined fragments of a world without distinction or identity:

le plus souvent c'est un endroit sans plan ni limite et dont il n'est jusqu'aux matériaux qui ne me soient incompréhensibles, sans parler de leur disposition. Et la chose en ruine, je ne sais pas ce que c'est, ce que c'était, ni par conséquent s'il ne s'agit pas moins de ruines que de l'inébranlable confusion des choses éternelles, si c'est là l'expression juste. (I, 58)

If the body has no inner consistency, or any distinctive attributes, it is because it is subject to a constant process of differentiation and erasure by language. Engulfment and expulsion are the twin terms between which the body is held. Thus *L'Innommable*:

Car aller plus loin, c'est m'en aller d'ici, me trouver, me perdre, disparaître et recommencer, inconnu d'abord, puis peu à peu tel que toujours, dans un autre endroit, où je me dirai avoir toujours été, dont je ne saurai rien, ne pourrai rien savoir, étant dans l'impossibilité de voir, de bouger, de penser, de parler, mais dont peu à peu, malgré ces handicaps, je saurai quelque chose, juste assez pour qu'il s'avère le même que toujours, celui qui a l'air fait pour moi et qui ne veut pas de moi, celui dont j'ai l'air de vouloir et dont je ne veux pas, au choix, celui dont je me saurai sans doute jamais s'il m'engloutit ou s'il me vomit. (III, 30–1)

The body in Beckett's trilogy is like the body of a failed act of birth, a body which finds it impossible to achieve separation from the maternal womb and reacts to this failure with an ambivalent mix of both fear and yearning. This ambivalence of response is mirrored in the rhetoric of paradox, aporia and indifference which Beckett elaborates throughout the trilogy. The threat of engulfment is something Beckett's writing both continually invites and yet struggles to keep at bay. Differences are multiplied as they are abolished. Oscillating to and fro between engulfment and expulsion, the body is an object, then, that, time and again, is expelled and ejected from itself, and Beckett's texts seem unable to incorporate in stable manner any of the names of their narrators or even that of their author.

There remains, for Beckett, as we have seen, the possibility of rewriting the name by reinventing and reinscribing it across a foreign language. The same chance exists for the body, which, paradoxically, may be re-embodied by being dramatised or enacted as a constant process of expulsion from sense. But what is thus expelled from sense is not the body as a renewed dwelling-place of being or presence, but the body as a form of writing and a text. In other words, the body in Beckett's trilogy finally dissolves into a writing, a writing that functions as a body, as a rhythm, a texture, a fabric of traces and as a discharge of affects. This body, like the fictional text it becomes, is not unchanging or static, but exists as a continual process of assertion and negation, affirmation and difference.

It is this that gives Beckett's prose its characteristic quality. It has less to do with the expression of ideas than the manipulation of verbal forms and Beckett's sentences persistently undo their meaning by the use of paratactic dispersion and false rhetorical symmetries, or by their zeal for dismantling and overturning set phrases. In the process of their articulation, Beckett's sentences take on the dynamism of a body It is a body which cannot be represented as a whole. It is more easily performed or produced, spoken aloud or acted. In exactly this way, some texts, notably *L'Innommable* and many of Beckett's later fragments, become radically unquotable. There exists no intentional message that may be extracted from the verbal motions of the text, and to read Beckett's novels becomes an exercise in breathing and in punctuation. What is expelled at the end, as the body seeks to embody its own expulsion, is the fragmentation of a text that needs continually to sign its own remnants as a means of leaving a stain, a trace, a mark, on the world.

7
EXPERIMENT AND FAILURE

Il y eut donc une fois quelque chose. Il faut croire que oui, mais
savoir que non, jamais rien, que l'abandon. D'avoir dit abandonner
on dit abandon, sans le penser.

'Textes pour rien'

One widespread and influential account of Beckett's situation at
the end of writing *L'Innommable* has it that the writer was in an
impasse, confronted with an aporia that was physical or strategic as
well as rhetorical. After *L'Innommable*, no literary progress or
escape seemed possible. The only prospect, the conclusion runs,
was authorial silence or the formal disintegration of the work, and
to a large degree these have remained the dominant terms in which
most of Beckett's narrative prose since the trilogy has been
received. One result of this largely negative horizon of expectation
has been that the numerous prose texts written since the trilogy,
short and fragmented as some of them are, have come to be seen
largely as exercises in reduction or controlled disintegration.

There are dangers in adopting this point of view. Whatever its
initial descriptive coherence, it endorses a misleading teleological
approach to Beckett's literary project, and thus reduces the
dynamic of experimentation in Beckett's writing to the idea of a
perpetual quest where what is desired or sought is a last, inexpressible – and therefore necessarily unavailable – state of truth or
essential being. The end result is an excessively tidy, domesticated
portrait of the writer's last, and most inventive period of writing.

Nevertheless, it is clear, despite the dangers of lapsing into a
teleological approach, that ending *L'Innommable* left Beckett in a
difficult aesthetic predicament. In what was his first major interview, with Israel Shenker in 1956, Beckett was unambiguous on the
point: 'At the end of my work', he is reported as saying, 'there's
nothing but dust – the namable. In the last book – *L'Innommable* –
there's complete disintegration. No "I", no "have", no "being".

121

No nominative, no accusative, no verb. There's no way to go on.'
He also made the point that, since *L'Innommable*, he had written
nothing that, for him, seemed to be 'valid'.[1]

Beckett's work proceeds more by process of exhaustion than by
cumulative progression. The economy of writing, for Beckett, is
not an economy of the accumulation and retention of resources, but
of recycled wastes and dilapidation. He is rarely an author, in this
respect, for whom the terms of an aesthetic statement can be taken
for granted or assumed in advance and it is not necessarily the case
that one method of reading which fits one text will do for another.
Several consequences flow from this, which concern Beckett's own
writing as well as the problems of reading Beckett. The most
important relates to the question of what direction to take after
L'Innommable, what to do in a situation where, as Estragon and
Vladimir had popularised it, there was 'rien à faire' (which the
author, mindful that aporia was more than a question of mere
boredom or inertia, emphatically refused to have translated as
*'Nothing to do').

In the same way, in his *Three Dialogues* with Georges Duthuit in
1949, apropos of Bram van Velde, Beckett also shuns the temptation of turning the aporia of language – what he describes in his
account of van Velde as the 'incoercible absence of relation, in the
absence of terms' (*P*, 125) – into a pretext for a series of stable
rhetorical statements (a danger which other writers of the period,
Ionesco, for example, were arguably less assiduous in avoiding).
The discussion ends with Beckett arguing as follows:

> I know that all that is required now, in order to bring even this horrible
> matter to an acceptable conclusion, is to make of this submission, this
> admission, this fidelity to failure, a new occasion, a new term of relation,
> and of the act which, unable to act, obliged to act, he makes, an expressive
> act, even if only of itself, of its impossibility, of its obligation. I know that
> my inability to do so places myself, and perhaps an innocent, in what I
> think is still called an unenviable situation, familiar to psychiatrists. (*P*,
> 125–6)

What Beckett refuses here is the dialectical sleight-of-hand by
which negativity is converted into deferred positivity and the failure
of rhetoric into a rhetoric of failure. For Beckett, the rhetoric of
impasse is nothing if it does not also entail the impasse of rhetoric.
Earlier, the narrator of *Malone meurt* had asserted the principle in
the form of a dictum which, by abysmal reflection, also demonstrates the truth it seems to contain. What he wrote down – or
quoted – was the favourite phrase: '*Rien n'est plus réel que rien*' (II,

32). If nothing, in this way, was to remain real for Beckett and actively fail to become the positive 'thing' it tended always to turn back into, as etymology demanded, then Beckett had to circumvent – aporetically – the risk of falling back into empty rhetoric and sterile repetition. After *L'Innommable*, a new strategy of writing had to be devised. This was evidently not going to be easy for a writer whose work till now had turned on the dynamic challenge to meaning posed by repetition, sterility and the void of aporetic language.

Despite the difficulty of the predicament, Beckett in the 1950s can be found exploring a number of different literary tactics. The point of the endeavour was not to overcome the aporia arrived at in the trilogy by an act of dialectical mastery, for this would be tantamount to abolishing it, transforming it merely into a superior form of rhetoric. Beckett's project rather takes the form of trying to generate, by way of the process of writing itself, enabling forms which would, in turn, allow writing to take place. This no doubt accounts for the fact that many of Beckett's subsequent prose texts of the 1960s are concerned with describing, surveying, plotting, in words, a series of impossible, evanescent, aporetic places having neither entry nor exit.

Prior to this, during the 1950s, Beckett's work seems to have advanced, experimentally, on three main fronts. It is difficult, as always, to gauge the degree of premeditation or prior calculation involved in the process, which may well have entailed much trial and error on Beckett's part. But it is likely that Beckett's work evolved rather as a series of specific moves in response to local needs rather than as a pre-formed plan (and the category of need is one to which Beckett continually returns, witness the essay fragment of the 1930s, 'Les Deux Besoins', now collected in *Disjecta*).[2] The texts of the 1950s and 1960s can almost be read as protocols, as records of experiments whose outcome, however, cannot be other than indeterminate. The purpose of literary experimentation, unlike scientific experimentation, is not the production of knowledge but the generation of fictional texts. It is therefore implicit in Beckett's project that no external discourse, like, say, that of scientific validity, is at hand to legislate on the question of success or failure. Beckett's writing, more than ever, proves irreducible to such a stark binary alternative and one object of Beckett's work after *L'Innommable* was no doubt to explore, according to the terms available, what artistic failure might possibly signify, or what human failure might be like. Such issues, aporetic and imponderable as they are, patently provide the backdrop to a play like *Fin de partie*, or *Krapp's Last Tape* with its mutually self-cancelling images of fire and dark, black and white, body and spirit, desire and renunciation, eroticism and constipation, which, together with the uncertain greying gloom of admixture, penetrate every small detail of both the staging and the text.[3]

The first major area of experimental inquiry to attract Beckett's attention was no doubt the choice of language. During the 1950s, Beckett began a slow move back to the English language, not used since completing, or abandoning, the novel, *Watt*, in 1944. At the outset, this return to English may have been prompted by a demand for translations of his French work, notably *En attendant Godot*. At any rate, in 1956, an English *Waiting for Godot* was available in print and, by 1959, *Molloy*, *Malone meurt* and *L'Innommable* had also all appeared in English in translations mainly due to Beckett himself. 1956 and 1958 had, respectively, seen the first productions of *All That Fall* and *Krapp's Last Tape*. Both plays were written originally in English and appear to contain much more directly autobiographical material than either of the preceding French plays, *En attendant Godot* and *Fin de partie*. In 1957, the broadcast reading of the fragment *From an Abandoned Work* revealed that Beckett had also turned to writing narrative prose in English.[4]

As the title explains, this last text is only a fragment. But as such, it is of considerable importance, for its publication inaugurated what, by the end of the next two decades, had become an extensive collection of short and fragmentary prose texts. Indeed, the use of textual fragmentation was the second tactic Beckett began to explore experimentally as a means of extricating himself from the apparent impasse. In 1958, *From an Abandoned Work* was joined, in French, by the 'Textes pour rien', which appeared in the volume *Nouvelles et textes pour rien* together with the three stories from 1945. Like *From an Abandoned Work*, the 'Textes pour rien' were also in the form of fragments, at least to the extent that they were made up of thirteen short pieces the unity of which was, at best, sporadic, and more the consequence of the reliance on first-person narrative and on a set of loosely similar thematic preoccupations than the mark of any strong narrative continuity. As in the case of the thirteen poems of the poetry collection, 'Echo's Bones', twenty years earlier, the number thirteen was an indication of an attempt to arbitrate equally within the structure of the work between unity and dispersion, completion and incompletion, using for that the fateful, treacherous number of the Last Supper (also to be found, of course, in the thirteen chapters of *Murphy*).

Both *From an Abandoned Work* and 'Textes pour rien' are visibly attempts to negotiate the question of moving on beyond *L'Innommable*. Though both texts explore fragmentation, they do so in differing ways. The title, 'Textes pour rien', indicates a musical pause, or 'mesure pour rien', in which silence and sound are indistinguishable from one another (one remembers the famous 'Beethoven pause' of *More Pricks Than Kicks*). Fragmentation, in the 'Textes pour rien', is treated chiefly as a mode of structural intermittence. The text shuttles back and forth from silence to speech and from speech to silence again and this oscillation, coming and going, characteristic of much of Beckett's writing, is thematised extensively in the narrative which, in this respect at least, closely resembles that in the trilogy. In *From an Abandoned Work*, on the other hand, beyond the fact that the story is suspended before it really begins, fragmentation is more a question of rhythm or phrase structure, with Beckett composing some of his most violent or manically disconnected prose since parts of *Watt* (the style of the piece is also somewhat reminiscent of the breathless verbal texture of the radio play, *Embers*). The staccato effect of discontinuity that results suggests deep turbulence barely contained or sublimated:

Extraordinary still over the land, and in me too all quite still, a coincidence, why the curses were pouring out of me I do not know, no, that is a foolish thing to say, and the lashing about with the stick, what possessed me mild and weak to be doing that, as I struggled along. (136)

As they proceed, both the 'Textes pour rien' and *From an Abandoned Work* also rehearse a number of motifs or themes borrowed from earlier texts. To this extent, their fragmentary structure is also a reiterative one, and Beckett no doubt continues exploring the effects of repetition as part of the strategy of fragmentation. The 'Textes pour rien', for instance, which at other times cannibalise material from earlier (witness the allusion to the blue tie with the star design first encountered in 'La Fin' [147]), begin by recalling the end of *L'Innommable*. They continue in a place which is mostly reminiscent of that evoked in the opening pages of *Molloy*, and, with the narrator finding his familiar position in the lee of a rock, it is clear that the site is a textual as well as topographical one:

Brusquement, non, à force, à force, je n'en pus plus, je ne pus continuer. Quelqu'un dit, Vous ne pouvez pas rester là. Je ne pouvais pas rester là et je ne pouvais pas continuer. (127)

For its part, *From an Abandoned Work* begins in similar vein, by exploring once more the ambivalent egress and regress of journeying. Though possessed of its own peculiar power, which derives from its driving speech rhythms and strong physical imagery, the text details a now familiar family melodrama, one in which the narrator-protagonist is leaving home, to the sight of his mother 'in the window waving, waving me back or on I don't know, or just waving, in sad helpless love' (130), and with the realisation that his journey is without object or destination and that, as he puts it, 'I have never in my life been on my way anywhere, but simply on my way' (129) (and here, as elsewhere in the text, Beckett conveys much with his gestural but indeterminate use of prepositions of place). Later, the narrator's mother is declared dead, as too is his father, and this latter event seems to have deprived him of speech as well as leaving him with a guilty conscience:

All this talking, very low and hoarse, no wonder I had a sore throat. Perhaps I should mention here that I never talked to anyone, I think my father was the last one I talked to. My mother was the same, never talked, never answered, since my father died. (132)

And some moments later he returns to the theme to ask:

My father, did I kill him too as well as my mother, perhaps in a way I did, but I can't go into that now, much too old and weak. The questions float up as I go along and leave me very confused, breaking up as I am. (133)

If *From an Abandoned Work*, like the 'Textes pour rien', remembers the past in this way, it does so, paradoxically, in order to dismember memory. Memory, in the texts of the 1950s, as Beckett shows in *Krapp's Last Tape*, is used less as a way of securing identity than of subdividing and fragmenting it. In turn, writing itself becomes less a means of recording the past than effacing it. The narrator of *From an Abandoned Work* is left to turn over in his mind his fascination with the emblematic indifference or blankness of the colour white, a lack of distinction it shares with his favourite object, a horse, as well as the sheets and walls he recalls and, finally, his own death: 'White I must say', avers Beckett's protagonist, 'has always affected me strongly, all white things, sheets, walls and so on, even flowers, and then just white, the thought of white, without more' (131). Four pages later, the allusion is to him being 'bitten and bled to death, perhaps sucked white, like a rabbit' (134). But after a few promising, if by now predictable moves of this kind, the published text leaves off, leaving the narrator's body 'doing its best without me' (137).

In addition to this use of fragmentation and the partial return to writing in English, probably the most significant development in Beckett's work during the 1950s was his involvement in the theatre. Stage and radio represented a whole new arena of experimentation for Beckett and it is striking that between *L'Innommable* in 1953 and the publication of his next novel, *Comment c'est*, in 1961, no fewer than eight works for the stage or for radio were produced or published, together with a further batch of drafts or sketches, many of which have been published since.[5] Beckett's interest in the theatre also overlaps considerably with the rediscovery of English, with the result that of the work for the theatre after 1953 only one major play, *Fin de partie*, was originally written in French.[6]

As the title suggests, *Fin de partie* operates as an enactment of aporia and impasse, for which it provides theme and variation. To do this, like many of Beckett's other works, it explores a series of unstable dual relationships (between Hamm and Clov, say, or Nell and Nagg, or between Hamm–Clov and Nell–Nagg, and so on) and is organised as a network of recurrent self-cancelling motifs. Time is a central concern of the text and the play manages to fill or occupy the stage by means of a time scheme in which all progression is countered by circularity, effacement and erasure. One item after another – bicycles, gruel, nature itself – is evoked, only to be declared lost, absent, impossible. In the theme of gaming, playing, shamming, acting, which runs through *Fin de partie*, there are shades of *Malone meurt* with its discovery that games do not produce clarity or presence, but lapse into absence and darkness. In *Fin de partie*, likewise, the rules of enactment which seem to regulate the play turn out to be aporetical, arbitrary and inconsequential, and the whole game, or play, ends up like Hamm's toy dog, missing crucial identifying parts, botched and incomplete.

The theme of lop-sidedness and incompletion is important. For the play cancels out the possibility of stage presence surviving as a means of overcoming or eluding the aporetic impasse. Reviewing *En attendant Godot* in 1953, Alain Robbe-Grillet claimed the central theme of the play was presence: 'Le personnage de théâtre *est en scène*' (Robbe-Grillet's italics), he wrote, 'c'est sa première qualité: il est *là*'.[7] But, in *Fin de partie*, the stage is no longer allowed to function as a space in which presence operates – as Robbe-Grillet's account suggests – as a residual form of self-sufficiency or self-identity. This was no doubt a response, in part, to interpretations of *En attendant Godot* which, showing a more zealously reductive approach than Robbe-Grillet, had taken the play to be using presence on stage as a metaphor for the human condition at large. To read the play as though stage presence were merely a symbol which could be decoded in universalising fashion was a move which made short work of the play's textual indeterminacy. And it is no doubt indicative of a wish to prevent his work being manhandled in this way that, while working on *Fin de partie* in 1956, in a letter to Alan Schneider, Beckett should speak of wanting a text that was 'more inhuman than *Godot*'.[8]

Beckett's rejection of stage presence as a potential source of recuperative stability is also clearly evident from his interest in radio drama.[9] Of *All That Fall*, his first work for the medium, it is sometimes argued that it is Beckett's most (and only) 'naturalistic' play, which draws extensively on memories of Ireland and, notably, Foxrock station (near Dublin, where Beckett spent his childhood). However, the play makes this mimetic concession to the audience only on condition – or at the cost – of the play also remaining unseen, unstaged, spectral, and finally a sham. With its assorted rural sounds ('Sheep, bird, cow, cock, severally, then together' [12]), or Mrs Rooney's 'way of speaking' which she finds 'very . . . bizarre' (13), the play is written in such a way that actual performance (which Beckett insists should be on radio or, at the very least, behind drawn stage curtains) challenges its representational credibility by turning the play into a theatre piece for ghosts. Rather than a faithful depiction of a small Irish community, the play dramatises the impossibility of depiction and offers a pointed commentary on the discontinuity between what may be believable and what is not, between the sluggish banality of everyday life and the shocking violence lurking in the play, as this culminates in the death, or, more likely, murder of a child, that, for being unconfirmed and unseen at the end, taxes the credulity of the audience to the limit. The play ends on this gap between the familiarity of the representation and the disruptive force of the enactment.

Something analogous is at work in *Krapp's Last Tape*. Here, too, there is a gulf between representation and performance, between the words of the younger Krapp, expressed in the confident thoughts consigned to the tape recorder on his thirty-ninth birthday, and the very different sound these words have for the older Krapp as, thirty years on, he listens to his former self. The two layers of memory and personality belong to different moments but are edited together in the play. Contemptuous of their professed autonomy in this way, the play challenges the permanence of identity as well as any notion of fulfilment in the progressive march of time. Juxtaposed by the act of performance, the two texts, Krapp past and Krapp present, rub against one another discordantly like the two sides of a chiastic analogy, and it is impossible to resolve, therefore, whether the play records the superiority of age over youth or the failure of age to match the enthusiasms of youth, or vice versa.

In *Krapp's Last Tape*, as in *Fin de partie*, there is no dominant central presence or unity (save the character of Krapp himself, who is neither fully present nor unified), but rather a series of layers of language, gesture, silence, elements of staging, which interact with each other in discordant or self-echoing ways. What theatrical performance contributes to Beckett's work is a repertoire of effects which break up the homogeneity of the written text. Any production of *Krapp's Last Tape* will thus rely more on such gambits or motifs of disturbance than on any attempt to sustain theatrical illusion. Among the play's disruptive techniques are: the use of pause, hesitation or silence to create ambiguity and to limit or question the power and meaning of words; erasing parts of the text so that communication is suspended in hypothesis and understanding becomes problematical; juxtaposing different voices or different temporal layers within the same voice for dramatic contrast or as a source of ironic interference; undercutting the seriousness of the text by interspersing it with elaborate routines of trivial stage business; the symbolic use of space and of lighting effects to carry implicit ironic messages that cut across the text or magnify its pathos; the use of discordant registers of speech in the text, ranging from the sentimental to the vulgar, from the elegiac to the vituperative; the use of costumes to interact with the text or to accentuate its symbolic overtones. The result is a complexity of nuance and idiom that makes *Krapp's Last Tape* into one of Beckett's most precisely orchestrated and economical pieces. And it is worth noting that the techniques of fragmentation which Beckett uses in the play serve not to create arbitrary disorder and meaninglessness but are a major source of dramatic energy. Indeed, it is through fragmenting the text that the play's theatrical economy and impact are achieved.

The active principle in all Beckett's work for the theatre after *Fin de partie* lies in this constant dichotomy between representation and performance, put crudely, between the 'what' and the 'how' of theatre, between narrative or text, say, on the one hand, and situation or enactment, on the other. Typically, in this way, Beckett's plays come to exploit more and more the interaction between narrative and situation than the possibilities of situation alone. Gone, largely, are those moments, partly derived from music-hall, in *En attendant Godot*, for instance, which resemble unscripted improvisations, where characters struggle to fill the emptiness of the stage with words or to ward off the threat of absence by making the most of their own fitful presence.[10] Emphasis shifts to characters reciting, inventing, producing stories, stories that are often held at a distance, as though they were fabrications or concerned someone else (who, as in Krapp's case, may simply be the same speaker, but viewed as someone else). At the same time, the circumstances or dramatic situations in which these narratives are delivered or performed become increasingly abstract or austere, and almost entirely anti-representational or self-reflexive. Works like *Play*, in 1963, or, from 1972, *Not I*, are prime instances of this. In both pieces, staging blocks easy comprehension of the text, and the words are exploited more as raw material for a rhythmic, musical and bodily enactment than as a vehicle for ideas or thoughts. A non-verbal language of gesture and rhythm takes over the words in the text and remodels their function. The result is a theatrical idiom whose main priority is more like the enactment of intensity than the production of meaning.

In these plays, then, representation, in the shape of story or text, is constantly being challenged, displaced, transformed and fragmented by the dynamics of performance. The interaction between the two is crucial. This is no doubt why Beckett, in the 1970s, was increasingly drawn to directing his own plays. When doing so, Beckett is always known to have attached extreme importance to the precise rhythms of performance. Speaking of *Not I* in this regard, Beckett professed not to mind if the audience failed to understand the words, preferring to rely on affecting them more directly by way of the nerve-endings he hoped his production would expose.

But if performance, in Beckett's plays, is somehow antagonistic to representation, the reverse is evidently also true, and in the plays, characters' stories are often in blatant contradiction with the contexts in which they are forced to recount them (though also, in more recent works like *A Piece of Monologue*, or *Ohio Impromptu*, the split is more apparent than real, and is constructed so that, by aporetic doubling, the performance mirrors and displaces the representation – and vice versa – often by way of a change in pronoun from first person to third). In *Play*, the austere intensity of the staging is offset, at times with unexpected comical effects, by the very banality of the tales the three characters tell (though these stereotypical remnants of ordinary life do also serve as a welcome threshold of familiarity for the disoriented audience). In *Happy Days*, too, much of the pathos derives from the discrepancy between Winnie's grim persistence in the idea that 'this will have been another happy day!'[11] and the evidence of the strange and unreal stage set which forces her to perform in a world totally unlike that of which she seems to speak.

While representation and performance are mutually antagonistic, they are also, necessarily, mutually self-implying. Representation requires a performative act just as performance, in turn, entails some measure of representation in order for it to take place. This is true not only in the theatre but of speech acts in general. Pure performance is an illusion that Beckett discards, but, equally, his plays, even when they are made up mainly of narrative text (like *A Piece of Monologue*), are inseparable from the fact and manner of their staging or performance. The interaction between representation and performance is often complicated by the fact that the two levels constantly contaminate each other. In such instances the distinction between the two becomes precarious. Does the stage set in *Happy Days*, say, serve mainly as a function of performance or does it not rather constitute an additional layer of representation and of fictionality alongside the world of the 'old style' (16) that, verbally, Winnie still inhabits? Beckett's plays have little time for stable hierarchies, and between the 'old style' and the mound in which Winnie now lies half-buried it is impossible to tell which is real and which is metaphor, which is fictitious and which is not, or, if both are equally fictitious, what the difference, if any, between them might be.

At work here is a by now familiar logic of chiastic reversal. Performance challenges the credibility of representation, but is not stable nor does it remain identical with itself. It cannot deliver any stage presence which might serve as a foundation for ontological security. Instead presence is put in suspense, bracketed off by the fictionality of representation which suggests that presence is effect rather than origin ('Je n'ai jamais été là' [97], says Hamm, concluding his story in *Fin de partie*). Representation, for its part, is merely a fictional construct which depends on performance in order for it to take place. Thus, its credibility is entirely provisional. As a result, the theatre for Beckett becomes a place with neither performative presence nor representational credibility, a place without inside or outside, impossibly split between the one and the other, speech and scene, gesture and story, production and image, stasis and dynamism.

It is worth lingering on Beckett's experiments in the theatre in the late 1950s and early 1960s because they demonstrate how, increasingly, Beckett was concerned to incorporate within his texts, as a key signifying element, the materiality of the medium in which he was working. From this point on, the activity of writing becomes synonymous with performative enactment. This, largely, was the strategy that allowed Beckett to proceed, not so much beyond the impasse of *L'Innommable*, by dialectical means, as further into the impasse and into the aporia of embodiment. At stake in the question of enactment in Beckett's plays is the issue of whether it is possible to embody meaning – and thus signify the singularity of a body – by using as the basis for performance, as theme, occasion and expression, the material constraints specific to a given medium. In the early 1960s, the possibility of doing so manifested itself most clearly in a variety of dramatic texts to which Beckett gave oddly literal or generic titles, of the type Gérard Genette calls 'rhematic' (as opposed to 'thematic'), namely: *Words and Music*, *Play* and *Film*.[12] (Something of the same tendency is evident in a number of later titles, *Footfalls*, for example, or 'Pour finir encore', say, which name the performance taking place rather than, as is more usually the case, the scene being represented. What is striking here, though, in the late prose texts, and many of the late plays, too, is how the difference between representation and performance becomes tenuous, fragile, almost untenable.)

In the late 1950s and 1960s, experimentation in Beckett's work, then, is an attempt to reformulate, or re-elaborate, the thematics of embodiment and incorporation that already play a major role in *Malone meurt* or *L'Innommable*. What is often described as Beckett's progressively reductive or minimalist approach to human endeavours is, in fact, from the 1960s onwards, indicative more of a wish to rediscover the body as an opaque, dynamic entity, both as a difference and an indifference, that is to say, neither an object nor a subject, which resists representation and is also irreducible to performance. The body in Beckett is neither a presence which might be performed nor does it possess a coherence which might be represented. But while it is neither of these and has no identity with itself, it is still the prime support of a desire, a force, an energy which sustains the need to write and as such may at least be signed with a name. Beckett's concern with exploring rigorously – ascetically – the material constraints of aesthetic form is thus not a move

directed at reducing theatre to its underlying essence, but at rediscovering the body in the text and signing that body.

The paradox of Beckett's work, as I have suggested, is that the
body, having neither the fullness of presence nor the unity of
narrative coherence, cannot be signed with any name that is
already available. It is not that the body in Beckett is beyond
language, more that it inheres in language as non-identity, as
indifference (in the peculiarly Beckettian sense of the term). Consequently, it may be captured in textuality, but only as a movement of fragmentation, as a force of expulsion expelling the body
from itself and from performance and representation. This movement of expulsion is both active and passive, enacted and suffered
in equal degree, and is a central preoccupation in Beckett's plays.
It shows itself in the process by which Beckett's later texts, theatre
and narrative prose alike, strive to create, or locate, fictional
spaces within which the body might be held, only to realise that for
the body to be signed, or signified, it has to be fragmented and
hence ejected or expelled from its womb-like space towards what
is usually a violent confrontation with words or the blinding light
of representation and performance. This is what happens, say, to
the body of Winnie, in *Happy Days*, half-buried in a mound,
exposed to what she calls a 'holy light', a 'blaze of hellish light'
(11), or to the three protagonists of *Play*, up to their necks in urns,
forced to react to the inquisitorial spotlight of performance with
words which tell of someone's life, though their own are perhaps
more likely to be found in the violence of the play's enactment
than in the story of love, betrayal and abandonment of which each
speaks.

Beckett's theatre work is important for another reason. For by
exploring their own medium in this way, the plays of the early
1960s anticipate significantly the strategy adopted by Beckett in
several of his late prose texts. In 1961, when the involvement in
theatre was at its peak, Beckett published *Comment c'est*.[13] This
was his first novel since *L'Innommable*, and much of what I have
been arguing about the use of fragmentation and the chiastic
dichotomy between performance and representation in Beckett's
plays can be applied to *Comment c'est*, with the necessary proviso
that *Comment c'est*, like the later prose works, was not written for
theatrical performance. (In some instances, though, of which *Le
Dépeupleur* is one, one or other of the late prose works has been
produced on stage or on radio in the form of dramatic readings.
That this is possible at all is some indication of the slippage taking

place in Beckett's work between narrative prose and theatre, the representational and the performative.)[14]

Evidently, *Comment c'est* is not fragmentary in the sense that the novel is unfinished or incomplete, indeed a pre-publication extract of the subsequent English translation pointed this out by appearing under the humorous title, 'From an Unabandoned Work'. But the novel shows many signs of what might be termed active fragmentation. This is not a state of decay which could be taken to imply the existence of a unified whole of which the text we have is a failed version or a partial realisation. There is no text of *Comment c'est*, either real or ideal, which is not a fragmented text (and the point is nicely illustrated some twenty-seven years later, by the reissue – with minor textual variants – of a portion of the novel in the form of the short prose text, *L'Image*).[15] The question of fragmentation in Beckett's writing needs to be put beyond the dialectic of success or failure. It is not that *Comment c'est* fails, in any simple way, to achieve its positive aim, nor is it that failure becomes a mere form of words, with Beckett really succeeding in his artistic project (this is the formula Beckett condemns in the *Three Dialogues*), nor is it that the book intentionally fails, perversely, in order to be an artistic success.

Fragmentation is a process that cannot be determined in terms of the dialectical round of positive and negative. Its function, to borrow a word from Maurice Blanchot, is to be 'neutre', neuter, neither one nor other, neither same nor different. Neuter is what undermines dialectical closure, transgressing its determinations in the direction of indeterminacy. In Blanchot's account, the neuter is – insofar as identity can be ascribed to it at all – affirmation without assertion, difference without identity, and it is in these terms that Blanchot describes how it might be possible – or indeed might not be possible – to read a work like *Comment c'est*. In a piece republished in *L'Entretien infini*, Blanchot describes how the text radically disables criticism.[16] To praise *Comment c'est* as a work of art, he suggests, is to miss the point: it is to misread and betray the text by taking it for something it is not. But no longer to read it as a work of art is, of course, in one sense, Blanchot argues, no longer to read at all. It is rather to retrace, mutely, the act of inscription of the text itself and to affirm the force of the neuter in a merging together of the act of reading with the act of writing.

Blanchot neatly describes here the position of the reader of *Comment c'est*. The novel is a far from easy text to interpret and contains relatively little of the allusive density so important for making sense of *Molloy*, *Malone meurt* and *L'Innommable*. As Blanchot suggests, by depriving the reader of dialectical criteria for evaluating the text in terms of success or failure, the act of reading is itself put into crisis. It is almost as though *Comment c'est* wants to do without a reader. The reader is not so much addressed by the novel as absorbed into it and is given the task of embodying Beckett's text as a process of linguistic production rather than interpreting it as a set of meanings. By the very fact of reading *Comment c'est*, as a condition of understanding it, the reader is forced to relinquish the role of the linguistic consumer. Between reader and text, here, there is no communicational dyad at work and thus no two-way structure of address to support the position of the reader as an hermeneutic interpreter. The position of the reader is to be found not so much in front of the stage, as a member in the audience, but more, one might say, on the stage itself, as a joint performer of the text. Reading the text becomes something like a theatrical event, and this is one way in which Beckett's prose work reflects and extends the experimental work in the theatre during the preceding years.

Fragmentation is an active process that also reshapes Beckett's prose both grammatically and typographically, and, as readers quickly discover, *Comment c'est* is assembled as a text of uncertain provenance, consisting of a lengthy sequence of nomadic phrases and part sentences attributed to a voice without place or identity. The language fragments of which the text is composed range from single words, or noun lists, or the merest of prepositional units to adjectival expressions, and, at times, include whole periods and propositions. These language packets, as the French text calls them, with their bird-like grammar ('petits paquets grammaire d'oiseau' [94] runs the French phrase) are grouped together in strophic sequences, but apart from numerous typographical intervals there are no apparent or visible punctuation marks.

There is punctuation of a sort, however, as is clear from the ease with which, generally, the text can be understood. The distribution of the text on the page is itself a form of punctuation that instructs the reader to pause at specific moments. Punctuation is implicit, too, in the speech rhythms of spoken French which Beckett is careful to observe and exploit, and it is also preserved within the hierarchical structures of grammar. Indeed, syntax is far from abandoned by Beckett's text. There is, however, extensive grammatical ellipsis. In only a very few cases is it difficult to construct both punctuation and syntax as context demands. By and large, intelligibility in *Comment c'est* is maintained by grammatical reprises, repetition and by regularly recurring set phrases. But the necessity for the reader to construct the text grammatically as he or she reads is an important factor, since it means that reading *Comment c'est* is a dynamic process of creation or invention, a forging of relations (in both senses of the word) that is not far removed, in reality, from the process being described, fictionally, by the words on the page. The result, as Blanchot points out, is that to read the book is, in a real way, also to have to rewrite it.

Restoring what is implicit but has been expelled or eliminated from the text by active fragmentation means, in the main, supplying finite verbs, especially the verb 'être', to be, or specifying some of the hierarchical relations between clauses or phrases. This is not a random effect of Beckett's writing. It is indicative of what is at stake in the process of fragmentation in Beckett's work that it should primarily affect the copula and syntactic subordination, for what *Comment c'est* recounts, one could say, is, on one level, a crisis in hierarchy, whether narrative, textual, linguistic, or bodily, and, on another level, the elimination of the assumption that anything 'is' and that 'being' is an unproblematic attribute of words or voices. (The motif of elimination has also, as in the trilogy, a bodily meaning that the later prose texts go on to extend and radicalise still further.)

Repetition looms large in *Comment c'est* at all levels of the text, from the organisation of the narrative to the articulation of individual strophes. As well as the hypertrophy of meaning that inevitably results from constant repetition, the effect is to create an idiosyncratic but highly characteristic texture of language and writing. The writing of the novel is fragmented, yet it remains dynamic to the extent that the writing is not atomised or divorced from the bodily gesture which produced it (and this is exemplified in the recurrent phrase: 'brefs mouvements du bas du visage pertes partout' [9]). Rhythm is an important factor here and Beckett's attention to prosody is to a large degree responsible for preserving the textual dynamism of *Comment c'est*. Its language is made up consistently, though not mechanically so, of units of three or four syllables which dramatise the gradual production of the text and do produce within the French text the resonant effect of phantom – and often limping – alexandrines or octosyllabic lines. With the loss of traditional hermeneutic devices for the creation of suspense and dynamism, the non-semantic elements of the text, sound and rhythm, repetition and variation, take on a primary function.

The text of *Comment c'est* is, as a result, more performative than descriptive or representational. It enacts, in the theatrical sense of the term, more than it recounts. Much of the narrative content that the novel does stage is itself elaborated in order to mirror the production of the text. The theme of the journey, for example, which sustains the novel's overall narrative structure, is quite clearly exploited as a metaphor for the act of writing. By the use of similar expressions, equivalence is established between measures of distance and measures of discourse. Thus, if, at the outset, the phrase is: 'en avant jambe droite bras droit pousse tire dix mètres quinze mètres halte' (14), by the end it has become: 'quand ça cesse de haleter dix mots quinze mots tout bas à la boue' (164). Of the 'immense procession' (146) of bodies crawling through the mud, it is observed that they are moving from left to right, West to East, just like the words themselves crossing the page, while what the procession leaves behind as a trace of its passing is none other than the 'jerks and spasms' (in Beckett's translation) of bodily waste:

avec ça d'une lenteur extrême la procession on parle maintenant d'une procession se faisant par bonds ou saccades à la manière de la merde à se demander les jours de grande gaîté si nous ne finirons pas l'un après l'autre ou deux par deux par être chiés à l'air libre à la lumière du jour au régime de la grâce (150–1)

Finally, to underscore the analogy between the three stages of the story, the journey, the couple and the abandon, and the process of textual production, Beckett has it so that the major event in the epic is an act of inscription: the writing of a text on the body of another (by the name of Pim, just as one's own name is Pim) by means of finger-nails, fist, finger, and the two ends of a bottle-opener (and the reader is reminded here of Lemuel's tools of inscription at the end of *Malone meurt*).

Beckett's plays show how the performative dimension of a text exists only insofar as it has the support of some representational material. Accordingly, *Comment c'est* is not slow to devise a token, makeshift fictional arena for itself. Describing that arena is what enables the text to take place as a performance. The text gradually specifies actions, protagonists, circumstances, utensils, and so on, apparently for no better reason than for these elements to serve as a support for textual performance. One question might be: why these details and not others? The text replies: 'ces détails afin qu'il y ait quelque chose' (41). The reason given as to why the text is in three parts is of the same ilk: 'd'une seule éternité en faire trois pour plus de clarté' (29), the text declares, failing to point out that the gain in clarity relates more to writing the novel than to reading it. Representation becomes an exercise in self-conscious fabrication and the provisional character of such fiction-making may explain why so many objects in the fiction (like the tins of tunny fish and shrimps, for instance, or the tin-opener) have an air of gratuitous irrelevance about them. Objects of the sort are plainly indispensable for the human survival of the protagonists of the novel, but the novel is so wildly implausible and so bereft of human ordinariness as to make such considerations ludicrous and grotesque in the extreme.

If the text invites an allegorical reading by suggesting to readers that they construe the novel as a cosmological fiction, it does so only to disqualify in advance the possibility of doing so when, at the end, the whole fictional fabric of the novel is erased, leaving as its sole remainder the spectacle of a voice murmuring in the mud. The representational content of the novel turns into so much bric-à-brac which may at times have a semblance of symbolic significance, as does the sack perhaps with which the protagonist is mysteriously provided at the outset and which is vaguely reminiscent of the amniotic sac abandoned by him at birth and to which he possibly aspires to return ('quand il sera vide j'y mettrai la tête puis les épaules ma tête en touchera le fond' [13]). Generally, however, the fiction as a whole remains radically and disturbingly empty of apparent symbolic purpose.

Reading *Comment c'est*, then, is more a question of performance than interpretation. But the performative routines of the writing do not hold out the promise of a language of pure embodiment, for the text is inhabited, haunted, even, by the memory, or dream, what the text prefers to call the image (14), or fiction (20) of another stage or theatre which might even be a cinema or picture-house (39). These images gradually fade as the text proceeds, but only because they are superseded by the meeting with Pim (90).

The relation to Pim is a relation to language and the relation to language is a relation to another space, first described as life in the light, which seems not necessarily to have existed, 'la vie l'autre dans la lumière que j'aurais eue' (10). This space of the other life, which also constitutes the major topic of conversation between the protagonist and his victim, is populated by theatrical images or scenes, the first of which is the protagonist looking sidelong at himself in a mirror: 'vie dans la lumière première image un quidam quelconque je le regardais à ma manière de loin en dessous dans un miroir la nuit par la fenêtre première image' (11). Later, memories of childhood pass across this stage, as theatre curtains open and close in the mud. It is evident that what is at issue here is the capture of the protagonist's image in a series of fictional representations of birth, childhood, adolescence and sexual maturity (some of which recall images from other Beckett texts or even memories from the author's life).[17]

These images provide the basis for an alternative account of the protagonist's life in the mud but remain too fragmentary to figure in the text as more than screen memories which gesture at more material hidden in the text. The process of interpretation is stimulated by these scenes but, just as clearly, also stalled and disappointed. The pictures remain rather as an indispensable corollary to the performative movement of words which necessarily produces them. By their very existence they split the fictional universe of the novel into two interdependent but discontinuous layers of fictional representation, divided from each other, as light is from dark. Neither the life in the light nor the existence in the mud can lay total claim to the fractured body of the protagonist, which signs itself as a process of expulsion both from the light, which it refuses, and from the mud, which it leaves behind like a trail, as though, the novel suggests, it were just so much anal waste.

Indeed, in *Comment c'est* Beckett's fondness for anal imagery is much in evidence. The protagonist is once more the victim of an anal birth, as becomes clear when he raises the question of origins: 'question si toujours bonne vieille question si toujours comme ça depuis que le monde monde pour moi des murmures de ma mère chié dans l'incroyable tohu-bohu' (52). A few pages further on, the equation between the waste of words and bodily waste is put forward as an hypothesis with some enthusiasm:

vite une supposition si cette boue soi-disant n'était que notre merde à tous parfaitement tous si on n'est pas des billions en ce moment et pourquoi pas puisqu'on voilà deux on le fut des billions à ramper et à chier dans leur merde en serrant comme un trésor dans leurs bras de quoi ramper et chier encore maintenant mes ongles (65)

Written and murmured across the excrement, then, the words of *Comment c'est* exist as so many marks, traces, stains, smudges and inscriptions spelt out over the page, letter by letter. In this they resemble Pim's words to the protagonist, extorted from Pim in an act of sadistic anal violence in which the positions of subject and object, speaker and listener are confused and inverted. And it is, of course, in the same way that, when the protagonist listens to the voice of the text and claims only to be quoting from it, it is no longer certain what the source of the words is, inside or outside, self or other.

This difficulty in naming the protagonist of *Comment c'est* or in attributing to him even the role of speaker of his own words is symptomatic of the eclipse of the figure of the narrator in Beckett's text. Who is speaking this novel? For the first time in Beckett's fiction there is no narrator in the text, and thus no presence, no person, no unified body which might answer for it. Instead, there is a trail of bodily remnants, the remains of what has been expelled from a body in its attempt to sign its place in language. Consequently, there is no whole body in the text, and no place to embody the narrating subject. Embodiment, if it is to happen, is a process which must be enacted in the very act of expulsion, in the act of bodily passage which passes through the absence of passage in the aporetical movement of aporia itself. This is what is meant by an act of failure.

8

WRITING REMAINDERS

Say a body. Where none. No mind. Where none. That at least. A
place. Where none. For the body. To be in. Move in. Out of. Back
into. No. No out. No back. Only in. Stay in. On in. Still.

Worstward Ho

After *Comment c'est* in 1961 and its translation as *How It Is* in 1964,
Beckett is the author of an extensive number of shorter and
medium-length prose works. The majority of these pieces are
written in French, though there is a clear tendency for more of the
later texts (notably *Company* and *Worstward Ho*) to be in English,
like most of Beckett's work for the theatre over the same period.[1]
The prose works vary in length from a single paragraph or a few
pages in some cases to fully developed narratives of anything up to
fifty or eighty sparsely printed pages. Some texts, like *Assez*,
Company, *Mal vu mal dit*, could be said, to a degree, to resemble
completed short stories – even brief novels – while others, like one
or two of the *Foirades* ('Il est tête nue' or 'Horn venait la nuit'),
seem well on the way to becoming extended narratives in the same
vein. Other texts, however, remain avowedly fragmentary in that
they are unfinished or have been declared unfinishable by the
author, like *All Strange Away* or *Le Dépeupleur*, while a number of
the shorter pieces, *Bing* or *Sans*, say, are more like condensed
miniatures which have to be viewed, in some sense, at any rate, as
completed and sufficient in themselves.

Reading any of these different works is not straightforward.
Firstly, the texts conform to no one literary model or genre. It is
misleading in this respect to assume that they make up an homogeneous whole. Also, it is far from clear what generic rules or
conventions, if any, apply to individual texts. The effect is to block
interpretation and force readers to adopt strategies of their own
devising. In addition, certain texts, like *Mal vu mal dit*, by their
elliptical manner, purposely make the task of reading more one of

arduous decipherment than speedy comprehension. It is thus increasingly difficult to have an understanding of Beckett's overall project, and the concept of the literary œuvre as a meaningful whole is, accordingly, suspended or put into abeyance. Normative criteria such as success or failure lapse into aporetic indeterminacy, and the difficulties of evaluation described by Blanchot in relation to *Comment c'est* are, if anything, exacerbated further.[2]

In 1967, Beckett brought out two collections of shorter prose work, one in French and one in English. The French volume, containing 'D'un ouvrage abandonné' – in translation – 'Assez', 'Imagination morte imaginez' and 'Bing' ('Sans' was added in 1972), was called *Têtes-mortes*. In English, *No's Knife* appeared. As well as the early stories and the 'Texts for Nothing', this included the same work as *Têtes-mortes* and grouped together the more recent texts under the heading 'Residua'.

The two titles, *Têtes-mortes* and 'Residua', contain a number of parallel clues as to the status of the texts they name. The first, evidently, is a translation – though an unusual one – of the Latin 'caput mortuum', which Beckett had used punningly in 'Textes pour rien' to describe the narrator's physical appearance: 'cette tête livide, barbouillée d'encre et de confiture, caput mortuum d'une jeunesse studieuse, oreilles décollées, yeux révulsés, cheveu rare, bouche écumeuse, et mâchant [. . .] une glaire, une prière' (205–6). Here, with its associations of grotesque or exorbitant physical incapacity, the phrase (which the English text renders unchanged) describes a worthless remainder. In the dictionary, a 'caput mortuum' is defined as a chemical deposit, a residue left behind after the distillation or sublimation of a substance. The name, *Têtes-mortes*, revives this meaning but also recalls the English term, to 'deadhead', familiar to gardeners, which is to remove a finished flower head before it goes to seed. The phrase is also to be understood literally, as death's heads or skulls, thus: dead heads. Witness the closing words of 'Bing':

Tête boule bien haute yeux blancs fixe face vieux bing murmure dernier peut-être pas seul une seconde œil embu noir et blanc mi-clos longs cils suppliant bing silence hop achevé. (66)

'Residua', the term used by Beckett to name these texts in English translation, has a similar range of meanings. A residuum is a waste product in much the same way as a 'caput mortuum', though it can also name 'that which remains of an estate after all charges, debts, and bequests have been paid' (and in Beckett's work one is never very far from the work of grieving and its rituals). Now, in 1970 or 1971, when asked to explain what was meant by the residual character of these texts, Beckett glossed the word by writing to Brian Finney to the effect that the texts are:

residual (1) Severally, even when that does not appear of which each is all that remains, and (2) In relation to whole body of previous work.[3]

There are a number of paradoxes or contradictions at work here. First, the residues are described as the sole remaining remnants of a whole which, if it exists, is not available, but absent (and it is unclear whether by this Beckett means they are simply unpublished or still unwritten). But their status as residues is solely a function of that whole. If it is absent, their residual character cannot be instantiated or verified. It remains external to them. Without the author's titles or commentary, there would probably be little question of reading *Assez*, say, or *Imagination morte imaginez*, as anything other than fully realised texts in their own right. Their nature as residues is in some ways invisible, non-essential to their status, and some studies have concluded from this that Beckett's residua should be seen, not as waste products, but as quintessential achievements.[4]

Beckett's titles insist however that something has been removed from the texts to change them into waste residues. This could be taken to mean portions of text, or, more plausibly, if intangibly, it might refer to an essential substance which these residues no longer contain or enjoy or otherwise have at their disposal. If substance has been removed from the texts, leaving only waste matter behind, it is obviously problematic to characterise them as being somehow quintessential. For something to be a residue it must evidently forfeit its substance and essential worth. As residues, Beckett's residua renounce any claim they may have to embody an essence. They lose all identity either with themselves or with Beckett's other writings. But in turn, if the remnants have no identity or essence, it seems to be inevitable that this property – or absence of property – should begin to contaminate the absent or non-existent wholes of which the residua are said to be all that remains. If they have been removed, like a chemical residue, from the entities of which they were formerly an integral part, then those entities are no longer whole, and there is no longer any whole work or essential œuvre of which these writings are the dross. They are residues without essence of a work without essence.

This leads to the author's second remark. It is difficult to agree

with Beckett that his previous work has the character of a whole
body. Throughout all the preceding writings, the body is used as a
figure of aporia and fragmentation, of differences set down and
effaced, of parts of bodies no longer subordinated to their organic
function or purpose. Further, Beckett finds himself caught here in
the logic of the dangerous supplement that Derrida develops in *De
la grammatologie*.[5] If Beckett's work is a whole body, it evidently
must include the later residues, since otherwise it would cease to be
whole. If the residues, as the author suggests, are not part of this
whole body, then the whole body can no longer claim to be whole.
One could argue that Beckett does make a clear distinction here
between his previous and present bodies of work. Again, however,
if that is true, the whole body negates itself by dividing into two,
into a whole body proper, and a supplementary corpus improper,
part residual testament and part revisionary codicil. To do this
denies either body the attribute of wholeness. Thus if one maintains
the separation Beckett makes between the residua and his earlier
texts, one must reject the terms in which that separation is
formulated. The only whole body in evidence here is more like a
phantom or ghost than a fully present organic structure. Neither the
early nor the late bodies of work are whole, and if the residues have
no part in a whole body which expels or rejects them, it is not only
because they are residual or fragmentary in themselves but also
because, as fragments, they are an integral part of Beckett's work.

The paradox, as always in Beckett, has the structure of aporia.
With Beckett's late writings, there is no dialectic of the part and the
whole to differentiate between the essential and the incidental, the
substantial and the residual. What takes the place of such a
dialectic, as was seen in *Comment c'est*, is a force of original
fragmentation which has the effect of constantly divorcing
Beckett's work from itself according to the rhetoric of chiastic
inversion or aporetic indifference that Beckett puts into play from
the very outset. Original fragmentation transforms all Beckett's
writing into a residue. But if texts in themselves become
remainders, the process also must be seen as an active one. Writing
remainders, then, also as a verb. As a result, Beckett's late residua
function like a residue of a residue, as dispersed fragments of
writing and text which imply no whole save a fictitious or ghostly
one.

In 1976, in French, Beckett published a further volume of shorter
prose, entitled *Pour finir encore et autres foirades*. Some of these
pieces were recent, whereas a number of others were texts

retrieved, or recycled from the 1960s. The same year, an equivalent collection in English was brought out, under the title *For To End Yet Again and Other Fizzles*. Again, the titles are illuminating. The verb, 'foirer', means to expel excrement in liquid form and is used, by extension, to describe anything which is a lamentable failure. In this way, though the principal meaning of 'foirade' given by the dictionary is 'dreadful failure', the word refers in the first instance to something like a splutter of diarrhoea. In English, as the *OED* confirms, a 'fizzle', as well as meaning a failure or fiasco, is a breaking of wind without noise.

Two things are immediately worth noting. The first is the link between failure and anal excretion or farting. The analogy is not a new one in Beckett's work. As we have seen, Beckett continually exploits anality as a source of aggressive and self-defeating humour or as a figure for aporia and the erasure of sexual difference. In the case of the 'foirade' or 'fizzle', the lack of passage of which aporia is the outcome gives way to the passage of something – a fart or diarrhoetic splutter – which is of the body yet detached from the body, real yet insubstantial. Beckett reorganises the terms of the argument presented, implicitly, at any rate, by the term, 'residua'. Now, as a 'foirade' or a 'fizzle', the fragmentary, residual text crosses the limit or frontier between inside and outside, inscribing and effacing the line of separation in the process. In their pro-duction, texts move repeatedly between the phantom totality of which they are no longer a part and the waste deposit to which they are reduced. Beckett's writing both embodies and disembodies itself in one self-effacing enactment. The text is both a bodily fragment and an insubstantial trace, a mark and a self-eclipsing performance.

The question of the body is an issue that haunts all Beckett's writing. So it is, too, with his earliest residual text (if one excepts the fragment, 'From an Abandoned Work'). *Imagination morte imaginez* was first published in 1965, and its translation followed the same year. It was accompanied, in 1965, by a brief fragment in French and English, entitled 'Faux départs', and followed in 1979 by the prose text *All Strange Away*. These texts all derive from a project for a novel provisionally entitled 'Fancy Dead'.[6]

Hesitating or oscillating, in a fluctuating movement, between English and French, these texts begin, like most of the late prose works, by addressing the possibility of finding a space for a body, a space in which that body might perform or be present. Who that

body might be is not specified, or, rather, diverse and conflicting
answers are given according to text. Thus 'Faux départs':

> Plus signe de vie, dites-vous, dis-je, bah, qu'à cela ne tienne, imagination
> pas morte, et derechef, plus fort, trop fort, Imagination pas morte, et le
> soir même m'enfermai sous les huées et m'y mis, sans autre appui que les
> Syntaxes de Jolly et Draeger.

All Strange Away replaces this attempt at first-person narrative
with a third person – or 'last person' (117) as the text will have it –
who might, in turn, conceal an unspoken first person:

> Imagination dead imagine. A place, that again. Never another question. A
> place, then someone in it, that again. Crawl out of the frowsy deathbed and
> drag it to a place to die in. Out of the door and down the road in the old hat
> and coat like after the war, no, not that again. (117)

In *Imagination morte imaginez*, the third person, in turn, gives way
to an unnamed second person plural present only in the interroga-
tive or the imperative:

> Nulle part trace de vie, dites-vous, pah, la belle affaire, imagination pas
> morte, si, bon, imagination morte imaginez. Iles, eaux, azur, verdure,
> fixez, pff, muscade, une éternité, taisez. Jusqu'à toute blanche dans la
> blancheur la rotonde. (51)

Numerous textual elements circulate in varying combinations
from one writing to another, and the narrated subject, who may or
may not be the same as the narrating subject, also undergoes
various permutations. More important than the terms in which he
or she – he and she in *All Strange Away* – is represented in each
writing is the movement by which the writing explores and discards
these possibilities. A body, or pair of bodies is outlined in diagrammatical fashion and effaced. Places or spaces – a stall, a box, a cube,
a womb, a rotunda – are posited then cancelled. As the various
fragments, or versions of text follow each other, one after another,
they place and displace the human subject from being a narrator
('Faux départs'), the man, then woman, then couple, of whom the
story is told in the third person, and which culminates in the
different–indifferent couple at the crux of *Imagination morte
imaginez*. The bodies described in this final text are left without
any proper personal pronoun. The text refers only to parts of
bodies in diagrammatical projection ('contre le mur la tête à A, le
cul à B, les genoux entre A et D, les pieds entre D et B, blanc aussi
à l'égal du sol, le partenaire' [56]), or has recourse to the
impersonal third person plural. It is left unsaid, of course, how that

plural form itself relates, if at all, to the other second person plural addressed by the writing.

The end comes, in *Imagination morte imaginez*, both diegesis and text, with the statement that 'la vie s'achève et non, il n'y a rien ailleurs, et plus question de retrouver ce point blanc perdu dans la blancheur' (57). Apparent in these last words is the disappearance or dissolution of the bodies in the womb-like rotunda into the quiet turmoil and still frenzy of indifference, dramatised once again as lack of desire as well as lack of identity, and figured here by the image, or theme of blankness upon blankness: 'voir s'ils sont restés tranquilles au fort de cet orage, ou d'un orage pire, ou dans le noir fermé pour de bon, ou la grande blancheur immuable' (57).

Indeed, the major part of the text is devoted to describing in detail the rhythmic rise and fall of the heat and light as the text goes through a familiar Beckettian spectrum of white, grey, and dark:

Vide, silence, chaleur, blancheur, attendez, la lumière baisse, tout s'assombrit de concert, sol, mur, voûte, corps, 20 secondes environ, tous les gris, la lumière s'éteint, tout disparaît. (52)

The body in Beckett's text is represented here as being the subject or victim of fluctuating differences in the environment, differences that are constantly marked then effaced according to a pulsating rhythm of oscillating extremes. As in *Comment c'est*, this is not an attempt at allegory on Beckett's part. Representing the body in this way is part of a strategy for treating the body as a surface of inscription or a theatrical stage. In this, the body is not a seat of organic identity but a locus of performative intensity. It is represented, therefore, in *Imagination morte imaginez* and a number of the other residues, as a series of undifferentiated parts of limbs and scraps of flesh which in themselves have no identity or essential being. But this is in order that the unrepresentable rhythmic pulse of the body may be enacted as an intensity and a difference beyond essence or being.

To this extent, *Imagination morte imaginez* continues to exploit the aporetic dichotomy between representation and performance at work in the theatre pieces of the early 1960s and in *Comment c'est*. But the performative emphasis of *Imagination morte imaginez* is not limited to its thematic content. From the opening lines, Beckett adapts some of the language characteristics of an experimental protocol as the basis for making fictional hypotheses and turning these, in turn, into hypothetical fictions:

Par terre deux corps blancs, chacun dans son demi-cercle. Blancs aussi la voûte et le mur rond hauteur 40 centimètres sur lequel elle s'appuie. Sortez, une rotonde sans ornement, toute blanche dans la blancheur, rentrez, frappez. (51)

The use of imperative verbs is striking here. They function rather like axiomatic statements referring to circumstances in a possible world irrespective of whether the existence of such a world can be verified or not. Beckett's writing has a theatrical dimension, too, that is occasionally reminiscent of the rhetoric of stage directions, as in the imperious statement: 'A la lumière qui rend si blanc nulle source apparente, tout brille d'un éclat blanc égal, sol, mur, voûte, corps, point d'ombre' (51–2).

The performance which the text stages, however, is not one that may be realised outside of the world posited by the text as the one needed for the text to take place. In this respect Beckett's text is quite circular. The reason for this is the reliance on paradox or blatant self-contradiction: 'Pas d'entrée, entrez, mesurez' (51). What is at stake here is the text's capacity as a verbal performance to defy the impasse of a represented space in which inside and outside are not in communication with each other. By way of paradox or self-contradiction, however, the residual text carries out the impossible act of crossing from one to the other. The text subscribes to its own representation, but also contradicts and denies its existence. What the text inscribes is immediately effaced and this dualistic – chiastic – rhythm of a mark and counter-mark is a technique Beckett uses widely in subsequent texts. In *Mal vu mal dit*, it takes the form of playing one expression off against another to redefine, if not defeat its meaning, as in the recurrent motif: 'comment dire? comment mal dire?' (20). In *Worstward Ho* the same tactic is used more radically. Here Beckett forms, or reforms, a long chain of binary neologisms which, by apposing side by side a trace and counter-trace, or mark and counter-mark, in effect invent for the text a cryptic language of its own devising: 'First try fail better one. Something there badly not wrong. Not that as it is it is not bad' (21).

By dramatising contradiction in this way, *Imagination morte imaginez*, like other late texts, instantiates itself as a residual work by both implying a representational whole (the closed space of the rotunda) and denying the whole any validity by not being bound by its constraints or by the limits it has set. Like the closed space it describes, Beckett's text poses the whole as a phantom possibility, but subtracts itself from that whole. As it does so it writes itself, but only as a text which is unable to account for its own existence. Imperative verbs necessarily leave the identity of the speaker (if one exists) indeterminate and considerable problems of attribution arise. The question of the identity of the narrator of *Imagination morte imaginez* is in some respects an uninteresting one, since it is clear the text has no narrator whom the reader can identify. However, the very fact that the source of the text cannot be named within the terms provided by the text is indicative of the extent to which the text is contradictory, illegitimate, residual and aporetic. (And in other late texts one finds Beckett working more and more on this question of the impossibility of attribution and experimenting with different methods of achieving it.)

The relationship between *All Strange Away* and *Imagination morte imaginez* and 'Faux départs' is curious. These different versions, or fragments, are like parts of an absent whole which ghost one another but do not coincide except in piecemeal fashion, when they are describing the position and characteristics of the bodies in all the texts or on the level of specific turns of phrase (like the title phrase). A situation of original fragmentation obtains both in respect of the relation of the different pieces to the phantom whole of which they are all somehow a part and in respect of the relationship each text has with the others. There is no essential project existing outside of the dispersion of individual textual fragments and the incompletion that this entails. And this is no doubt how, in the author's view, they acquire their residual status.

Between 1966 and 1970 three more residua appeared, *Bing*, *Sans*, and *Le Dépeupleur*. The last of these seems quite unlike the other, much shorter texts of the period. Yet the relationship between *Bing* and *Le Dépeupleur* is, the author tells us, a very close one. To the notebooks containing the manuscript versions of these two texts Beckett appends a brief description which states:

> Though very different formally these two MSS belong together. *Bing* may be regarded as the result or miniaturisation of *Le Dépeupleur* abandoned because of its intractable complexities.[7]

Elsewhere, however, in correspondence with Brian Finney, Beckett has it that *Bing* is 'a separate work written after and in reaction to *Le Dépeupleur*'.[8]

If these two notes are read in conjunction with one another, it is clear that the relation between the two texts is, simultaneously, one of reduction and reversal. How this comes about can be plotted from the working drafts of *Bing*, ten of the typescripts for which are

published by Raymond Federman and John Fletcher in the appendix to their early bibliography of Beckett's work.[9] From these it
appears as though *Bing* began as a gloss on *Le Dépeupleur* as well
as, to some extent, a part of it. In the initial versions, therefore,
Bing seems to be devoted to exploring or detailing what it might be
possible to say about a body's life in the niches described in *Le
Dépeupleur*. These are dotted about the upper walls of the cylinder
and are much sought after by the searchers in *Le Dépeupleur* who
use them, paradoxically, it would seem, to gain some respite from
the search.

Gradually, however, this referential narrative link between the
two manuscripts seems to have given way to a more complex
textual relationship, by which *Bing* separates itself, stylistically,
from *Le Dépeupleur* and becomes more like a dramatic enactment
of life in the niches, almost as though its purpose is to refute *Le
Dépeupleur* and the language of the larger text. But Beckett is
plainly unconcerned with representational conformity and, as *Bing*
develops, he abandons all mention of the cylinder and its niches or
ladders. The emphasis falls instead on onomatopoeic expressions,
like 'paf' (in the initial draft), or 'hop' and 'bing' (which take over
after version two and five, respectively, but then, in the final
English version of the text, are both collapsed into the one term,
'ping').[10]

The recourse to onomatopoeia is only one element in a concerted
attempt at writing a text which, like *Imagination morte imaginez*, is
more performative than representational. Having no conceptual
content, the terms 'bing' and 'hop' function more like verbal
gestures than words and, though they are not pure embodiments of
sound or rhythm, being coded as words or pseudo-words of French
(which is one reason why Beckett has to translate them), they tend
to change the writing of *Bing* into something physically more
dynamic and theatrical than *Le Dépeupleur* which, for its part, on
the surface, as most readers have acknowledged, preserves the
decorum traditionally associated with descriptive or narrative
prose.

Other techniques are used in *Bing* to produce a similar gestural
effect. Rhythm is a key consideration and Beckett develops the
idea of word packets devised in *Comment c'est* into a distinctive
idiom in which syntactic relations, in the absence of finite verbs,
take the form of lists of nouns and qualifiers with the occasional
adjectival participle. The narrative function is taken over by
sequencing of strategic word groups. This naming of elements in

recurrent series serves to create a number of dynamic but mimetically indeterminate scenes or events. The reader knows that something is happening but would be hard pressed to say what that something is. If the reader wishes to continue understanding the text, he or she is compelled to decipher it dynamically and collaborate in the text's complex construction or enactment. Narrative development is provided by way of the onomatopoeic expressions, 'hop' and 'bing'. Though neither term has any precise denotational value, both have meaning of a sort, deriving from the body position required to produce them as sounds. The first, therefore, in French, translates an eructation, a glottal convulsion which explodes from the lips, while the other, inversely, could be seen as an ejaculatory release of tension resounding into the nasal passages. As the text proceeds, these non-words function as events, thus breaking up the closed fictional space the text is describing. Different verbal associations attach themselves to the terms and create narrative interest. Each occurrence of 'hop' is followed, more or less immediately, by the word 'ailleurs', so that, after a few moments of reading, the one begins to stand for the other. The sound, 'bing', for its part, is accompanied by a cluster of words which grows in size, rhythmically, as the work unfolds, so that, by the end, the phrase is no longer just: 'Tête boule bien haute yeux bleu pâle presque blanc bing murmure bing silence' (62), but: 'Bing jadis à peine peut-être un sens une nature une seconde presque jamais bleu et blanc au vent ça de mémoire plus jamais' (66). The final appearance of both terms, together for the first time, brings the performance to an end by effacing it in the customary fashion:

Lumière chaleur tout su tout blanc cœur souffle sans son. Tête boule bien haute yeux blancs fixe face vieux bing murmure dernier peut-être pas seul une seconde œil embu noir et blanc mi-clos longs cils suppliant bing silence hop achevé. (66)

Though 'bing' and 'hop' have no prior meaning, they nonetheless acquire, in the course of the work, by virtue of these accretions, a textual significance. To this extent, they perform or enact the meaning that they come to embody. In the same way that the terms speak of the possibility of there being some other place, elsewhere, and of there being an exit from the closed space of the text, perhaps into nature, meaning, or time, so the terms themselves move beyond the closed system of language or the dictionary to embody their own idiomatic meaning as an effect of the textual act which produces them. 'Bing' and 'hop' acquire here the status of a signature, or a private cryptic name. It comes as no surprise to find therefore that both these pseudo-words repeat and rewrite the authorial name circulating within the writing ·of the trilogy. That name, it will be remembered, at one point takes the form of a sequence of phonemes, /m/ or /b/, followed by /g/ or /k/, exactly as written (if not quite pronounced) in the title: *Bing*. More importantly, if the cryptic name is taken to be a gesture more than a code-word, more a process of verbal expulsion than a stable sign, then, here, it can be identified with the sound that produces it. Its form, then, is like an ejaculation – bing! – or a vomiting – hop! – of language, even like a blow struck across the head if one cares to disinter the onomatopoeic 'paf' which in the drafts precedes 'bing' (and is a common onomatopoeia in French, though its near homophone, the word 'baffe' means a blow to the head, around the ears).

The scene which writes itself through *Bing* can be likened to a further attempt at fictional embodiment on the part of the writer. In *Bing*, however, as in *Comment c'est*, there is no present moment of self-identity to be found in textual embodiment. This lack of being manifests itself powerfully in the total absence from the text of finite verbs. If 'bing' is a bodily or mental spasm, it is a spasm that expels itself from any verbal present. All the verb forms in *Bing* are past participles. For the body in the box, then, the end has already taken place and what is left are the remains of that closure. Those remains remain as written remainders, expelled bits, parts of language and body strewn across the page as though their existence was to be 'traces fouillis signes sans sens gris pâle presque blanc' (61). Words here are like the residues of an effort of embodiment that ends, as it necessarily must, in disembodiment, verbal fragmentation and the indistinction of grey, almost white.

If *Le Dépeupleur* is a matrix, engendering a smaller, miniature version of itself (as Beckett puts it), then *Bing* leaves by the back passage, as a waste deposit, not a spiritual legacy. As *Bing* expels itself from the inclusive fictional space of the precursor text, it breaks the closure of that space. The appropriate – if improper – figure, in this case, however, ought not to be the metaphor of trespass but rather of the text breaking wind, passing like breath and an insubstantial trace from inside to out, a bodily remainder or fizzle without essence or identity. If *Bing* is a performative text, what it performs is the process of its own bodily expulsion. And the aporetic non-space into which it is expelled is the space of indifference, of limbs separated only to be sewn together again, of eyes opened only to close again, of lips unclenched only to fall silent, of a body revealed only to merge into the blankness of the background. Compared to *Bing*, *Le Dépeupleur* seems dry and detached. This is one reason why the work is often read as a cosmological allegory. To do so is to take the view, as Brian Finney puts it, that the work can be understood as a 'model in miniature of man's condition.'[11] This entails interpreting the text purely as a representation, not a performance. However, the continual presence of discursive markers in the text, in the form of words like 'peut-être' ('leur séjour va peut-être finir' [71]), 'comme si' ('comme si à un moment donné [11]), expressions of doubt ('il est douteux' [11]) or opinion ('il n'y a qu'à considérer' [12]), to mention only a few, together with many evaluative terms ('plus ou moins' [8] or 'pas tout à fait' [12], for instance), make this a difficult argument to sustain. Evidently, as several critics have suggested, if the text is an allegory, it is more an allegory of its own fabrication or textual production than of any stable view of human endeavours.[12]

What is fundamentally at issue is the question of the identity of the narrator of *Le Dépeupleur*. Interpretations of the text vary according to how the question of the narrative voice is resolved. It is, naturally enough, not a simple task to identify the narrator because, firstly, no narrator is ever named in the text. This is not unusual in Beckett's later prose works. All the fiction texts since *Comment c'est*, without exception, suffer from such problems of attribution and it is one of the chief methods Beckett uses to destabilise his fictions, even, or especially, when, as with *Le Dépeupleur*, the fictional world appears on the surface to possess an internal harmony and order working overtime to keep aporia at bay.

The success of this is only apparent. If *Le Dépeupleur* were a solitary text, it might be able to impose itself as a text having an authority beyond question. But *Le Dépeupleur*, too, the author makes clear, has residual status in Beckett's work. It is a remainder, an incomplete text. Even if readers were not aware of the publishing history of *Le Dépeupleur* (abandoned in 1966, published in bits and pieces over the years immediately following, and finally brought out as a separate volume, with the closing paragraph added, in 1970), there would still be at least one tell-tale trace of its residual status. The name of that trace is *Bing*, or it might be any of Beckett's other residual works. The fact that the residual works are many, and that they differ widely from one another are in themselves important factors in challenging the textual stability of each of the works in turn.

But it is not only *Bing* and other residua which remain behind as a symptom of the fragmentary nature of *Le Dépeupleur*. At one point in *Le Dépeupleur* the narrative itself addresses the question of harmony, and therefore of its own structure. Speaking of the place and distribution of the niches, the text states that:

Elles sont disposées en quinconces irréguliers savamment désaxés ayant sept mètres de côté en moyenne. Harmonie que seul peut goûter qui par longue fréquentation connaît à fond l'ensemble des niches au point d'en posséder une image mentale parfaite. Or il est douteux qu'un tel existe. Car chaque grimpeur a ses niches de prédilection et évite autant que possible de monter dans les autres. (11)

The only agency who might be thought to have a perfect mental image of the niches and thus an idea of the harmony existing in the cylinder is the narrator, who demonstrates such superior knowledge *a contrario*, in the very act of denying the existence of any climber who might have similar insight. But, by calling into doubt the likely existence of such a figure, the narrator also calls into question the authority of the narrative itself. The narrative voice revokes one of its own conditions of existence. It cannot account for itself within the terms of the fiction it presents. Its position becomes therefore self-contradictory and stricken with illegitimacy.

The difficulty is not limited to speculation about the harmony of the niches. Some pages later the narrative turns to the question of whether it is possible that a way out from the cylinder exists. This is an occasion for the narrative voice to rehearse the ideas of the two rival belief systems prevalent in the cylinder. The first holds that the way out is via a secret passage, while the other maintains that a trap-door leads to a flue 'au bout de laquelle brilleraient encore le soleil et les autres étoiles' (17). The text observes, however, that from one opinion to the other,

Les revirements sont fréquents dans les deux sens si bien que tel qui à un moment donné ne jurait que par le tunnel peut très bien dans le moment qui suit ne jurer que par la trappe et un moment plus tard se donner tort de nouveau. Ceci dit il n'en est pas moins certain que de ces deux partis le premier se dégarnit au profit du second. Mais de façon si lente et si peu suivie et bien entendu avec si peu de répercussion sur le comportement des uns et des autres que pour s'en apercevoir il faut être dans le secret des dieux. (17)

The logic of Beckett's text is circular. It is clear that in order to be privy to something which is a secret of the gods one must already be party to that secret. In the circumstances, in *Le Dépeupleur*, that is tantamount to being blessed with the knowledge of a god. The question arises whether the evidence of the cylinder will allow divine status to be conferred on the narrator in this way. After all, the narrator is not a source of absolute knowledge. What *Le Dépeupleur* has to report is constantly hedged with reservations, the most important of which is no doubt the leitmotif: 'si cette notion est maintenue'. But if one accepts, with the text, that the narrator is not divine, then the position of the narrative voice is made more vulnerable still.

It falls subject to an aporetic contradiction. If, in terms of the narrative, the narrator is able to observe events within the cylinder, the narrator's position must be inside the cylinder. But the possibility of there being a vantage point which would afford an all-embracing, inclusive view of the inside seems questionable in the light of the conditions of speculative uncertainty which prevail in the cylinder. Outside the cylinder lies only mystery, the reader is told: 'seul le cylindre offre des certitudes et au dehors rien que mystère' (38). For the narrator to be able to speak of the world outside in this way, even if momentarily, or to express doubts as to its nature, is at least to know an outside exists and thus have limited access to it. To know this, the narrator must enjoy a privileged position. This cannot be inside, it must be outside. If the narrator is inside the cylinder, the narrator must be outside it. But it seems unclear whether there is an outside. There is no passageway guaranteed to exist between the inside and the outside. The narrator's position must reside therefore in either the one or the other. If it cannot be outside, it must be inside. The narrative voice is faced with an aporetical impasse: if in, then out; if out, then in.

This might be the epitaph not only of *Le Dépeupleur* but all the other residua, too. Impossibility threatens each of the texts from within. It is evident here that the representational coherence of *Le Dépeupleur* fails in respect of the unspoken and unanswerable question of its production. If what the text says can be accepted as a fictional representation, then its own writing becomes an impossibility. The narrative cannot account for itself within the terms of its own fiction. The narrator is a figment of his (or her?) own imagination. The text of *Le Dépeupleur* becomes therefore an allegory of its own impossibility. Its difficulty, in Beckett's word, is intractable, and the writing founders on the question of attribution.

Performance is self-contradictory. The text turns into a remainder, a remnant and a residue of itself, a monument to its inability to exist as a representation. Cosmology therefore is impossible.

This is not an isolated occurrence. The crisis it provokes is endemic to all Beckett's later texts. This can be seen from the effect on a very different prose work, though one to which Beckett also gives residual status: the story, *Assez*. *Assez* is usually thought to be somewhat unusual among the later prose works because it still adheres to the convention of first-person narrative and does have a plot, even if only a sketchy one. In recent years, on occasion, the piece has been done successfully on stage, in tandem with *Not I*, as a monologue for female voice. Paradoxically, though, this theatrical performance of the text, especially in English, serves more to conceal the turbulence which is apparent in the writing of *Assez*.

The central issue here, and one which has given rise to some controversy, is the question of the gender identity of the narrator figure who recounts the story in the first person. However, the text published in the collection, *Têtes-mortes*, in 1967 is careful to avoid attributing specific gender identity to the narrator in the writing. There are no adjectives used to qualify the narrator, no pronouns, except for the ungendered first person singular. And the text has no verb forms which, in French, might necessitate gender agreement. In the course of the fiction, though, it is true that a number of anatomical traits are specified by the text, and which, on the surface, by conventional expectation, seem to make the narrator into a woman. The narrator speaks, for instance, of performing fellatio on the older man who is the major character in the story (33–4), while at the end, in similar manner, the narrator refers to having breasts (47).

Critical assumptions about sexual behaviour in Beckett's texts have meant that *Assez* has usually been taken to be a narrative told by a woman. But when *Assez* was first published by the Editions de Minuit as a separate limited edition in 1966, the text, as Brian Finney reports, had one minor difference. In paragraph sixteen (corresponding to p. 41 of the *Têtes-mortes* version), the text read: 'si je m'étais retourné' (in place of 'en me retournant'). By the effect of a single word, even a single letter or the absence of a letter, it was revealed that the narrator was male.[13]

Various issues arise here in consequence. First, it is important to realise that neither variant can be taken as though its purpose was to discount the other. That the gender of the narrator in the second version is not marked as male or female does not imply that the narrator in the first version was not really a man but a woman, nor does the earlier reading signify that the narrator of the second version is, in reality, a man. But the existence of these variants cannot mean either – as some have wished to conclude – that the gender issue is of negligible importance for Beckett's text or that the narrator of *Assez* can be seen as male or female – or androgynous – according to critical or theatrical preference.

It is not difficult to imagine reasons why Beckett may have revised the text. Was it by inadvertence or in error that Beckett, a non-native speaker of French, had written 'si je m'étais retourné' in the first place? Beckett makes other minor changes to published texts. He had to admit at one stage that the mathematical calculations in his 1972 translation of *Le Dépeupleur, The Lost Ones*, were also wrong and corrected them in later editions of the text. It could be objected, of course, that there is a difference between a change made to a translation and one made to an original text. But, in reality, whether the reason for the change is that it was a mistake on Beckett's part, a momentary lapse, or a lapsus, is not important. What is important, however, is that the gender identity of the narrator cannot be secured or guaranteed by the story he or she is telling. The text, as a result, loses its authority. It falls victim to a disturbing indeterminacy.

This indeterminacy takes the form of a powerful identificatory ambivalence. The story begins, as we have seen, with a description of the narrator's dependence on the older man in matters of desire, sexuality and need. Towards the end, while wedged together, the two turn over. They do this, the story says, 'comme un seul homme' (46). But as it spells out this fantasy of communion, the text is stricken with duality and repetition. Fusion is contradicted by an uncontrollable process of doubling. Most events in the story are recounted twice over, and the two occurrences the narrator picks out as forming the beginning and end of the tale are both moments of separation. The event of the narrator's adoption ('je devais avoir dans les six ans quand il me prit par la main' [35]) is marked by the older man and the narrator walking hand in hand, like parent and child, yet each wearing a glove to stop their bodies from touching and to defend against identification. The end arrives when the narrator is disgraced and told to go, but whether this is momentary or permanent the narrator is unable to decide. Crucial distinctions are left vague and ambivalent. In due course, the years between these incidents, which correspond to the time of growing up, are described by the narrator as years of engulfment, as 'ces années englouties' (43).

The theme of engulfment is a recurrent one in Beckett's work, and in *Assez* it seems to have as one of its corollaries the erasure of the narrator's gender identity. Or, to put it more accurately, one would have to say that, while the narrator's gender identity is engulfed, the indeterminacy of gender is not left to one side as an issue without importance. On the contrary, it returns forever in Beckett's text as an unsecured enigma, a puzzle which cannot even be properly framed. Witness the last lines of the text of *Assez*:

Nous étions dans l'ensemble calmes. De plus en plus. Tout l'était. Cette notion de calme me vient de lui. Sans lui je ne l'aurais pas eue. Je m'en vais maintenant tout effacer sauf les fleurs. Plus de pluies. Plus de mamelons. Rien que nous deux nous traînant dans les fleurs. Assez mes vieux seins sentent sa vieille main. (47)

The effect of indeterminacy on the gender structure of French is striking here. *Assez* ends suspended between masculine breasts in the plural, that may belong to a woman, and a rhyming feminine hand in the singular, which is meant to belong to an aged man. Is this enough? the narrator seems to ask. What is enough? Enough for what? Enough, of course, means: just enough, barely enough, as when referring to some lack or shortage adequately contained. Or it means: more than enough, plenty, more than required, as when dealing with an excess contained with difficulty. At the end of Beckett's text, then, as it inspects the gender pattern of words – and of its own narrator – it finds either a lack or an excess. In either case, whichever it is, it is impossible to decide whether enough is enough. 'Je ne peux pas beaucoup à la fois' (33), the narrator says at the beginning. Beckett translates: 'Too much at a time is too much' (139). Not much is too much. Whether or not it is enough is, naturally enough, not said or even sayable.

Assez, then, is neither enough nor not enough. No doubt this is what is implied by its status as a residue. If the purpose is to grieve for the loss of the paternal companion and compensate for his rejection of the narrator (34), then the text is a failure, for all it can do is to mourn the loss by repeating it. For the real relationship between the narrator and his companion is arguably not between two lovers but, more clearly, if more provocatively, between a son and his father: 'Il ne devait plus en avoir pour longtemps', the narrator explains. 'Moi en revanche j'en avais encore pour long-temps. J'étais d'une tout autre génération' (34–5).

As though to confirm the fact, this scene of father and child, the one hand in hand with the other, plodding around the globe like two forlorn searchers, begins again, in texts entitled *Company* and *Worstward Ho*, which, in turn, begin recycling themes and motifs from *Watt* or *Malone meurt*. Thus *Company*, in 1980:

> You are an old man plodding along a narrow country road. [...] Sole sound in the silence your footfalls. [...] You listen to each one and add it in your mind to the growing sum of those that went before. You halt with bowed head on the verge of the ditch and convert into yards. On the basis now of two steps per yard. So many since dawn to add to yesterday's. To yesteryear's. To yesteryears'. [...] The giant tot in miles. In leagues. How often round the earth already. Halted too at your elbow during these computations your father's shade. In his old tramping rags. (18–19)

Thus, too, Beckett's last prose text, *Worstward Ho*, in 1983:

> Hand in hand with equal plod they go. In the free hands – no. Free empty hands. Backs turned both bowed with equal plod they go. The child hand raised to reach the holding hand. Hold the old holding hand. Hold and be held. Plod on and never recede. Slowly with never a pause plod on and never recede. Backs turned. Both bowed. Joined by held holding hands. Plod on as one. One shade. Another shade. (13)

The father's ghost, the bowed head, the plodding body, the being apart while being together, writing as a circular journey shuttling to and fro from birth to death and back: once again these are the terms of reference Beckett's writing chooses for itself. If the fate of writing is to create residues, it seems, it is because writing is an act of mourning which is never complete. Birth, death, embodiment are the issues it confronts and finds impossible to resolve or lay to rest. By the metaphor of the liquid stool or the botched fart that gives them their name, Beckett's 'foirades', or 'fizzles' make this more explicit still. The putting together of abandoned fragments dating from the 1960s with the two recent texts of 1975, 'Pour finir encore' and 'Still' ('Immobile', as it is in the French translation) rehearses further the impossibility both of the beginning and of the end.

'Pour finir encore', like many of Beckett's texts, deals again with birth as an expulsion and the body is portrayed, once more, as 'l'expulsé raide debout parmi ses ruines' (10). The body here, like in *Sans*, is expelled into a place which is thematised as a ruin, as a remnant of space filled with the dust of engulfment: 'Sable fin comme poussière ah mais poussière en effet profonde à engloutir les plus fiers monuments qu'elle fut d'ailleurs par-ci par-là' (10). It is possible, perhaps, that the dust in Beckett's text, into which its characters, such as they are, are irremediably sinking, is a memory of that dust of the namable to which the author once referred when interviewed by Israel Shenker. But if this is so, dust hardly proves more distinct or differentiated than what it replaces.

Indeed, in Beckett's last works, major efforts are made to make words into their own residues. Words are used increasingly to dramatise the indifference, the lack of identity and the plurality of sense which they embody or rather – the paradox is necessary as well as Beckettian – fail to embody. In the end, words disembody what it is they embody, and embody what they disembody. If 'Still' means stasis, it also means continuation, if peace, also repetition. Words squint at themselves and divide into antagonistic doubles of each other, the one meaning postponing the other, contradicting it, making it different, losing its own stability in the process.

If words are unceasing, then it is necessary to bear witness to their difference–indifference. While the texts in *Pour finir encore* deal with the fiasco of birth, the last works – *Company*, *Mal vu mal dit* and *Worstward Ho* – seem to be about valediction and grieving. In *Company*, in particular, countless motifs familiar from earlier works return: precise evocations of Ireland, the mother's 'cutting retort' (13), first mentioned in the story, 'La Fin' (83) or *Malone meurt* (II, 179), the bathing scene from *Embers*, the father's green topcoat, the names and initials of previous texts, and many other motifs which turn *Company* into a kind of cryptic memorial to all the texts that have gone before. The words are, once more, however, attributed to another, to a voice that cannot be made present and which disperses into a multiplicity of idiom from which unity, in the shape of the first-person pronoun, has been removed, detached, subtracted:

Use of the second person marks the voice. That of the third that cankerous other. Could he speak to and of whom the voice speaks there would be a first. But he cannot. He shall not. You cannot. You shall not. (9)

In 'Pour finir encore', the dust engulfing everything is said to be all that remains of formerly proud monuments (Beckett's translation calls them: 'haughtiest monuments'). The monuments have become dust. The dust of words, one might say, is both monumental and yet bereft of all substance, form or essence. It coincides only with its own dispersion. It is a remainder which remains solely as a remainder. The metaphor seems aptly coined by Beckett to serve as a basis for his last prose texts. Beckett seems there to be striving for monumentality. This is at any rate the effect created by the valedictory memorialising of the voice in *Company*.

But in Beckett's texts, monumentality must somehow do without its monument. Writing remainders, it does not erect or edify. What it leaves behind are formless ruins, sand or dust. Those ruins are like stone ruins, memorials to dead relatives or loved ones, say, but they are made of words, words which have become like dust, which cannot preserve, but only engulf memories in indifference just as, once before, grief and loss engulfed words in their turn. Memories turn to dust. So, however, do words and it is by tracing words in the indifferent dust that a monument may be written to what long ago engulfed all words. Thus, perhaps, in *Mal vu mal dit*, one can understand the old woman – the maternal figure of Beckett's last texts – as she visits her own stone memorial, the grave, no doubt, of a loved one, and how in Beckett's prose she somehow becomes changed into that stone figure in dust, just as, earlier, by the ambiguities of grammar and the slippery nature of pronouns, she also becomes almost indistinguishable from the evening star of Venus, the moon, or the worn stone on her step. At the end, then, is this:

Les revoilà à côté l'une de l'autre. Sans se toucher. Frappées de biais par encore les derniers rayons elles jettent vers l'est-nord-est leurs longues ombres parallèles. C'est donc le soir. Un soir d'hiver. Ce sera toujours le soir. Toujours l'hiver. Sauf la nuit. La nuit d'hiver. Plus d'agneaux. Plus de fleurs. Les mains vides elle ira voir la tombe. Jusqu'à ne plus y aller. Ou ne plus en revenir. C'est décidé. Les deux ombres se ressemblent à s'y méprendre. Mais l'une pour finir comme d'un corps mieux opaque l'emporte en densité. En fixité. Dès que l'autre sous l'œil qui s'acharne finit par frémir. Pendant tout le temps de cette confrontation arrêt du soleil. C'est-à-dire de la terre. (56–7)

Here, in *Mal vu mal dit*, as in *Worstward Ho*, too, Beckett reaches something that, in *L'Innommable*, was already thématised as being something like the end of language, both its purpose and its effacement: the indifference of words, the infinity of difference in words, of words no longer same, but other, ghosting the same with the thrill not of trespass but of return, of grief, calm, peace, joy, ecstasy.

INDIFFERENT WORDS

The themes of Beckett's writing are those of other modern or postmodern texts: the body, language, sexuality, repetition, memory, law, humour, Christianity, difference, paradox, transmission, aporia. Beckett's originality is to treat these themes as modes of language, as positions of enunciation, as points of singularity within discourse. He distributes them simultaneously across a multiplicity of languages, French and English, English and French, sometimes German. Beckett's writing is not made of intentions, but intensities. It expresses no theses, no philosophical positions, makes no statements. The author professes no religion, but bears witness instead to the dissolution of embodied religion and the slow return of the questions it once addressed – of language, sexuality, and filiation – in the form of a series of textual conundrums.

From beginning to end, Beckett's work pursues one end, which is the end of language. The end of language, however, never comes. Or rather it has always already taken place. Beckett writes in the name of something which has no name, but to which he struggles to give a name. That something is what throughout this book, for my part, I have named: indifference. Yet indifference is not stasis. It is the infinity of difference, the erasure of identity and the still turbulence at the centre of language and the body.

Indifference, in Beckett's work, has many guises. It is the space of poor Belacqua Shuah's 'Beethoven pause' and the purgatorial oscillation which takes him back and forth between egress and regress, being born and dying, laughter and tears; it is the intensity of indecision and indeterminacy experienced by the man Murphy when on his rocker; it is the dark enigma of proliferating incoherence and engulfment plotted by Watt within Knott's paternal abode. It is a name for the turmoil of indistinction discovered by the narrators of *Molloy*, *Malone meurt* and *L'Innommable*, who by inspecting its verbal motions and diabolical sabbath, are somehow able to hold it up against the murk to see how it compares to the design of their own uncertain lives. And indifference, too, names the dispersion of fragments that in the later residua or fizzles Beckett leaves behind him like a trace across the world's surface.

Indifference threatens dissolution, but it also holds a promise of ecstasy and of communion infinitely deferred. The man who claims his name is Molloy finds this out in a garden belonging to the woman he calls Lousse. What kind of place is this? Is it even a place? It is somewhere without mystery and which cannot be reached by going there. As the narrator discovers, it is not an object but a loss of object, a space where things collapse, dissolve and disperse, where boundaries and limits yield to something else without name, and submit to an end that cannot take place but everywhere leaves a trail of fragmentation and text (I, 58–9).

In Lousse's garden, as in other such places, Beckett's writing explores the fragility of boundaries and both the fear and the tranquillity of effacement, the dread and joy of illegimacy or expulsion. The questions of Beckett's writing are questions of negativity, and the fate of Beckett's texts hangs, quite uniquely, on the issue of how the power of the negative in his work is understood. Indeed, the history of reception of Beckett's texts could be written in terms of the different interpretations put forward as to the force and significance of the negative. It leads one to believe that the single most important reason for Beckett's success, with critics and audiences alike, is in the questions his work raises as to the shape and character of the negative, the different, the other, the something without name that haunts not only the words and rhythms of Beckett's writing, but also the words with which audiences, too, strive to pattern their lives.

According to this book, negativity in Beckett's work does not allow redemption. The issues it raises cannot be resolved by dialectical decision, by the covert imposition of a body of beliefs or doctrines. The force of indifference in Beckett's writing cannot be incorporated. That is its definition. This is why, for this book at least, there is no exit from the labyrinth.

The heavens, however, continue to gleam and one may still get a sight of the sun and other stars.

NOTES

1 Murphy's law

1 The idea, to some extent, originates with the author, who, in the poem, 'Gnome', from 1934, spoke of 'politely turning / From the loutishness of learning'. The poem is reprinted in Beckett's *Collected Poems in English and French* (London, John Calder, 1977), p. 7. Influential and characteristic among first accounts of Beckett's early fiction is Raymond Federman's study, *Journey to Chaos: Samuel Beckett's Early Fiction* (Berkeley, University of California Press, 1965). Federman refers to Beckett 'purifying the traditional novel' (p. 7), and maintains that the continuity of Beckett's work lies in the 'gradual disintegration of form and content' (p. vii).

2 Beckett's 'Dante. . . Bruno. Vico. . Joyce', together with most of his other early or later occasional critical pieces, has now been usefully reissued in the anthology, *Disjecta*, edited by Ruby Cohn (London, John Calder, 1983). The literature dealing with Beckett's relationship with Proust is extensive. A cross-section of opinion can be found in the following: Lawrence E. Harvey, *Samuel Beckett: Poet and Critic* (Princeton, Princeton University Press, 1970); John Pilling, 'Beckett's *Proust*', *Journal of Beckett Studies*, 1 (1976), 8–29, and *Samuel Beckett* (London, Routledge and Kegan Paul, 1976); Steven J. Rosen, *Samuel Beckett and the Pessimistic Tradition* (New Brunswick, Rutgers University Press, 1976); Hans-Hagen Hildebrandt, *Becketts Proust-Bilder: Erinnerung und Identität* (Stuttgart, J.B. Metzlersche Verlagsbuchhandlung, 1980). A more recent account is by the Proust specialist, Bernard Brun, 'Sur le *Proust* de Beckett', in Jean-Michel Rabaté (ed.), *Beckett avant Beckett* (Paris, Editions de l'E.N.S., 1984). The assumption that in his book on Proust Beckett was giving voice to his own deeply personal opinions is widespread, but, beyond the expectations of critics, there seems to be little factual evidence for it. Steven J. Rosen goes so far as to assert that Beckett 'used the study of Proust as an occasion for voicing [pessimistic] commonplaces, though attributing them to Proust sometimes required distortion' (p. 125). Rosen seems to be unaware of how much Beckett is paraphrasing, even parroting Proust in the essay, and Rosen's argument seems to fail as a direct result. Beckett, in the main, shows himself a fastidious reader of

Proust, though he clearly lacks Proust's enthusiasm for redemption or for any epiphanic or religious justification of art. Hans-Hagen Hildebrandt claims, somewhat unnecessarily, that Proust is an integral presence in Beckett and proceeds to read the whole of Beckett's work as a rewriting or countering of Proust. Evidence for this seems, at best, somewhat patchy.

3 The piece was first published in the journal, *transition*, as part of a collection of essays all devoted to *Work in Progress*, largely, it seems, under Joyce's personal direction. On the background to the essay, see Dougald McMillan, *transition: The History of a Literary Era 1927–38* (London, Calder and Boyars, 1975).

4 A rough sampling of passages taken at random from Beckett's *Proust* and compared with the text of Proust's *A la recherche du temps perdu*, in the version edited by Pierre Clarac and André Ferré, 3 vols (Paris, Gallimard, Pléiade, 1954) – not, of course, the edition used by Beckett himself in 1931 – reveals the following concordances:

1. Beckett, 11–12: Proust, III, 1045–6;
2. Beckett, 23–4: Proust, I, 666–7;
3. Beckett, 26–7: Proust, II, 133–4;
4. Beckett, 32: Proust, I, 890;
5. Beckett, 41–2: Proust, II, 756–7;
6. Beckett, 49–50: Proust, II, 364–5;
7. Beckett, 74–5: Proust, III, 872–3;
8. Beckett, 79–80: Proust, I, 81–2;
9. Beckett, 87–8: Proust, III, 895.

This list is naturally far from exhaustive. It becomes clear that while there are times when Beckett quotes directly (in his own English translations) from Proust's text and signals the fact by the use of quotation marks, it is more usual to find Beckett translating or paraphrasing Proust in silence, almost as a token of his respect for the Proustian text and his detachment from it.

5 See Jacques Derrida, *La Dissémination* (Paris, Editions du Seuil, 1972), pp. 71–197.

6 Samuel Beckett, *More Pricks Than Kicks* (London, Calder and Boyars, 1970). All references will be to this edition and will be given directly in the text.

7 Blanchot is the author of two outstanding essays on Beckett. The first, a review of *L'Innommable*, can be found in *Le Livre à venir* (Paris, Gallimard, 1959), pp. 256–64, while the second, on *Comment c'est*, is collected in *L'Entretien infini* (Paris, Gallimard, 1969), pp. 478–86. On the 'neutre' in Blanchot's work, see Françoise Collin, *Maurice Blanchot et la question de l'écriture* (Paris, Gallimard, 1971).

8 Samuel Beckett, *Murphy* (London, Calder and Boyars, 1963). All further references will be to this edition and will be given directly in the text.

9 See, in turn, Samuel Mintz, 'Beckett's *Murphy*: a "Cartesian" novel', *Perspective*, 11 (Autumn 1959) 156–65; Robert Harrison, *Samuel Beckett's 'Murphy': A Critical Excursion* (Athens, Ga., University of Georgia Press, 1968); Sighle Kennedy, *Murphy's Bed* (Lewisburg, Bucknell University Press, 1971); Hugh Kenner, *Samuel Beckett: A Critical Study* (Berkeley, University of California Press, 1961). Discussion of *Murphy* often takes place under the aegis of Beckett's alleged Cartesianism. For a survey of Cartesian motifs, see Edouard Morot-Sir, 'Samuel Beckett and Cartesian Emblems', in Edouard Morot-Sir et al. (eds.), *Samuel Beckett: The Art of Rhetoric* (Chapel Hill, North Carolina Studies in Romance Languages and Literatures, 1976). A useful compendium of recurring motifs is provided in Rubin Rabinovitz, *The Development of Samuel Beckett's Fiction* (Chicago, University of Illinois Press, 1984). On paradoxes in Beckett's early work, see Rolf Breuer, *Die Kunst der Paradoxie: Sinnsuche und -scheitern bei Samuel Beckett* (Munich, W. Fink, 1976).

10 See Jean-Michel Rabaté, 'Quelques figures de la première (et dernière) anthropomorphie de Beckett', in *Beckett avant Beckett*, 135–52 (p. 138). Beckett began analysis with Bion in 1934. On some of the background, see Deirdre Bair's (much disputed) biography, *Samuel Beckett: A Biography* (London, Jonathan Cape, 1978), p. 177.

11 These punning derivations are suggested by Ruby Cohn in her *Samuel Beckett: The Comic Gamut* (New Brunswick, Rutgers University Press, 1962), p. 54.

12 In his study of techniques of *mise en abyme* in the novel, *Le Récit spéculaire* (Paris, Editions du Seuil, 1977), Lucien Dällenbach points out that, while there is a strong tendency for reflexive textual metaphors to take on the role of a central pivot, there is often a reluctance for this to result in a situation of perfect symmetry. Whence the fact that a *mise-en-abyme* chapter is commonly found immediately after the middle of a narrative or, as in the case of *Murphy*, just before it.

2 The loss of species

1 Samuel Beckett, *Watt* (London, John Calder, 1963). All references to the novel will be to this edition and will be given directly in the text. In 1956, Beckett recalled the circumstances of his return to France in an interview with Israel Shenker. This is reprinted in Lawrence Graver and Raymond Federman (eds.), *Samuel Beckett: the Critical Heritage* (London, Routledge and Kegan Paul, 1979), pp. 146–9.

2 See, for example, the now classic account of *Watt* and Wittgenstein in Jacqueline Hoefer's article, '*Watt*', reprinted in Martin Esslin (ed.), *Samuel Beckett: A Collection of Critical Essays* (Englewood Cliffs, N. J., Prentice Hall, 1965), pp. 62–76; on Beckett's early intellectual background see the useful account by John Pilling, *Samuel Beckett*. Other useful discussions of *Watt* may be found in : Ruby Cohn, *Samuel*

Beckett: The Comic Gamut; Olga Bernal, *Langage et fiction dans le roman de Beckett* (Paris, Gallimard, 1969); John Chalker, 'The Satiric Shape of *Watt*', in Katherine Worth (ed.), *Beckett the Shape Changer* (London, Athlone Press, 1975); Rubin Rabinovitz, *The Development of Samuel Beckett's Fiction*; Michel Beausang, '*Watt*: logique, démence, aphasie', in *Beckett avant Beckett*, pp. 153–72; and Ann Beer, '*Watt*, Knott and Beckett's bilingualism', *Journal of Beckett Studies*, 10 (1985), 37–75.

3 The theme of incorporation in Beckett's work is a recurrent concern which involves a number of different, at times contradictory layers. In her paper, 'Deuil *ou* mélancolie', in the collection of essays by Nicolas Abraham and herself, *L'Ecorce et le noyau* (Paris, Aubier-Flammarion, 1978), Maria Torok draws the useful distinction between the concept of *incorporation* and the concept of *introjection*, proposed by Ferenczi, and developed by Freud in 'Mourning and Melancolia' in 1917. Introjection refers to the process by which an object from the outside world is taken up into the self as a symbolic signifier. If introjection is a process, incorporation, Torok argues, needs to be seen as an unconscious representation, a fantasy. It corresponds to the idea of literally taking the object into the body, orally, as real or imaginary food, but only so in response to the loss of that object. Incorporation is a reaction to unspeakable grief, what Torok describes as 'un deuil inavouable' (p. 267), a grief, therefore, which is not worked through and accepted. It is thus a response to a failure of introjection, a failure to accomplish grieving and accept loss. It attempts to economise on grief and compensate for loss by taking the lost object directly into the body. Torok explains that for the fantasy of incorporation to take the place of introjection in this way, the main requirement is that the loss of the object should put in jeopardy the capacity to communicate the loss. 'Il ne peut s'agir', she writes, 'que de la perte soudaine d'un objet narcissiquement indispensable, alors même que cette perte est de nature à en interdire la communication' (p. 264). She points out that 'absorber ce qui vient à manquer sous forme de nourriture, imaginaire ou réelle, alors que le psychisme est endeuillé, c'est *refuser le deuil* et ses conséquences' (p. 261). But if the object is incorporated and its loss therefore denied, the lost object continues to live on, not as a real presence, but as a ghost, locked away in a cryptic vault, as a series of unconscious or obsessional words, images, or memories. At times, these ghosts return to haunt the subject, and it seems clear that one of the ways this may happen is in a literary text, as Derrida suggests in his commentary on Genet in *Glas* (Paris, Galilée, 1974). It follows, too, from Torok's analysis that if incorporation is an attempt to defer incommunicable loss, it must always remain vulnerable to the renewed knowledge or experience of loss. Torok acknowledges incorporation is a utopian fantasy: 'la fantasmatique de l'incorporation ne fait que trahir le vœu utopique: puisse le souvenir de ce qui fut secousse, n'avoir

jamais été, ou, au plus profond, n'avoir pas eu à secouer' (p. 270). In Beckett's work, clearly, everywhere that it is attempted, incorporation ends in failure, and this is often expressed by a series of other physical symptoms (vomiting, defecating, etc.). It seems nonetheless evident that, in Beckett's writing, the thematics of incorporation do represent an identification with the father and a desire for fusion, one which is also counterbalanced with a fear of engulfment. It is the latter which predominates in *Watt*, and this also seems to function as a response to definitive and unspeakable loss. But the emphasis on incorporation in Beckett's writing shifts as his work proceeds. Accordingly, in later chapters discussion tends to centre more on the theme of embodiment. The key emblem of embodiment is perhaps the Christian Eucharist, a moment when, by oral incorporation, body and spirit, word and flesh, become momentarily as one and the son is united with the father. This desire for embodiment is closely related to the fantasy of incorporation, and might be described as a desire for unity between body and language, between name and flesh. In many ways, Beckett's work is an exploration of the possibility or impossibility of carrying out such a project, and one understands here how for Julia Kristeva, for instance, Beckett's plays and novels are an enactment of the end of Christianity, and that his texts, for her, come more under the heading of the religious or the 'sacred' than the strictly literary. See Julia Kristeva, *Polylogue* (Paris, Editions du Seuil, 1977), pp. 137–47.

4 On this aspect of the play, see Bert O. States, *The Shape of Paradox* (Berkeley, University of California Press, 1978).

5 The allusions can be found, in turn, in *Collected Shorter Plays* (London, Faber and Faber, 1984), p. 61; in *L'Innommable* (Paris, Editions de Minuit, 1953), p. 36; in the English version of *The Unnamable*, the phrase is: 'I invented love, music, the smell of flowering currant, to escape from me', *Molloy, Malone Dies, The Unnamable* (London, Calder and Boyars, 1959), p. 307, where what is notable is the echoing of the text of *Watt* by the translation of 'groseiller' as 'flowering currant'. In French, 'gooseberry' (the version in *Krapp's Last Tape*) is 'groseille à maquereau', which is how Beckett translates it himself in *La Dernière Bande* (Paris, Editions de Minuit, 1959), p. 25, and it is perhaps superfluous to note the sexual connotations of 'maquereau', meaning, of course, both 'mackerel' and 'pimp'. Conversely, in colloquial British English, a 'gooseberry' is a chaperon and it seems not to have escaped Beckett's attention that while the role of a 'maquereau' is to facilitate sexual encounters that of a 'gooseberry' is precisely to forestall them. Promiscuity in one language is offset by deferral in another. One begins here, perhaps, to get some idea of how Beckett's text incorporates its own bilingualism as a network of word associations existing at a subterranean level within the text. Incidentally, the word 'groseiller' seems to be a mistake or a misprint. The usual French form is 'groseillier'.

6 See, respectively, Samuel Beckett, *Nouvelles et textes pour rien* (Paris, Editions de Minuit, 1958), p. 49; *Malone meurt* (Paris, Editions de Minuit, 1951), pp. 97–9; 'From an Abandoned Work', in: *Collected Shorter Prose 1945–1980* (London, John Calder, 1984), p. 135; *Collected Shorter Plays*, p. 229; *Company* (London, John Calder, 1980), p. 31; and *Mal vu mal dit* (Paris, Editions de Minuit, 1981), p. 27.

7 Ruby Cohn, *Samuel Beckett: The Comic Gamut*, p. 70. In her psychoanalytically inspired thematic analysis of Beckett's fiction Fernande Saint-Martin makes a similar point. See Fernande Saint-Martin, *Samuel Beckett et l'univers de la fiction* (Montreal, Presses de l'Université de Montréal, 1976), p. 45.

8 Samuel Beckett, *Premier Amour* (Paris, Editions de Minuit, 1970), pp. 11–12.

9 The phrase recurs in Beckett's work, notably in *Comment c'est* (Paris, Editions de Minuit, 1961), pp. 32, 57, and 153.

10 Deirdre Bair, *Samuel Beckett: A Biography*, p. 3. The event is replayed, so to speak, in *Company*, pp. 15–18.

11 See J. M. Coetzee, 'The Manuscript Revisions of Beckett's *Watt*', *Journal of Modern Literature*, 2 (1972), 472–80. It is interesting to note, in this context, that in Beckett's fiction the figure of the father is rarely rooted, always nomadic, always walking, always 'abroad', and one may recall that, by profession, Beckett's own father was a surveyor. This association of the term 'abroad' (in its various possible meanings) with the figure of the father in Beckett's work is strangely resonant, of course, with Beckett's own migration out of Ireland. On the MS of the novel, further useful information is given by Ann Beer, '*Watt*, Knott and Beckett's bilingualism'. The phrase, 'never been properly born', is usually taken as a reference to C. G. Jung's 1935 Tavistock Lectures, one of which Beckett is known to have attended. See Deirdre Bair, *Samuel Beckett: A Biography*, p. 208. Beckett himself makes a similar attribution in *All That Fall*. See *Collected Shorter Plays*, p. 36.

12 See Samuel Beckett, *Pour finir encore et autres foirades* (Paris, Editions de Minuit, 1976), pp. 47–8 and p. 50; *Collected Shorter Prose 1945–1980*, p. 136.

13 See Nicolas Abraham and Maria Torok, *Cryptonymie: le verbier de l'homme aux loups* (Paris, Aubier-Flammarion, 1976); and Samuel Beckett, *Pour finir encore*, pp. 38–40 and 47–50.

14 On literary bilingualism, see Leonard Forster's useful survey, *The Poet's Tongues* (London, Cambridge University Press, 1970); and Abdelkebir Khatibi (ed.), *Du bilinguisme* (Paris, Denoël, 1985).

15 The first quotation comes from Nabokov's first novel in English, *The Real Life of Sebastian Knight* (Harmondsworth, Penguin, 1964), p. 17, which deals – not inappropriately – with a fictitious writer of fiction, the brother and *alter ego* of the narrator. The second extract is from Nabokov's postface to *Lolita* (Harmondsworth, Penguin, 1980), pp. 309–15. Nabokov recalls the circumstances of his knowledge of

English in *Speak, Memory!* (Harmondsworth, Penguin, 1967). On Nabokov's self-translations (many of which were done in collaboration with the author's son, Dmitri Nabokov), see Jane Grayson, *Nabokov Translated* (London, Oxford University Press, 1977). Though both Nabokov and Conrad are very different cases from Beckett, their bilingualism seems similarly inseparable from their fiction writing. In the case of Nabokov, as the example of the late novel *Look at the Harlequins!* (Harmondsworth, Penguin, 1964) suggests, it is as though different languages – Russian, English and French – correspond to different lyrical or erotic experiences as well as different landscapes. Conrad's novels, on the other hand, are deeply informed by a simultaneous excess and paucity of language and languages. There are simply too many words – or too few – to cope with the opaquely inexpressible centre around which language is forced to revolve. This I take to be the main issue, in, say, *Lord Jim*.

16 Ludovic Janvier, *Samuel Beckett par lui-même* (Paris, Editions du Seuil, 1969), p. 18. A helpful anthology of this and other statements by Beckett on the reasons why he took up French can be found in Ruby Cohn, *Back to Beckett* (Princeton, Princeton University Press, 1973), pp. 58–9.

17 Hugh Kenner, *Samuel Beckett: A Critical Study*, p. 56.

18 This is demonstrated in extraordinary fashion by the uses to which bilingualism is put by Louis Wolfson, the New York schizophrenic who writes in French (and currently lives in Montreal). See his own account of his use of French (and other languages) in *Le Schizo et les langues* (Paris, Gallimard, 1969).

19 This is particularly the case with recent psychoanalytic critical writing on Beckett's work. See, for example, Patrick Casement, 'Samuel Beckett's Relationship to His Mother-Tongue', *International Review of Psycho-Analysis* (1982), 9, 35–44; and Didier Anzieu, 'Un soi disjoint, une voix liante, l'écriture narrative de Beckett', *Nouvelle Revue de psychanalyse*, 28 (Autumn 1983), 71–85. Both Casement and Anzieu, somewhat unfortunately, take Deirdre Bair's biography of Beckett as a reliable and sufficient account of the life and largely tend to give Bair's biography more prominence in their description of Beckett's work than Beckett's actual writings themselves.

3 The trilogy translated

1 Samuel Beckett, *Molloy* (Paris, Editions de Minuit, 1951); *Malone meurt* (Paris, Editions de Minuit, 1951); *L'Innommable* (Paris, Editions de Minuit, 1953). Throughout this and following chapters, references to Beckett's three novels will be to these editions and given in the text. Beckett's three novels have never appeared in French explicitly as a trilogy, and it is only recently that they have done so in English. None the less, the convention is a useful one and I shall be using it here. My

references to the corresponding English translation of the three novels will be to the one-volume edition, *Molloy, Malone Dies, The Unnamable* (London, Calder and Boyars, 1959).

2 See Eoin O'Brien, *The Beckett Country* (London, The Black Cat Press with Faber and Faber, 1986).

3 Sigmund Freud, 'Das Unheimliche', in *Gesammelte Werke*, 17 vols. (London, 1940–52), 12, 229–68; *Standard Edition of the Complete Psychological Works of Sigmund Freud*, vol. XVII (London, Hogarth Press, 1955), 217–56.

4 See Brian T. Fitch, 'The Status of Self-Translation', *Texte*, 4 (1985), 111–25. Fitch has written extensively on the formal implications of the question of translation in Beckett's work. See also Brian T. Fitch, 'L'Intra-Intertextualité interlinguistique de Beckett: la problématique de la traduction de soi', *Texte*, 2 (1983), 85–100; 'La Problématique de l'étude de l'œuvre bilingue', *Symposium*, 38 (1984), 91–112; and 'The Relationship between *Compagnie* and *Company*: one work, two texts, two fictive universes', in Alan Warren Friedman, Charles Rossman and Dina Sherzer (eds.), *Beckett Translating/Translating Beckett* (Pennsylvania, Pennsylvania State University Press, 1987). The critical literature on this aspect of Beckett's work is large, if piecemeal. Useful accounts are: Anthony Jones, 'Samuel Beckett's Prose Fiction: A Comparative Study of the French and English Versions', unpublished Ph.D. dissertation, University of Birmingham, 1972, and 'The French *Murphy*: from "rare bird" to "cancre" ', *Journal of Beckett Studies*, 6 (Autumn 1980), 37–50; and Harry Cockerham, 'Bilingual Playwright', in *Beckett the Shape Changer*, pp. 141–59.

5 Beckett's bilingual textual variations in one instance are neatly illustrated by James Knowlson in his parallel edition of *Happy Days / Oh les beaux jours* (London, Faber and Faber, 1978). The study of variants in Beckett's work, from one version to another, one finished text to another, one language to another, is an increasingly fruitful line of inquiry. Beckett's working practice in this regard, as far as some of his theatre texts are concerned, is usefully analysed in S.E. Gontarski, *The Intent of Undoing in Samuel Beckett's Dramatic Texts* (Bloomington, Indiana University Press, 1985).

6 The translation from Joyce, much revised by a variety of hands, eventually appeared in *La Nouvelle Revue française*, 212 (May 1931). The French version of *Murphy*, largely completed by 1939, first appeared in Paris in 1947, published by Bordas.

7 This is taken from Nabokov's own – rather choleric – translator's preface to Aleksandr Pushkin, *Eugene Onegin*, translated with a commentary by Vladimir Nabokov, 4 vols. (New York, Bollingen Foundation, 1964), I, vii. On the relationship between Nabokov's own theory and practice of translation, see Jane Grayson, *Nabokov Translated*.

8 There is an illuminating discussion of the translations of *Premier Amour*

and *Mercier et Camier* in Steven Connor, *Samuel Beckett: Repetition, Theory and Text* (Oxford, Basil Blackwell, 1988), pp. 88–114.

9 *All That Fall* was translated as *Tous ceux qui tombent* (Paris, Editions de Minuit, 1957) by Robert Pinget, while *Cendres* (published with *La Dernière Bande* [Paris, Editions de Minuit, 1959]) is credited to Pinget and Beckett. 'L'Expulsé' and 'La Fin', among the *Nouvelles*, were done jointly with Richard Seaver, while the French *Watt* (Paris, Editions de Minuit, 1968), like 'D'un ouvrage abandonné', in *Têtes-mortes* (Paris, Editions de Minuit, 1972), was done in collaboration with Ludovic and Agnès Janvier. Ludovic Janvier reports on his collaboration with Beckett in 'Au travail avec Beckett', *La Quinzaine littéraire*, 16–28 February 1969.

10 Paul de Man, *The Resistance to Theory* (Manchester, Manchester University Press, 1986), pp. 81–2. De Man's remarks are by way of a commentary on Walter Benjamin's famous essay, 'Die Aufgabe des Übersetzers' (The Task of the Translator), written in 1923 (see below, n.11). Benjamin's text has been the subject of extensive commentary in recent years. In addition to De Man's piece, other important contributions to the debate are: Carol Jacobs, 'The Monstrosity of Translation', *Modern Language Notes*, 90 (1975), 755–66; and Jacques Derrida, 'Des tours de Babel', now available in: *Psyché* (Paris, Galilée, 1987), pp. 203–36. Derrida's essay first appeared in English, in Joseph F. Graham (ed.), *Difference in Translation* (Ithaca, Cornell University Press, 1985). Some of the implications of the debate are addressed by Andrew Benjamin in his *Translation and the Nature of Philosophy: A New Theory of Words* (London, Routledge, 1989) and I am grateful to the author for drawing them to my attention.

11 Walter Benjamin, 'Die Aufgabe des Übersetzers', in *Gesammelte Schriften*, edited by Rolf Tiedemann and Hermann Schweppenhäuser, 6 vols. (Frankfurt, Suhrkamp, 1974), 4:1, pp. 9–21 (p. 18). The text is available in English in Walter Benjamin, *Illuminations*, translated by Harry Zohn (London, Fontana, 1973), pp. 69–82.

12 On Beckett's involvement in the German language versions of his texts and productions of his plays, see Dougald McMillan and Martha Fehsenfeld, *Beckett in the Theatre I* (London, John Calder, 1988).

13 The argument is explored further, in relation to *Finnegans Wake*, by Jacques Derrida in *Ulysse gramophone* (Paris, Galilée, 1987).

14 Ruby Cohn, *Back to Beckett*, p. 112.

15 There are many versions of this thesis, from the full-blown to the mildly cautious. In their book, *The Testament of Samuel Beckett* (London, Faber and Faber, 1966), probably little read today, Josephine Jacobsen and William R. Mueller argue that beneath all the first-person narrators of the trilogy lies a single, indefinable identity or consciousness, whom they describe as 'the Beckett protagonist: this unique figure of which all alter egos are the mask [...]. This omnipresent figure should be referred to as Malone, Molloy, Estragon, Watt, etc., only in specific

contexts. In its omnipresent whole it contains their composite identities' (p. 21). The relationship between the texts is seen as one of underlying unity; and unity is finally located in consciousness, or nothingness, beyond language. A similar, if more prudent interpretation can often be found at work in early Cartesian readings of Beckett's trilogy. Thus Hugh Kenner in *Samuel Beckett: A Critical Study*: '*The Unnamable* is the final phase of a trilogy which carries the Cartesian process backwards, beginning with a bodily *je suis* and ending with a bare *cogito*. This reduction begins with a journey (Molloy's) and a dismemberment of the Cartesian Centaur; its middle term (*Malone Dies*) is a stasis, dominated by the unalloyable brain; and the third term [...] concerns itself endlessly to no end with a baffling intimacy between discourse and non-existence' (p. 128). Similar implications are evident when Ruby Cohn, in *Samuel Beckett: The Comic Gamut*, argues that 'the Unnamable, as nearly a pure mentality as has appeared in fiction, derives from the Cartesian definition of man as "a thing that thinks" ' (p. 117). The 'naming' of a character as 'the Unnamable' seems to derive more from a wish to find continuity in the three novels (in the form of a theme of 'progressive decay') than from careful attention to the text. Finally, a more refined variation on the thesis is presented by Olga Bernal when, rebutting Kenner and Cohn, she argues that, in *L'Innommable*, 'le personnage ne reprend à son compte aucun cogito. Ce qui, par contre, a lieu dans ce roman, c'est un *cogitare* sans pronom personnel fixe' (*Langage et fiction dans le roman de Beckett*, p. 101). Reading Beckett through the eyeglass of Cartesian philosophy implies, inevitably, the positing of language as equivalent to consciousness and the assumption therefore that, in Beckett's work, as Descartes tries to argue, language has true being (no matter how much deferred or displaced) as its ultimate goal or final raison d'être. This book takes the opposing view that both suppositions are put out of circulation in Beckett's work by the writing itself.

16 The titles of fictional works now have their Linnaeus in the person of Gérard Genette. See his account of titles in *Seuils* (Paris, Editions du Seuil, 1987), pp. 54–97.

17 The idea that Molloy and Moran are, at bottom, one person seems to have originated with Edith Kern in her essay, 'Moran–Molloy: the Hero as Author', in J.D. O'Hara (ed.), *Twentieth-Century Interpretations of Molloy, Malone Dies, The Unnamable* (Englewood Cliffs, N.J., Prentice-Hall, 1970), pp. 225–35. The suggestion that there is a third narrator, embracing both the one called Molloy and the one who calls himself Moran, is expounded in greatest detail by Angela B. Moorjani in 'A Mythic Reading of *Molloy*' in Edouard Morot-Sir and others (eds.), *Samuel Beckett: The Art of Rhetoric*, pp. 225–35.

18 See Maurice Blanchot, *Le Livre à venir*, p. 259.

4 Duality, repetition, aporia

1 Samuel Beckett, *Mercier et Camier* (Paris, Editions de Minuit, 1970). Further references will be to this edition and given in the text. The book was written around 1946 and it shows Beckett still exploring the possibilities of the intermittent or spasmodic heterodiegetic narrator used in *Watt*. The book begins with a sentence in the first person singular and thus a first-person narrator, but there is no further mention of this narrator in the novel. The effect is of a fiction which is simultaneously legitimated (by a narrator) and delegitimated (by the immediate disappearance of the narrator).

2 See Samuel Beckett, *More Pricks Than Kicks*, pp. 39–49.

3 Much detective work has been done, at various times, in tracking down Beckett's many indirect allusions. One useful trawl is that presented in Philip H. Solomon's study, *The Life After Birth: Imagery in Samuel Beckett's Novels* (Mississipi, Romance Monographs, 1975).

4 On the derivation and understanding of aporia for the purposes of this discussion I am indebted to Sarah Kofman's excellent essay, *Comment s'en sortir?* (Paris, Galilée, 1983).

5 On repetition in general in Beckett's work, see Steven Connor, *Samuel Beckett: Repetition, Theory and Text*; for a view influenced by Kleinian psychoanalysis, see Angela B. Moorjani, *Abysmal Games in the Novels of Samuel Beckett* (Chapel Hill, North Carolina Studies in the Romance Languages and Literatures, 1982).

6 Samuel Beckett, *Company*, p. 15.

7 See Dina Sherzer, *Structure de la trilogie de Beckett: Molloy, Malone meurt, L'Innommable* (Paris–The Hague, Mouton, 1976). It is perhaps odd that except for Sherzer's diligent opening survey so little methodical critical attention has ever been paid to narrative structure in the trilogy. Like a number of other important aspects of Beckett's work, it has been almost entirely overshadowed by the preoccupation with philosophical discussion or the emphasis on thematic concerns.

8 For a detailed theoretical account of what is most likely at issue in verbal rejection in Beckett's work, see Julia Kristeva, *La Révolution du langage poétique* (Paris, Editions du Seuil, 1974), pp. 101–50.

9 Olga Bernal, *Langage et fiction dans le roman de Beckett*, p. 164.

10 Readers may recognise here the effect exerted on much avant-garde literary thinking by the metaphysics of presence diagnosed and analysed by Jacques Derrida in *De la grammatologie* (Paris, Editions de Minuit, 1967) and *L'Ecriture et la différence* (Paris, Editions du Seuil, 1967).

5 Fables of genealogy

1 Samuel Beckett, *Fin de partie* (Paris, Editions de Minuit, 1956), p. 91.

2 The critical literature on mythological allusions or mythic patterns in

Beckett's work is extensive. See, for instance, Dieter Wellershoff, 'Failure of an Attempt at Demythologisation: Samuel Beckett's Novels', in Martin Esslin (ed.), *Samuel Beckett: A Collection of Critical Essays*, pp. 99–107; David Hayman, '*Molloy* or the Quest for Meaninglessness', in Melvin Friedman (ed.), *Samuel Beckett Now* (Chicago, University of Chicago Press, 1970), pp. 129–56; Edith Kern, 'Moran–Molloy: the Hero as Author', *Twentieth-Century Interpretations of Molloy, Malone Dies, The Unnamable*, pp. 35–45; Philip H. Solomon, *The Life After Birth: Imagery in Samuel Beckett's Trilogy*; Angela B. Moorjani, 'A Mythic Reading of *Molloy*', Edouard Morot-Sir and others (eds.), *Samuel Beckett: The Art of Rhetoric*, pp. 225–35; Alda Tagliaferri, *Beckett et la surdétermination littéraire*, translated by Nicole Fama (Paris, Payot, 1977).

3 Sigmund Freud, 'Das Unheimliche', *Gesammelte Werke*, 12, 229–68; *Standard Edition*, 17, 224. 'Unheimlich', writes Freud, reporting the verdict of Schelling, 'sei alles, was ein Geheimnis, im Verborgenen bleiben sollte und hervorgetreten ist.' ('"Unheimlich" is the name for everything that ought to have remained ... secret and hidden but has come to light.')

4 Interestingly, Mercier and Camier, when they get ready to leave, find that their bicycle is a lady's model, with no freewheel mechanism, *Mercier et Camier*, p. 29. One might speculate, of course, as to whether this is the same bicycle as the one in *Molloy*. Janet Menzies gives a different view on bicycles in Beckett's writing in 'Beckett's Bicycles', *Journal of Beckett Studies*, 6 (Autumn 1980), 97–105.

5 Samuel Beckett, *Collected Poems in English and French*, p. 18. On some of the cryptic meanings of the poem, see Lawrence E. Harvey, *Samuel Beckett: Poet and Critic*, pp. 138–48.

6 From Beckett's 'Letters on *Endgame*', first published in *The Village Voice* in 1958. They are reprinted in Samuel Beckett, *Disjecta*, pp. 106–10.

7 On the anal charge behind the letter 'g', see Ivan Fónagy, 'Les Bases pulsionnelles de la phonation', *Revue française de psychanalyse*, 34: 1, January 1970, 101–36. Fónagy refers explicitly to this instance in *Molloy* in his paper (pp. 122–3). A critical view is taken up by Jacques Derrida in *Glas*, pp. 111–12 and *passim*.

8 Samuel Beckett, 'L'Expulsé, in *Nouvelles et textes pour rien*, p. 23. Further references to the story will be to this edition and will be given in the text. In English translation the story appears in *Collected Shorter Prose*, pp. 21–33.

9 In 'All That Fall', in *Collected Shorter Plays*, pp. 9–39. All references to the play will be to this edition and will be given in the text.

10 Compare the first volume of Michel Leiris's autobiography, *Biffures* (Paris, Gallimard, 1948), p. 192, where Leiris recounts how, because of his own name – which he explains is not a Jewish name – he was for some time attacked with the term, 'youdi', by gangs of anti-semitic schoolboys.

One may remember that, for Adorno, the dustbins in *Fin de partie* were emblematic of the rebuilding of culture after Auschwitz ('Becketts Mülleimer sind Embleme der nach Auschwitz wiederaufgebauten Kultur'). See Adorno's essay on Beckett, 'Versuch, das Endspiel zu verstehen', in *Noten zur Literatur II, Gesammelte Schriften*, edited by Rolf Tiedemann (Frankfurt, Suhrkamp, 1974), vol. II, pp. 281–321 (p. 311).

6 Naming the body

1 On this problematic of names and naming in the literary text, see Derrida's treatment of the writing of Jean Genet in *Glas*. Derrida writes: 'Un texte n'"existe", ne résiste, ne consiste, ne refoule, ne se laisse lire ou écrire que s'il est travaillé par l'illisibilité d'un nom propre' (p. 41). The argument is pursued in Derrida's *La Vérité en peinture* (Paris, Flammarion, 1978) and *Signéponge* (New York, Columbia University Press, 1983).

2 The relevance of the meaning of the names, Lemuel and Samuel, for Beckett's work seems to have been first expounded by Kenneth and Alice Hamilton in *Condemned to Life: The World of Samuel Beckett* (Grand Rapids, Michigan, Eerdman's, 1976), pp. 34 and 216. The study also contains a useful discussion of Beckett's relationship to the Bible.

3 On the relation between Beckett and Christianity and the Bible, see Julia Kristeva, *Polylogue*, pp. 137–47.

4 Deirdre Bair, *Samuel Beckett: A Biography*, p. 7.

5 Ruby Cohn, *Just Play* (Princeton, Princeton University Press, 1980), p. 169.

7 Experiment and failure

1 Lawrence Graver and Raymond Federman (eds.), *Samuel Beckett: The Critical Heritage*, pp. 146–9.

2 Samuel Beckett, *Disjecta*, pp. 55–7.

3 In this and the following chapter all references to Beckett's plays in English, unless otherwise indicated, will be to the volume of *Collected Shorter Plays* (London, Faber and Faber, 1984) and will be given in the text. On the use of images of light and dark in *Krapp's Last Tape*, see James Knowlson, *Light and Darkness in the Theatre of Samuel Beckett* (London, Turret Books, 1972). Knowlson is also the editor of the useful volume on the play in the Theatre Workbook Series: *Theatre Workbook I: Samuel Beckett: 'Krapp's Last Tape'* (London, Brutus Books, 1980). Much is sometimes made of Beckett's use of Manichean patterns of antithesis and admixture in *Krapp's Last Tape*. They seem to have served the author principally as a means of organising the text around chiastic inversions and collapsing contraries. Exploiting the rhetoric of

purgatorial admixture and separation in this way should not necessarily be taken to imply a belief in Manicheism. On this, see Kenneth and Alice Hamilton, *Condemned to Life: The World of Samuel Beckett*, pp. 51–8.

4 In this and the following chapter all references to Beckett's shorter prose works in English, unless otherwise indicated, will be to the volume of *Collected Shorter Prose 1945–1980* (London, John Calder, 1986). Reference to the original French text of the 'Textes pour rien' will be to the volume, *Nouvelles et textes pour rien*, and will be given in the text.

5 *Fin de partie* (1956), *Acte sans paroles I* (1956), *Acte sans paroles II* (1956), *All That Fall* (1957), *Krapp's Last Tape* (1958), *Embers* (1959), *Words and Music* (1961), *Happy Days* (1961). Various drafts or sketches from the period are now available in: *Pas, suivi de quatre esquisses* (Paris, Editions de Minuit, 1978) and, in English, in the *Collected Shorter Plays*, pp. 65–89 and 105–24.

6 Samuel Beckett, *Fin de partie* (Paris, Editions de Minuit, 1957). All references will be to this edition and will be given in the text.

7 Alain Robbe-Grillet, *Pour un nouveau roman* (Paris, Editions de Minuit, 1963), p. 95. The review was first published in *Critique* in 1953.

8 Samuel Beckett, *Disjecta*, p. 107.

9 On Beckett's work for radio, see Clas Zilliacus, *Beckett and Broadcasting* (Åbo Akademi, Åbo, 1976).

10 That Beckett carried on experimenting with that format is clear from the sketches of the late 1950s or early 1960s in the volume, *Pas, suivi de quatre esquisses*.

11 Samuel Beckett, *Happy Days* (London, Faber and Faber, 1963), p. 47. All references will be to this edition and will be given in the text.

12 See Gérard Genette, *Seuils*, pp. 78–87.

13 Samuel Beckett, *Comment c'est* (Paris, Editions de Minuit, 1961). In recent years the Editions de Minuit have reissued the novel in a larger (more attractive) format than in the original edition. All references to the novel, however, will be to this first printing and will be given in the text. The translation, *How It Is*, appeared in 1964.

14 On the theatrical performance or adaptation of Beckett's non-theatrical texts, see Ruby Cohn, *Just Play*, pp. 206–29.

15 'From an Unabandoned Work', consisting of an extract from the first drafts for *How It Is*, was published in *Evergreen Review*, IV (Sept.–Oct. 1960), 58–65. Beckett's *L'Image* (Paris, Editions de Minuit, 1988) reprints a piece that was first published in the journal *X*, 1:1 (November 1959), 35–7. The text corresponds, with changes, to the sequence on pp. 33–8 of *Comment c'est*. The text of 'L'Image' does not have the division into strophes.

16 Maurice Blanchot, *L'Entretien infini*, pp. 481–2,

17 See for example the photograph of Beckett as a child reproduced by Ludovic Janvier in *Samuel Beckett par lui-même*, p. 6, showing Beckett in the pose described in *Comment c'est*, p. 19.

8 Writing remainders

1 The texts discussed in this chapter are as follows: (in French), 'Assez', 'Imagination morte imaginez', 'Bing', and 'Sans', all collected in: *Têtes-mortes, Le Dépeupleur* (Paris, Editions de Minuit, 1970), *Pour finir encore et autres foirades* (Paris, Editions de Minuit, 1976), *Mal vu mal dit*. Texts in English are all contained in: *Collected Shorter Prose 1945–1980*, bar *Company, Worstward Ho* (London, John Calder, 1983). Unless otherwise indicated, all references will be to these editions and will be given in the text.

2 Despite the difficulties, however, the critical literature on the late texts has grown considerably. Among the more informative accounts are: Brian Finney, *Since 'How It Is'* (London, Covent Garden Press, 1972); James Knowlson and John Pilling, *Frescoes of the Skull* (London, John Calder, 1979); James Acheson and Kateryna Arthur (eds.), *Beckett's Later Fiction and Drama: Texts for Company* (London, Macmillan, 1986). For a fresh account of the late theatre texts, see also Enoch Brater, *Beyond Minimalism: Beckett's Late Style in the Theatre* (New York, Oxford University Press, 1987).

3 Brian Finney, *Since 'How It Is'*, p. 10. In 1978, in English, Beckett brought out 'From an Abandoned Work', 'Enough', 'Imagination Dead Imagine', 'Ping', 'The Lost Ones', and 'Lessness' as the volume *Six Residua* (London, John Calder, 1978).

4 Laura Barge, for instance, writing of the residua, maintains that they are not 'something extraneous or what is left over as dregs when the main substance is removed. In spite of their stripped form and condensed wording, these pieces are the concentrated essence, the quintessence, of the entire Beckettian canon'. See her article '"Coloured Images" in the "Black Dark": Samuel Beckett's Later Fiction', *PMLA*, 92 (1977), 273–84 (p. 285). It is curious – and somewhat ironical – that, in subscribing to an essentialist view of Beckett's texts in this way, Barge should end up flatly contradicting even the author's notion of writing as a remainder.

5 Jacques Derrida, *De la grammatologie*, pp. 203–34.

6 On 'Fancy Dead', see James Knowlson and John Pilling, *Frescoes of the Skull*, pp. 136–49. 'Faux départs', unlike the two other pieces, has never been republished and is sometimes not even mentioned in bibliographies. It consists of what are most likely earlier, discarded versions of the beginning of the two other texts, some in French and some in English. It appeared in the first issue of the magazine *Kursbuch*, 1 (1965), 1–3. It could be argued, no doubt, that the text ought not to be given the same status as 'Imagination morte imaginez' and 'All Strange Away', both of which have been fully acknowledged by the author and republished a number of times. But how does one distinguish here between incidental, circumstantial writings and other, canonic writings? Which is the residue of which?

7 The note is reproduced by Richard Admussen, *The Samuel Beckett Manuscripts: A Study* (Boston, G. K. Hall and Co., 1979), p. 22.

8 Brian Finney, *Since 'How It Is'*, p. 11.

9 The typescripts of *Bing* are reproduced in an appendix by Raymond Federman and John Fletcher, *Samuel Beckett: His Work and His Critics* (Berkeley, University of California Press, 1970), pp. 325–43. Further manuscript material is reproduced in Richard Admussen, *The Samuel Beckett Manuscripts: A Study*, pp. 132–48.

10 The reasons why Beckett translates *Bing* as *Ping* are interesting ones. First, it was no doubt essential that the words used to render 'hop' and 'bing' should not take on unwanted meanings. In English, however, 'hop' is a word for springing a short way in a leap (or an ingredient for beer), while 'bing' is the name of a famous crooner. Phonetically, the value of /b/ in French and in English is different, as is the sound /i/, French not distinguishing between short and long (try to say 'ship' and 'sheep' with a French accent). The English sound /ping/ is to this extent probably closer to the French sound /bing/ than the English */bing/. Elsewhere, in *Ill Seen Ill Said* (London, John Calder, 1982), the translation of *Mal vu mal dit*, 'bah' in the French text (p.48) is rendered as 'pah' (p. 39). The rule, however, is not respected in 'Imagination Dead Imagine' which gives the French 'pah' (*Têtes-mortes*, p. 51) as . . . 'pah' (p. 145). Also, *Ping* uses only one pseudo-word where *Bing* uses two. The reason for this seems to be, not so much the greater economy of the English text (as alleged by some critics), as the result of a further collapse or erasure of difference, of 'hop' and 'bing', therefore, dissolving into 'ping'. The change also made it unnecessary for Beckett to have to devise a totally different onomatopoeia for the English text, one that would be similar to 'hop' but distinct from it for the reason given above.

11 Brian Finney, *Since 'How It Is'*, p. 12. The view is a common one among earlier critics of the text.

12 See Susan Brienza, '*The Lost Ones*: the Reader as Searcher', *Journal of Modern Literature*, 6: 1 (February 1977), 148–68. Eric P. Levy comments that '*The Lost Ones* concerns the limitations of narration far more than the torment of bodies in a cylinder. The story becomes a symbol or means of representing the movement of the narrator behind it, and only by remembering this will we discover what necessity drives the Lost Ones', *Beckett and the Voice of Species* (Totowa, N.J., Gill and Macmillan, 1980), p. 98.

13 Brian Finney, *Since 'How It Is'*, p. 44 note. It is plainly not enough to argue here, as does Paul Lawley, that 'Beckett meant the narrator to be taken as sexless.' See his essay on the text, 'Samuel Beckett's "Art and Craft": A Reading of "Enough"', *Modern Fiction Studies*, 29: 1 (Spring 1983), 25–41 (p. 30).

BIBLIOGRAPHY

Abraham, Nicolas, and Maria Torok, *Cryptonymie: le verbier de l'homme aux loups*, Paris, Aubier-Flammarion, 1976
L'Ecorce et le noyau, Paris, Aubier-Flammarion, 1978
Acheson, James, and Kateryna Arthur (eds.), *Beckett's Later Fiction and Drama: Texts for Company*, London, Macmillan, 1986
Admussen, Richard, *The Samuel Beckett Manuscripts: a Study*, Boston, G.K. Hall and Co., 1979
Adorno, T.W., *Noten zur Literatur II, Gesammelte Schriften*, vol. II, edited by Rolf Tiedemann, Frankfurt, Suhrkamp, 1974
Anzieu, Didier, 'Un soi disjoint, une voix liante, l'écriture narrative de Beckett', *Nouvelle Revue de psychanalyse*, 28 (Autumn 1983), 71–85.
Bair, Deirdre, *Samuel Beckett: a Biography*, London, Jonathan Cape, 1978
Barge, Laura, ' "Coloured Images" in the "Black Dark": Samuel Beckett's Later Fiction', *PMLA*, 92 (1977), 273–84
Beckett, Samuel, *Disjecta*, edited by Ruby Cohn, London, John Calder, 1983
Proust and Three Dialogues, London, Calder and Boyars, 1965
Collected Poems in English and French, London, John Calder, 1977
More Pricks Than Kicks, London, Calder and Boyars, 1970
Murphy, London, Calder and Boyars, 1963
Watt, London, John Calder, 1963
Mercier et Camier, Paris, Editions de Minuit, 1970
Premier Amour, Paris, Editions de Minuit, 1970
Molloy, Paris, Editions de Minuit, 1951
Malone meurt, Paris, Editions de Minuit, 1951
En attendant Godot, Paris, Editions de Minuit, 1952
L'Innommable, Paris, Editions de Minuit, 1953
Fin de partie, Paris, Editions de Minuit, 1956
Tous ceux qui tombent, translated by Robert Pinget, Paris, Editions de Minuit, 1957
Nouvelles et textes pour rien, Paris, Editions de Minuit, 1958
Molloy, Malone Dies, The Unnamable, London, Calder and Boyars, 1959
La Dernière Bande, Paris, Editions de Minuit, 1957

Comment c'est, Paris, Editions de Minuit, 1961
Happy Days, London, Faber and Faber, 1963
How It Is, London, Calder and Boyars, 1964
'Faux départs', *Kursbuch*, 1 (1965)
Têtes-mortes, 2nd edition, Paris, Editions de Minuit, 1972
Le Dépeupleur, Paris, Editions de Minuit, 1970
Pour finir encore et autres foirades, Paris, Editions de Minuit, 1976
Pas, suivi de quatre esquisses, Paris, Editions de Minuit, 1978
Company, London, John Calder, 1980
Mal vu mal dit, Paris, Editions de Minuit, 1981
Ill Seen Ill Said, London, John Calder, 1982
Worstward Ho, London, John Calder, 1983
Collected Shorter Plays, London, Faber and Faber, 1984
Collected Shorter Prose 1945–1980, London, John Calder, 1984
L'Image, Paris, Editions de Minuit, 1988
'Stirrings Still', *The Guardian*, 3 March 1989
'Comment dire', *Libération*, 1 June 1989
Soubresauts, Paris, Editions de Minuit, 1989
Beer, Ann, '*Watt*, Knott and Beckett's bilingualism', *Journal of Beckett Studies*, 10 (1985), 37–75
Benjamin, Andrew, *Translation and the Nature of Philosophy: A New Theory of Words*, London, Routledge, 1989
Benjamin, Walter, *Gesammelte Schriften*, edited by Rolf Tiedemann and Hermann Schweppenhäuser, 6 vols., Frankfurt, Suhrkamp, 1974–84
Illuminations, translated by Harry Zohn, London, Fontana, 1973
Bernal, Olga, *Langage et fiction dans le roman de Beckett*, Paris, Gallimard, 1969
Blanchot, Maurice, *Le Livre à venir*, Paris, Gallimard, 1959
L'Entretien infini, Paris, Gallimard, 1969
Brater, Enoch, *Beyond Minimalism: Beckett's Late Style in the Theatre*, New York, Oxford University Press, 1987
Breuer, Rolf, *Die Kunst der Paradoxie: Sinnsuche und -scheitern bei Samuel Beckett*, Munich, W. Fink, 1976
Brienza, Susan, '*The Lost Ones*: the Reader as Searcher', *Journal of Modern Literature*, 6: 1, February 1977, 148–68
Casement, Patrick, 'Samuel Beckett's Relationship to His Mother-Tongue', *International Review of Psycho-Analysis*, 9 (1982), 35–44
Coetzee, J.M., 'The Manuscript Revisions of Beckett's *Watt*', *Journal of Modern Literature*, 2 (1972), 472–80
Cohn, Ruby, *Samuel Beckett: The Comic Gamut*, New Brunswick, Rutgers University Press, 1962
Back to Beckett, Princeton, Princeton University Press, 1973
Just Play, Princeton, Princeton University Press, 1980
Collin, Françoise, *Maurice Blanchot et la question de l'écriture*, Paris, Gallimard, 1971
Connor, Steven, *Samuel Beckett: Repetition, Theory and Text*, Oxford, Basil Blackwell, 1988

Dällenbach, Lucien, *Le Récit spéculaire*, Paris, Editions du Seuil, 1977
de Man, Paul, *The Resistance to Theory*, Manchester, Manchester University Press, 1986
Derrida, Jacques, *De la grammatologie*, Paris, Editions de Minuit, 1967
   L'Ecriture et la différence, Paris, Editions du Seuil, 1967
   La Dissémination, Paris, Editions du Seuil, 1972
   Glas, Paris, Galilée, 1974
   La Vérité en peinture, Paris, Flammarion, 1978
   Signéponge, New York, Columbia University Press, 1983
   Ulysse gramophone, Paris, Galilée, 1987
   Psyché, Paris, Galilée, 1987
Esslin, Martin (ed.), *Samuel Beckett: A Collection of Critical Essays*, Englewood Cliffs, N.J., Prentice Hall, 1965
Federman, Raymond, *Journey to Chaos: Samuel Beckett's Early Fiction*, Berkeley, University of California Press, 1965
Federman, Raymond, and John Fletcher, *Samuel Beckett: His Work and His Critics*, Berkeley, University of California Press, 1970
Finney, Brian, *Since 'How It Is'*, London, Covent Garden Press, 1972
Fitch, Brian T., 'L'Intra-Intertextualité interlinguistique de Beckett: la problématique de la traduction de soi', *Texte*, 2 (1983), 85–100
   'La Problématique de l'étude de l'œuvre bilingue', *Symposium*, 38 (1984), 91–112
   'The Status of Self-Translation', *Texte*, 4 (1985), 111–25
Fónagy, Ivan, 'Les Bases pulsionnelles de la phonation', *Revue française de psychanalyse*, 34: 1, January 1970, 101–36
Forster, Leonard, *The Poet's Tongues*, London, Cambridge University Press, 1970
Freud, Sigmund, *Gesammelte Werke*, 17 vols., London, S. Fischer, 1940–52
Friedman, Alan Warren, Charles Rossman and Dina Sherzer (eds.), *Beckett Translating/Translating Beckett*, Pennsylvania, Pennsylvania State University Press, 1987
Genette, Gérard, *Seuils*, Paris, Editions du Seuil, 1987
Gontarski, S. E., *The Intent of Undoing in Samuel Beckett's Dramatic Texts*, Bloomington, Indiana University Press, 1985
Graham, Joseph F. (ed.), *Difference in Translation*, Ithaca, Cornell University Press, 1985
Graver, Lawrence, and Raymond Federman (eds.), *Samuel Beckett: The Critical Heritage*, London, Routledge and Kegan Paul, 1979
Grayson, Jane, *Nabokov Translated*, London, Oxford University Press, 1977
Hamilton, Kenneth, and Alice Hamilton, *Condemned to Life: The World of Samuel Beckett*, Grand Rapids, Michigan, Eerdman's, 1976
Harrison, Robert, *Samuel Beckett's 'Murphy': A Critical Excursion*, Athens, Ga., University of Georgia Press, 1968
Harvey, Lawrence E., *Samuel Beckett: Poet and Critic*, Princeton, Princeton University Press, 1970

Hildebrandt, Hans-Hagen, *Becketts Proust-Bilder: Erinnerung und Identität*, Stuttgart, J. B. Metzlersche Verlagsbuchhandlung, 1980

Hill, Leslie, 'The Name, the Body, *The Unnamable*', *Oxford Literary Review*, 6: 1 (1983), 52–67.

'Reading Beckett's Remainders', *French Studies*, 38: 2 (April 1984), 173–87

Jacobs, Carol, 'The Monstrosity of Translation', *Modern Language Notes*, 90 (1975), 755–66

Jacobsen, Josephine, and William R. Mueller, *The Testament of Samuel Beckett*, London, Faber and Faber, 1966

Janvier, Ludovic, *Samuel Beckett par lui-même*, Paris, Editions du Seuil, 1969

Jones, Anthony, 'The French *Murphy*: from "rare bird" to "cancre"', *Journal of Beckett Studies*, 6 (Autumn 1980), 37–50

Joyce, James, *Ulysses*, London, The Bodley Head, 1960

Finnegans Wake, London, Faber and Faber, 1964

Kennedy, Sighle, *Murphy's Bed*, Lewisburg, Bucknell University Press, 1971

Kenner, Hugh, *Samuel Beckett: A Critical Study*, Berkeley, University of California Press, 1961

Khatibi, Abdelkebir (ed.), *Du bilinguisme*, Paris, Denoël, 1985

Knowlson, James, *Light and Darkness in the Theatre of Samuel Beckett*, London, Turret Books, 1972

Knowlson, James (ed.), *Theatre Workbook I: Samuel Beckett, 'Krapp's Last Tape'*, London, Brutus Books, 1980

Knowlson, James, and John Pilling, *Frescoes of the Skull*, London, John Calder, 1979

Kofman, Sarah, *Comment s'en sortir?*, Paris, Galilée, 1983

Kristeva, Julia, *La Révolution du langage poétique*, Paris, Editions du Seuil, 1974

Polylogue, Paris, Editions du Seuil, 1977

Lawley, Paul, 'Samuel Beckett's "Art and Craft": A Reading of "Enough" ', *Modern Fiction Studies*, 29, 1 (Spring 1983), 25–41

Leiris, Michel, *Biffures*, Paris, Gallimard, 1948

Levy, Eric P., *Beckett and the Voice of Species*, Totowa, N.J., Gill and Macmillan, 1980

Lyotard, Jean-François, *Des dispositifs pulsionnels*, Paris, Union Générale d'Editions, 1973

La Condition postmoderne, Paris, Editions de Minuit, 1979

McMillan, Dougald, *transition: The History of a Literary Era 1927–38*, London, Calder and Boyars, 1975

McMillan, Dougald, and Martha Fehsenfeld, *Beckett in the Theatre I*, London, John Calder, 1988

Menzies, Janet, 'Beckett's Bicycles', *Journal of Beckett Studies*, 6 (Autumn 1980), 97–105

Mintz, Samuel, 'Beckett's *Murphy*: a "Cartesian" novel', *Perspective*, 11 (Autumn 1959), 156–65

Moorjani, Angela B., *Abysmal Games in the Novels of Samuel Beckett*, Chapel Hill, North Carolina Studies in the Romance Languages and Literatures, 1982

Morot-Sir Edouard, et al. (eds.), *Samuel Beckett: the Art of Rhetoric*, Chapel Hill, North Carolina Studies in Romance Languages and Literatures, 1976

Musil, Robert, *Gesammelte Werke*, 9 vols., Hamburg, Rowohlt Verlag, 1978

Nabokov, Vladimir, *The Real Life of Sebastian Knight*, Harmondsworth, Penguin, 1964

Speak, Memory!, Harmondsworth, Penguin, 1967

Lolita, Harmondsworth, Penguin, 1980

Look at the Harlequins!, Harmondsworth, Penguin, 1964

O'Brien, Eoin, *The Beckett Country*, London, The Black Cat Press with Faber and Faber, 1986

O'Hara, J. D. (ed.), *Twentieth-Century Interpretations of Molloy, Malone Dies, The Unnamable*, Englewood Cliffs, N.J., Prentice-Hall, 1970

Pilling, John, 'Beckett's *Proust*', *Journal of Beckett Studies*, 1 (1976), 8–29

Samuel Beckett, London, Routledge and Kegan Paul, 1976

Proust, Marcel, *A la recherche du temps perdu*, edited by Pierre Clarac and André Ferré, 3 vols., Paris, Gallimard, Pléiade, 1954

Pushkin, Aleksandr, *Eugene Onegin*, translated with a commentary by Vladimir Nabokov, 4 vols., New York, Bollingen Foundation, 1964

Rabaté, Jean-Michel (ed.), *Beckett avant Beckett*, Paris, Editions de l'E.N.S., 1984

Rabinovitz, Rubin, *The Development of Samuel Beckett's Fiction*, Chicago, University of Illinois Press, 1984

Robbe-Grillet, Alain, *Pour un nouveau roman*, Paris, Editions de Minuit, 1963

Rosen, Steven J., *Samuel Beckett and the Pessimistic Tradition*, New Brunswick, Rutgers University Press, 1976

Saint-Martin, Fernande, *Samuel Beckett et l'univers de la fiction*, Montreal, Presses de l'Université de Montréal, 1976

Sherzer, Dina, *Structure de la trilogie de Beckett: Molloy, Malone meurt, L'Innommable*, Paris–The Hague, Mouton, 1976

Solomon, Philip H., *The Life After Birth: Imagery in Samuel Beckett's Novels*, Mississippi, Romance Monographs, 1975

States, Bert O., *The Shape of Paradox*, Berkeley, University of California Press, 1978

Tagliaferri, Alda, *Beckett et la surdétermination littéraire*, translated by Nicole Fama, Paris, Payot, 1977

Wolfson, Louis, *Le Schizo et les langues*, Paris, Gallimard, 1969

Worth, Katherine (ed.), *Beckett the Shape Changer*, London, Athlone Press, 1975

Zilliacus, Clas, *Beckett and Broadcasting*, Åbo Akademi, Åbo, 1976

INDEX

185

Cambridge Studies in French

General editor: MALCOLM BOWIE

Also in the series

MITCHELL GREENBERG
Corneille, Classicism, and the Ruses of Symmetry

HOWARD DAVIES
Sartre and 'Les Temps Modernes'

ROBERT GREER COHN
Mallarmé's Prose Poems: A Critical Study

CELIA BRITTON
Claude Simon: Writing the Visible

DAVID SCOTT
*Pictorialist Poetics: Poetry and the Visual Arts in
Nineteenth-Century France*

ANN JEFFERSON
Reading Realism in Stendhal

DALIA JUDOVITZ
*Subjectivity and Representation in Descartes: The Origins
of Modernity*

RICHARD D. E. BURTON
Baudelaire in 1859: A Study in the Sources of Poetic Creativity

MICHAEL MORIARTY
Taste and Ideology in Seventeenth-Century France

JOHN FORRESTER
The Seductions of Psychoanalysis: Freud, Lacan and Derrida

JEROME SCHWARTZ
Irony and Ideology in Rabelais: Structures of Subversion

DAVID BAGULEY
Naturalist Fiction: The Entropic Vision